**Blackstone's**
**Crime Invest**
**Handbook**

# Blackstone's
# Crime
# Investigators'
# Handbook

Tony Cook
Steve Hibbitt
Mick Hill

OXFORD
UNIVERSITY PRESS

# OXFORD
UNIVERSITY PRESS

Great Clarendon Street, Oxford, OX2 6DP,
United Kingdom

Oxford University Press is a department of the University of Oxford.
It furthers the University's objective of excellence in research, scholarship,
and education by publishing worldwide. Oxford is a registered trade mark of
Oxford University Press in the UK and in certain other countries

© Oxford University Press 2013

The moral rights of the authors have been asserted

First Edition published in 2013

Impression: 1

British Library Cataloguing in Publication Data

Data available

ISBN 978-0-19-966293-7

Printed in Great Britain by
Ashford Colour Press Ltd, Gosport, Hampshire

# Preface

This book is aimed primarily at police officers, particularly detectives and any other persons or agencies involved in tackling or studying crime investigation. The contents follow the general principles of the National Occupational Standards for policing and law enforcement by covering topics within prescribed units and elements. It should therefore greatly assist those who are seeking accreditation at PIP level 2 and not only help those who are in training or going through and/or maintaining accreditation, but also those who wish to increase their knowledge and enhance their skills.

An overarching objective has been to compile a comprehensive handbook that contains lots of 'hands on' practical advice and essential information for performing the role and duties of a crime investigator. The book has been deliberately designed in an easy-to-carry, read and accessible size and format. It contains sufficient essential material for making important decisions and applying the best procedures and processes to help solve crimes. The inclusion of checklists and keypoints have been added to ensure essential details are summarised and highlighted. These are, however, intended to be guidelines not tramlines.

The handbook contents include necessary elements that relate to most if not all the fundamental aspects of crime investigation. The chapter headings and sections have been carefully chosen to ensure all the most important topics are covered. These should reinforce and build upon knowledge provided by the College of Policing and Authorised Professional Practice.

There is no vagueness within these pages, nor academic terminology, complicated words or abstract theories. The book quite simply aims to develop investigative creativity whilst applying proven and recognised models and

## Preface

techniques. The depth of content has been deliberately
organised so that sufficient information is supplied around
the wealth of topics included. Because of the nature of some
of the subjects covered, the book could very easily have
developed into a further volume with even greater detail,
but then the objective of producing one single 'reach for'
reference book would have failed.

Our sincere wish is that crime investigators find this
handbook both practical and convenient. Hopefully the
contents should help professionalise performance and
overall success in investigations and benefit not just the
police service and criminal justice system, but also those
who have become victims through the commission of
criminal offences.

Tony Cook
Steve Hibbitt
Mick Hill

# Contents

## Contents

# Contents

# Contents

# Contents

# Contents

# Contents

# Contents

# Contents

# Contents

# Abbreviations

| | |
|---|---|
| 5WH | Who? What? Where? When? Why? How? |
| ABC | Assume nothing, Believe nothing, Challenge/check everything |
| ABE | Achieving Best Evidence |
| ACC | Assistant Chief Constable |
| ACPO | Association of Chief Police Officers |
| AFI | Accredited Financial Investigators |
| AFO | Authorised Firearms Officer |
| AKA | also known as |
| ALTE | apparent life-threatening event |
| ANPR | Automatic Number Plate Recognition System |
| AO | Authorising Officer |
| AOABH | assault occasioning actual bodily harm |
| AQ | Al-Qaeda |
| ATM | Automatic Telling Machine |
| AYR | Are You Ready? |
| BCU | Basic Command Unit |
| BIA | Behavioural Investigative Adviser |
| BPA | Blood Pattern Analysis |
| BT | British Telecom |
| CACDP | Council for the Advancement of Communication with Deaf People |
| CAP | common approach path |
| CATCHEM | Centralised Analytical Team Collating Homicide Expertise and Management |
| CAU | Crime Analysis Unit |
| CCRC | Criminal Cases Review Commission |
| CDI | Communications Data Investigator |
| CDOP | Child Death Overview Panel |
| CEOP | Child Exploitation and Online Protection Centre |
| CHIS | covert human intelligence source |

## Abbreviations

| | |
|---|---|
| CIA | Community Impact Assessment |
| CID | Criminal Investigation Department |
| CISO | Crime Investigative Support Officers |
| CJA | Criminal Justice Act 1967 |
| CJPO | Criminal Justice and Public Order Act 1994 |
| COD | cause of death |
| COS | Crime Operational Support |
| CPA | crime pattern analysis |
| CPD | continuous professional development |
| CPIA | Criminal Procedure and Investigations Act 1996 |
| CPS | Crown Prosecution Service |
| CSC | Crime Scene Coordinator |
| CSE | Crime Scene Examiner |
| CSI | Crime Scene Investigator |
| CSM | Crime Scene Manager |
| CT | counter-terrorism |
| CTC | Counter Terrorism Command |
| CTU | Counter-Terrorism Unit |
| CWB | Central Witness Bureau |
| DCC | Deputy Chief Constable |
| DIDP | Detective Inspectors Development Programme |
| DIR | Dissident Irish Republicans |
| DNA | Deoxyribonucleic acid |
| DPP | Director of Public Prosecutions |
| DSU | Dedicated Source Unit |
| DV | domestic violence |
| EAW | European Arrest Warrant |
| ECHR | European Convention on Human Rights |
| EI | emotional intelligence |
| EO | Exhibits Officer |
| ESDA | Electrostat Document Apparatus |
| fDNA | familial DNA searching |
| FDR | firearms discharge residue |
| FLC | Family Liaison Coordinator |
| FLO | Family Liaison Officer |
| FME | Force Medical Examiner |

| | |
|---|---|
| FOI | Freedom of Information Act 2000 |
| FSID | Foundation for the Study of Infant Death |
| FSP | Forensic Service Provider |
| GHB | Gamma Hydroxyburate |
| H-2-H | house-to-house enquiries |
| HBV | honour-based violence |
| HOLMES | Home Office Large Major Enquiry System |
| HP | high priority |
| HSE | Health and Safety Executive |
| HTA | Human Tissue Act 2004 |
| ICIDP | Initial Crime Investigators Development Programme |
| IED | improvised explosive device |
| ILOR | International Letter of Request |
| IMEI | International Mobile Station Equipment Identity |
| IMSC | Initial Management of Serious Crime Course |
| IO | Investigating Officer |
| IP | Internet Protocol |
| IPCC | Independent Police Complaints Commission |
| IPLDP | Initial Police Learning and Development Programme |
| ISP | Identify, Secure and Protect (crime scenes) |
| ISP | Internet Service Provider |
| JDLR principle | 'just doesn't look right' principle |
| LCN | Low Copy Number DNA |
| LKP | last known position |
| LSCB | Local Safeguarding Children Board |
| LSD | Lysergic Acid Diethylamide |
| MAPPA | Multi-Agency Public Protection Arrangements |
| MAPPP | Multi-Agency Public Protection Panels |
| MARAC | Multi-Agency Risk Assessment Conference |
| MDMA | Ecstasy |

## Abbreviations

| | |
|---|---|
| MIM | *Murder Investigation Manual* (ACPO, 2006) |
| MIR | Major Incident Room |
| MIRSAP | *Major Incident Room Standardised Administrative Procedures Guidance Manual* (ACPO/Centrex, 2005) |
| MLO | Media Liaison Officer |
| MLOE | main lines of enquiry |
| MO | modus operandi |
| MOD | manner of death |
| MPB | UK Missing Persons Bureau |
| MPS | Metropolitan Police Service |
| MtDNA | Mitochondrial DNA |
| NABIS | National Ballistics Intelligence Service |
| NCA | National Crime Agency |
| NDM | National Decision Model |
| NDNAD | National DNA Database |
| NFRC | National Footwear Reference Collection |
| NID | National Injuries Database |
| NIM | National Intelligence Model |
| NOS | National Occupational Standards |
| NRPSI | National Register of Public Service Interpreters |
| NSA | National Search Adviser |
| NSPCC | National Society for the Prevention of Cruelty to Children |
| OCG | Organised Crime Group |
| OIA | Operational Intelligence Assessment |
| OIC | Officer in Charge |
| OP | Observation Post |
| OSC | Office of Surveillance Commissioners |
| OSRI | Open Source Research of the Internet |
| PACE | Police and Criminal Evidence Act 1984 |
| PAT | Problem Analysis Triangle |
| PCMH | Plea and Case Management Hearing |
| PCSO | Police Community Support Officer |
| PDF | Personal Descriptive Form |
| PDP | potentially dangerous persons |
| PED | Police Elimination Database |

| | |
|---|---|
| PHA | Protection from Harassment Act 1997 |
| PIB | pre-interview briefing |
| PII | Public Interest Immunity |
| PIP | Professionalising Investigations Programme |
| PNC | Police National Computer |
| PND | Police National Database |
| POCA 2002 | Proceeds of Crime Act 2002 |
| POI | persons of interest |
| POLKA | Police Online Knowledge Area |
| PolSA | Police Search Advisor |
| PPE | Personal Protection Equipment |
| PPO | persistent and priority offender |
| PST | Police Search Team |
| QUEST | Query Using Enhanced Search Techniques |
| RA | responsible authority |
| RA | Regional Advisers (NCA) |
| RARA | Remove, Avoid, Reduce, Accept |
| RAT | Routine Activity Theory |
| RIPA 2000 | Regulation of Investigatory Powers Act 2000 |
| ROVI | Record of Video Interview |
| RVP | rendezvous point |
| SARC | Sexual Assault Referral Centre |
| SCAS | Serious Crime Analysis Section |
| SIDS | sudden infant death syndrome |
| SIO | Senior Investigating Officer |
| SIODP | Senior Investigating Officer Development Programme |
| SOC | Specialist Operations Centre |
| SOCA | Serious Organised Crime Agency |
| SOCO | Scenes of Crime Officer |
| SOCPA | Serious Organised Crime and Police Act 2005 |
| SOS | Specialist Operational Support |
| SPoC | Single Point of Contact |
| SUDC | sudden and unexpected death of a child |

## Abbreviations

| | |
|---|---|
| SUDI | sudden and unexpected death of an infant |
| SWIT | significant witness |
| SWOT | Strengths, Weaknesses, Opportunities and Threats |
| TCG | Tasking and Coordinating Group |
| TIE | Trace, Interview, Eliminate |
| TTL | threats to life |
| UK | United Kingdom |
| VCCM | Volume Crime Management Model |
| VCSE | Volume Crime Scene Examiners |
| ViSOR | UK Violent and Sex Offenders Register |
| VPS | victim personal statement |
| WOFD | Warrant of Further Detention |
| XRW | extreme right wing |
| YJCEA | Youth Justice and Criminal Evidence Act 1999 |
| Y-STR | Y strand |

# Chapter 1

# Role of a Criminal Investigator

## 1.1 **Introduction**

The investigation of crime is continuously in the public spotlight. There is extensive coverage of the topic through news reporting, television programmes, documentaries, films, novels and magazines, the radio and social media sites. It also holds true that there are high expectations on investigators to use and apply their professional skills and expertise to solve crimes, support victims and help communities and the general public.

Modern day detectives are expected to possess a wide range of knowledge, not just of legislative powers and statutory offences, but also of scientific approaches, crime scene management, collection of physical evidence, investigative interviewing, case file preparation, disclosure and management of the administration of the investigative process. There are complex procedural and legal constraints, internal and external policies and politics, personal and professional challenges, resourcing and financial constraints, changing political landscapes, competing demands, structural reorganisations, long and unsocial working hours, dangerous and uncertain environments, emotional pressures (of the crime itself and those of the victim's families, as well as public expectations), extreme levels of accountability and media intrusion.

Judicial processes and internal and external review mechanisms pose added levels of accountability. Agencies such as the Independent Police Complaints Commission

## 1 Role of a Criminal Investigator

(IPCC) can also become involved and, not surprisingly, the manner in which crimes are investigated has undergone significant changes. One example is the emphasis on 'multi-agency' working, partnership and community policing; another is the shift from traditional suspect-centred approaches to those which are far more professionally and evidence-based.

Being a crime investigator is still one of the most enjoyable and rewarding roles in policing. A lot of thrill and satisfaction can be gained from uncovering facts and evidence, identifying and arresting offenders and taking cases successfully to court. So too is being able to inform victims that their crime has been solved and helping them gain a sense of justice to move on with their lives.

This handbook is directly aimed at giving practical help, advice and inspiration to those who are or intend to work in an investigative role. It will help remove conceptual barriers to learning and practising detective work and act as a practical, 'hands on' no nonsense guide. The first chapter now begins by outlining various requirements and elements that make up the crime investigator's role and sets the scene for the other chapters that follow.

## 1.2 Criminal Investigation and Investigator

### 1.2.1 Criminal investigation

Criminal investigations can be either proactive or reactive and until recently tended to be primarily the latter. The emphasis has now changed, with less emphasis on 'points to prove' and a shift towards a search for the truth (ie 'search for the truth not search for the proof'). Whereas 'points to prove' presupposes a crime or crimes, an offender or offenders and a prosecution case, a 'search for the truth' provides other possible outcomes, such as no crime having been committed or revealing suspects to be innocent.

A general definition of crime investigation might be as simple as 'the collection of information and evidence for identifying, apprehending and convicting suspected offenders'. It is, however, a lot more complex and embraces a wide range of functions and responsibilities, the majority of which make up the contents of this handbook.

There is no official definition of a criminal investigation except in statute such as in the Criminal Procedure and Investigations Act 1996 (CPIA) Code of Practice, Part II of which defines a criminal investigation as:

An investigation conducted by police officers with a view to it being ascertained whether a person should be charged with an offence, or whether a person charged with an offence is guilty of it. This will include:

- investigations into crimes that have been committed;
- investigations whose purpose is to ascertain whether a crime has been committed with a view to possible institution of criminal proceedings; and
- investigations which begin in the belief that a crime may be committed, for example when the police keep premises or individuals under observation for a period of time with a view to the possible institution of criminal proceedings.

Charging a person with an offence includes prosecution by way of summons.

### KEY POINT

Some investigations are affected by additional challenges, for example:

- lack of victim/offender close contact (eg fraud cases)
- badly contaminated or disturbed crime scenes
- high risk and/or vulnerable victims
- absence of evidence or information from witnesses, forensic or other sources
- lack of help and assistance from witnesses or communities
- multiple victims and series crimes

## 1  Role of a Criminal Investigator

- cases that attract widespread public/media attention
- drug- or gang-related crimes (eg so-called 'bad on bad' cases)
- absence of criminal pointers
- low or high information investigations
- critical incidents
- stringent time scales for preparing case papers for trial (eg forensic reports and delayed tests, communications data enquiries, passive data capture/viewing, witness statements)
- crimes involving trans-European or international victims and offenders
- use of social networking sites, global communication, travel networks and 'virtual' communities to facilitate criminality
- lack of resources, funding cutbacks and competing demands
- changing political landscapes and priorities

### 1.2.2  Criminal investigator

The term 'criminal investigator' tends to be a broad term that covers many activities and several types of specialists and professionals in law enforcement. It would include, for example, operational 'street' detectives within traditional Criminal Investigation Departments (CID), Crime Scene Investigators (CSIs), computer and communications data investigators, child protection experts and even forensic examiners and laboratory specialists. The list is not exhaustive and perhaps the most obvious and visible of the various alternatives is the police detective who follows up enquiries and information on crimes, such as developing leads, interviewing witnesses and suspects, and preparing prosecution case files.

The Oxford English Dictionary defines the term 'investigate' as: 'To carry out a systematic or formal enquiry to discover and examine the facts of an incident or allegation so as to establish the truth ...'; while an 'investigation' is: 'The action of investigating something or someone by formal or systematic examination or research.' The same source defines a detective as: 'A person, especially a police officer whose occupation is to investigate and solve crimes'; 'detection' is: 'The action or process of identifying the presence of something concealed''; and the noun 'crime' is simply defined as: 'An action or omission which constitutes an offence and is punishable by law' (C Soanes and A Stevenson (eds), *Oxford Dictionary of English*, (2nd edn, OUP, 2008)).

Part II of the CPIA Code of Practice defines the officer in charge of an investigation and what their role is within the Act as:

> the police officer responsible for directing a criminal investigation. S/he is also responsible for ensuring that proper procedures are in place for recording information and retaining records of information and material in the investigation.

The CPIA sets out duties for an investigator in relation to disclosure and also in respect of the investigation itself. Section 23 refers to the treatment and retention of material and information generated during such an investigation, and section 23(1)(a) contains a requirement for the police to carry out an investigation. It states:

> … where a criminal investigation is conducted all reasonable steps are taken for the purposes of the investigation, and in particular all reasonable lines of enquiry are pursued.

Apart from satisfying the requirements of the CPIA for recording and retaining all pertinent information, crime investigators have many other important duties and responsibilities. These include the following:

### Checklist—duties of an investigator

- Establish what happened through gathering facts and information
- Establish what type and category of crime, if any, has been committed
- Gather all available evidence
- Determine the objectives of the investigation
- Assess what factors might impact positively/negatively on the investigation

## 1 Role of a Criminal Investigator

- Plan and conduct an investigation
- Apply an investigative mindset to the examination of case circumstances
- Sceptically question and scrutinise
- Brief, task and debrief others for the investigation
- Develop, prioritise and pursue all reasonable lines of enquiry
- Identify, secure and protect crime scenes
- Establish the identity of offenders and arrest, interview, process and prosecute those who have committed offences
- Develop hypotheses and theories and keep them dynamically updated
- Develop and implement investigative strategies
- Locate and interview victims and witnesses and apply categorisation requirements (eg significant, vulnerable, intimidated or hostile)
- Acquire intelligence and turn it into evidence
- Plan, organise and conduct crime scene searches
- Recover stolen property or items
- Collect and accurately record available information and material that may be relevant to the investigation
- Protect the integrity of material or evidence gathered
- Identify and obtain necessary resources and expert and specialist support wherever appropriate
- Develop and apply overt and covert proactive tactics
- Keep appropriate stakeholders, eg supervisory officers, victims, witnesses and communities, updated on progress
- Relay to appropriate persons or departments any information or intelligence that may be relevant to other investigations
- Remain accountable to police organisations, colleagues, the judicial process, victims and communities for the professional conduct of the investigation

- Assemble prosecution files, liaise with the Crown Prosecution Service (CPS), present evidence in court/hearings
- Accurately record all decisions and actions taken

---

**KEY POINT**

One of the key roles of a crime investigator is to sceptically question and scrutinise, all information and material that is or becomes available.

---

## 1.3 Key Investigative Skills and Knowledge Areas

Investigators need a combination of skills and knowledge and the lists in sections 1.3.1 and 1.3.2 provide an outline. There are added responsibilities relating to management if performing in a supervisory role.

### 1.3.1 Investigative skills

- Investigative competence (eg formulating lines of enquiry and decision making)
- Ability to appraise information (eg interpreting and assimilating information, challenging assumptions, checking accuracy and relevance)
- Adaptability (ie being flexible to changing circumstances)
- Strategically (understanding the wider consequences) and tactically aware
- Innovative (being creative to achieve aims)
- Good communication skills (verbal and written)
- Strong problem-solving and decision-making skills
- Ability to manage time, prioritise and deal with competing demands
- Ability to work effectively and as part of a team
- Ability to recognise and work with diversity and cultural differences
- Ability to cope under pressure

## 1.3.2 Knowledge areas

- Awareness of covert and overt proactive tactics
- Theoretical knowledge. Investigators must keep up their continuous professional development (CPD) and conscientiously seek out, learn, appreciate and understand new knowledge and information applicable to the role. For example, current legislation and updates and changes, legal procedures, powers and definitions, organisational policies and requirements (eg in relation to race, diversity, human rights and health and safety), national guidelines, manuals and doctrines, crime categories and types, crime recording and processing methods, relevant police powers, forensic procedures, investigative and technological advances, nationally disseminated good practice and learning points, debrief reports, definitions of offences, points to prove, potential defences, case law, rules of evidence, public and community awareness, national and local force policies, priorities and performance targets etc
- Creative thinking. Expanding and drawing upon mental agility of self and colleagues, challenging existing knowledge and replacing it with better and improved information (ie looking at things from a different perspective to produce alternative methods and possibilities to achieve results)

### KEY POINTS

- 'Creative thinking' involves looking at problems from different perspectives and questioning assumptions to test the validity of theories and information. Investigators must continually question whether there might need to be another possible way or explanation (*Practice Advice on Core Investigative Doctrine* (2nd edn, ACPO/NPIA, 2012)).
- Creativity and bright ideas can come at odd times (eg when off duty, middle of the night, etc) and be triggered by unrelated activities and events. It is worthwhile having a means of noting them down so they can be recalled later and not easily forgotten.

- Investigative knowledge covers areas such as dealing with TIE subjects (Trace, Interview, Eliminate), suspects and significant witnesses; awareness of forensic examination techniques and crime-scene examination; procedures relating to exhibit recovery, packaging, storage, examination and review; 'fast-track' forensic tests; strategies for main lines of enquiry, eg communications data, passive data collection and analysis (eg CCTV footage); disclosure requirements, etc.
- Communication covers a wide spectrum. Investigators must be adept at communicating with a wide range of people and agencies at different levels and adapting to various styles; being able to speak, write, take notes quickly, coherently and intelligently, and to soak up information by active listening and recalling accurate detail and facts.

## 1.4 Professionalising Investigations Programme Levels and the National Occupational Standards

The Professionalising Investigations Programme (PIP) maps out the training and career path for crime investigators, while the National Occupational Standards (NOS) are the areas to cover that are contained within the training and development portfolios required in order to achieve the requisite PIP Accreditation. There are defined courses and programmes which are summarised in sections 1.4.1 and 1.4.2.

### 1.4.1 PIP core programmes

- Initial Police Learning and Development Programme (IPLDP)—PIP level 1

## 1 Role of a Criminal Investigator

- Initial Crime Investigators Development Programme (ICIDP)—PIP level 2
- Initial Management of Serious Crime Course (IMSC)—PIP level 2
- Detective Inspectors Development Programme (DIDP)—PIP level 2
- Senior Investigating Officer Development Programme (SIODP)—PIP level 3
- PIP level 4 (strategic coordination)

These can be supplemented by 'add on' courses, a sample of which are contained in section 1.4.2.

### 1.4.2 Specialist training programmes

- Core skills in communications data
- Financial investigation
- Specialist Child Abuse Investigator Development Programme—PIP level 2
- Investigative interviewing
- Family liaison
- HOLMES (Home Office Large Major Enquiry System)
- Sexual offences investigation
- Child abuse/death investigation

## 1.5 Motivation, Confidence and Optimism

A most important asset of any criminal investigator is one of personal motivation. Motivated individuals are always more productive due to their sheer enthusiasm, commitment and conscientiousness, good attributes that rub off onto others. Very little happens without these star qualities, yet they are not easily taught.

Positive thinking is a method of increasing confidence and ensuring any problems and obstacles are approached more favourably. Negative and pessimistic attitudes are not going to help and almost become self-fulfilling. Optimistic attitudes allow tasks to be approached with greater vigour, energy and vitality; focusing on what can be achieved and not what cannot. Those who constantly raise problems to solutions, play the 'devil's advocate' and destroy rather than construct need to be tasked with balancing their negative views with positive ones. The 3P principle is one to remember:

```
POSITIVE
POSITIVE
POSITIVE
```

The main benefits of motivation, confidence and optimism is their contribution to resilience in the face of setbacks. Staying positive and remaining confident about achieving successful outcomes and not becoming easily defeated is a key mental attitude in all top performers, not just crime investigators. Focusing on positives rather than negatives helps maintain morale and sustain interest, which is what victims expect of those who are representing their interests in achieving justice. This should be balanced against being realistic and managing expectations.

## 1.5.1 Managing expectations

High expectations can become burdensome and difficult to manage. Communities, relatives, friends of victims, the media and internal supervision can place high demands and hopes on the individual and team performance of investigators. Personal morale and motivation levels can become adversely affected when under-delivering against highly expected, anticipated or promised results. Good results become compromised when they fall short of what has been promised. Long-term failure to meet expectations will almost certainly undermine an investigator's credibility and morale through loss of confidence and trust. Therefore it is wiser to *under-promise and over-deliver*. Only when certain and positive about a fact, piece of information or update should it be reported and made public. Predictions, estimates and speculative promises must be avoided, and events or information should not be allowed to assume a greater importance than their worth.

In some circumstances it can be tactically wise to withhold success stories or good news temporarily. This could prevent alerting suspects that vital evidence has been obtained or that they are to be arrested; or could avoid building false hopes in victims, or creating 'closed minds' from sources of information and/or communities from whom assistance is still required. In such a case, the reasons and justification for withholding the update and information would need to be recorded so they can be explained at any later stage.

## 1.6 **Preparation**

In addition to knowledge and skills, physical and mental energy and stamina are also useful assets to have when performing an investigator's role, particularly when working long hours or on difficult and protracted enquiries under arduous conditions. At regular stages investigators need to refresh themselves to prepare for these challenges.

Effective and professional crime investigation requires adequate preparation in readiness for spontaneously having to attend and take charge of cases and 'hitting the ground running'. The acronym 'AYR' is applicable:

> **A** Are
> **Y** You
> **R** Ready?

Good routines are good practice. One worth getting used to is having the right materials and equipment ready and available for when needed. The maxim 'failing to plan is planning to fail' holds true, meaning the basic requirements can and should be prepared and ready to go. Essential items should be readily available and accessible in a quick 'grab' or 'go bag'.

### Checklist—Crime investigator's basic kit

- A 'grab' or 'go' bag containing the essential items
- A reliable timepiece for accurately recording the times that events occurred
- A 'daybook' or notebook with reliable writing implements to record all information, details and decisions (or digital equivalent)
- Weatherproof clipboard (or similar) to rest on with sufficient writing/drawing paper
- Essential documents, such as witness statement forms and crime scene logs
- Mobile phone (fully charged) and charger lead (and/or spare battery)
- List of important contact numbers (eg CSI, Duty Senior Investigating Officer (SIO), Duty Officer etc)
- Police airwave radio, spare battery and list of channels
- Suitable and/or practical clothing (ie weatherproof and warm boots etc)
- Refreshments (food and drink)
- Maps (eg digital mapping or satellite navigation system)
- Torch/batteries
- Forensic gloves/overshoes
- Crime scene barrier tape and evidence bags/labels
- Suitable transport (if vehicle, sufficient fuel and notice to display saying whose it is)
- Money/loose change for emergencies
- Blackstone's Crime Investigators' Handbook

## 1.7 **Specialist Assistance**

Omni-competent and lone investigators have been replaced by those who have the advantage of being able to call upon a wide range of support, specialists and experts. It is accepted that one person alone cannot solve complex cases. There are specialist departments and units within the police family that assume responsibility for various elements of or types of investigation, and in some cases take overall responsibility. Units, squads and teams of various types and descriptions, such as major crime units (eg homicide), robbery, burglary, sexual offences, child protection, domestic violence, drugs, cyber crime, child abuse and financial investigation units, hold specific remits for particular investigations. They may also be able to offer advice or support, expertise, knowledge and specialist services even if not directly involved.

Other supporting roles can be provided by tactical advisers, colleagues and outside experts who perform diverse roles and functions. A key skill is not only drawing on one's own personal experience and knowledge but also that which is available from others to help form a strong investigation team. This is useful not only for carrying out significant actions or activities, but can also provide assistance and produce useful suggestions and solutions.

Highly trained and skilled Crime Scene Managers (CSMs)/ CSIs advise on scene preservation and forensic evidence recovery. Other specialists can also be called upon when required, such as ballistics experts, fire investigators, police search advisors (PolSA), geographic and behavioural investigative profilers and advisers, trained analysts, media liaison officers, forensic specialists and advisors, specialist interview advisers, communications data investigators, community awareness and family liaison specialists. There are lots of 'ologists' to choose from depending on the circumstances, such as biologists, palynologists, entomologists, gastroenterologists, forensic anthropologists and so on.

Various units and departments within each force or agency, such as specialist firearms units or covert operations teams, can provide advice and guidance on a variety of techniques and tactical options. All these can at some stage form part of the investigation team.

---

**KEY POINT**

An important rule is not to step outside the boundaries of one's own training and expertise. It is better to seek assistance from those who have the necessary skills and ability to perform a function than run the risk of making poor mistakes by covering up for lack of knowledge.

---

National assets can be worthwhile sources of advice, such as the National Crime Agency (NCA) Crime Operational Support and Specialist Operations Teams, Homicide Working Group, databases such as CATCHEM (Centralised Analytical Team Collating Homicide Expertise and Management), National injuries Database and SCAS (Serious Crime Analysis Section) and the Police Online Knowledge Area (POLKA). These are resources worth knowing about and using, and usually come free of charge.

Several external agencies and bodies now share responsibilities with the police and have obligations to mount investigations themselves or assist certain crime investigations. Bodies such as local authorities, for instance, may be required to work in partnership with police investigators on cases such as child neglect or cruelty, or the Health and Safety Executive (HSE). These agencies sometimes refer cases to the police for investigation, which may be the first time a police investigator becomes involved.

## 1.8 **Welfare Management**

It is essential, no matter how experienced or professional a person is, to be able to cope physically and mentally under pressure, sometimes when fatigued or even when stressed. Planning to avoid, identify or effectively manage the symptoms is important.

Stress is highly counterproductive and is to be distinguished from enthusiasm and energy. Stress is a personal thing and manifests itself in different ways, eg loss of patience, arguing or inappropriate behaviour. There is always a cause for irrational behaviour and this should be remembered when the symptoms surface in oneself or colleagues to establish what may be causing the problem.

Emotional intelligence (EI) is the ability to identify, assess, manage and control the emotions of oneself, of others and of groups, and will help to make sense of and to survive a high pressure working environment. Coping mechanisms can include knowing one's own emotions, strengths, weaknesses, drives, values and goals and recognising their impact on others, using self regulation to control impulses and adapting to changing circumstances. Demonstrating good social and teamworking skills is important.

Tiredness and taking on too much can cause problems, so adopting basic principles of being well organised and managing time become critical, because being unable to complete all necessary and urgent tasks leads to increased pressure and stress. Busy and conscientious crime investigators must be ruthlessly efficient at prioritising their workloads and getting the most out of their valuable time. Some issues and individuals conspire to commandeer valuable time, which is when it is necessary to be firm and polite, pointing out what is more pressing and urgent. Planning and prioritising a working day and tasks is very important, whilst appreciating that events can and do change at a moment's notice.

It is important to be able to mentally 'switch off'. Sometimes it is difficult to concentrate on little else when engrossed in a fascinating or challenging case. Creating time to focus on unrelated matters and to pursue other interests can significantly help reduce mental anxiety and stress. A change of thought refreshes the mind and clears the head ready to refocus later. This method is a useful coping mechanism.

---

**KEY POINT**

Creating time to sit quietly and enjoy personal space to gather thoughts without interruption counteracts fatigue and pressure. Hamsters on a wheel are sensible enough to stop and get off when they are tired, and it is useful to do likewise. Putting something back into energy levels and the coping system by occasionally resting and concentrating on something completely different helps clear and refresh the mind and body.

---

## 1.9 **Ethical Standards and Integrity**

There are many legal rules, codes and guidelines that affect the work of a criminal investigator. There have been a number of high-profile cases of serious corruption and miscarriages of justice that placed questions of police ethics and integrity in the spotlight. Such high-profile cases have the potential to damage the reputation of the police, as do less serious, but more common, breakdowns in integrity that may impact negatively on service delivery and public perceptions. Ethical principles must prevail over any practices, preferences or other immoral external or internal cultures.

Fabricating information or evidence, conveniently ignoring material facts and evidence that don't fit with a convenient theory or showing preferential treatment towards particular persons for self-interest, personal convenience, profit or other extraneous motivation must never creep into an investigation or prosecution.

Public trust and confidence in investigations depend on honesty, transparency and integrity. Statutory regulations such as the Human Rights Act 1998, the Police and Criminal Evidence Act 1984 (PACE) and its Code of Practice, the code for victims, and bodies such as the Independent Police Complaints Commission (IPCC) have provided the public with ways of challenging police activities and actions. The media, through investigative journalism, make efforts to expose devious and unethical methods, and sometimes have their own creative ways of investigating public bodies. The TV documentary in 2003 entitled 'Secret Policeman' featured a BBC undercover journalist named Mark Daly, who infiltrated the police as a recruit to expose and covertly record racist behaviour. The Freedom of Information Act 2000 (FOI) and Criminal Procedure and Investigations Act 1996 (CPIA) also provide opportunities for a lot of hitherto protected material to be released upon request that may also reveal unprofessional and unethical processes.

Concepts known as 'tunnel vision' or 'closed mind syndrome' are unethical and must be avoided. Investigators should not focus on any individual (or individuals) or a particular line of enquiry at the exclusion of others without good reason. Any narrow-minded approach does not bode well for the integrity of the investigation and will always provide complications in the long term.

### KEY POINT—THE YORKSHIRE RIPPER

In the West Yorkshire Police 'Ripper' enquiry the SIO became fixated on letters and recorded messages from a person claiming to be the killer ('Wearside Jack'). Placing too much reliance on this individual led the team on a wild goose chase. Meanwhile, the real killer, Peter Sutcliffe, continued to murder more female victims. In March 2006, some 28 years after he had penned his first letter, hoaxer John Humble was convicted of perverting the course of justice and sentenced to eight years in prison.

Creativity and innovation from entrepreneurial detectives are one thing; deception of any kind that breaches the law is entirely another. This is to be distinguished from finding legal solutions to legal problems, which is a core skill of any good investigator.

## Checklist—role of a criminal investigator

- Modern day detectives are expected to possess a wide range of knowledge, not just of legislative powers and statutory offences
- The emphasis is on a 'search for the truth' not 'search for the proof'
- Apply the investigative mindset and sceptically question and scrutinise
- Be confident, positive and optimistic
- Planning and preparation are highly advisable (AYR)
- There is a wide range of support, specialists and experts available
- Don't step outside the boundaries of your own training and expertise
- Plan to avoid, identify and effectively manage the symptoms of stress
- Be well organised and efficient at getting the most out of valuable time
- Emotional intelligence helps survive a high pressure working environment
- 'Tunnel vision' or 'closed minds' are unethical and must be avoided

## References

*Practice Advice on Core Investigative Doctrine* (2nd edn, ACPO/ NPIA, 2012)

C Soanes and A Stevenson (eds), *Oxford Dictionary of English* (2nd edn, OUP, 2008)

# Chapter 2
# Investigation Management

## 2.1 Introduction

Effective management of crime enquiries helps to achieve successful outcomes. Even if the offence under investigation is of a minor nature, good management and administration of all the necessary processes remain equally important. Making an arrest, for example, is not the end of a sequence but the continuation of responsibilities for the investigator. Such events trigger other processes necessary to meet the requirements of a thorough, methodical investigation, prosecution and case disposal process.

Investigators must strive to demonstrate to victims, supervisors, the Crown Prosecution Service (CPS) and the courts that these responsibilities have been tackled with utmost professionalism and rigour. This will go a long way towards achieving faith and confidence in the investigation and investigator.

## 2.2 Stages of a Criminal Investigation

A well-known phrase states 'a chain is only as strong as its weakest link', and many stages link together sequentially to complete a criminal investigation. Crime investigators should be mindful of each element from start to finish that need approaching professionally. Individual or lead investigators often have responsibility for most of the various stages depending on what type and level of crime they are investigating. For example, the majority of volume crime investigations are managed and conducted almost entirely by the first attending officer and/or allocated crime investigator; while more serious or complex cases are led by an Investigating Officer (IO) or even Senior Investigating Officer (SIO).

The stages for most reported crimes are illustrated in Figure 2.1.

**Figure 2.1 Pyramid of investigation**

Briefly, the stages are:

1. Crime investigation instigation. Can originate from victims, via phone calls, to patrolling officers, enquiry counters or even online. Some are referred by other agencies or are 'cold cases'. Intelligence and proactive work also generates investigations. Delays in reporting can be detrimental, as offenders then have more time to conceal or destroy evidence, concoct alibis, escape, disappear, gain confidence and interfere with witnesses whose memories fade over time, and trace evidence may be lost or tampered with (eg vital CCTV may be recorded over).

2. Call handling and grading. Communications room incident logs contain factual information and decisions made, which become important to the investigation. The manner in which a call is dealt with, the quality of information gathered and grading are also highly significant.

3. Resource(s) despatch. Call takers/handlers are responsible for determining and arranging the resources required and the speed of deployment. Some minor crimes are dealt with entirely by telephone or online.

4. Initial response. Includes confirmation of incident grading and initial evaluation, a period when 'golden hour' tasks and fast-track actions are needed, eg safety and welfare of victims, preserving evidence, identifying and preserving crime scenes, conducting flash searches for suspects or obtaining witness accounts.

5. Crime scene(s) management. Encompasses identification, security and preservation of crime scenes and avoidance of destruction and contamination. Various phases for managing and processing (eg searching and exhibit recovery) then commence.

6. Further investigation. Lines of enquiry need to be identified or reviewed and the consideration of investigative strategies and tactics to progress the enquiry. This includes an evaluation of (un)available evidence and any information gaps.

7. Suspect management. Includes declaring suspect status, arrest, evidential processing and charge, and meeting an important primary investigation objective.

8. Case management. Work continues (sometimes increases) after phase (7) with the preparation of the prosecution case file and liaison with the CPS.

9. Court case. Plea and possible trial/court process take place, presentation of evidence, production of exhibits, witness management, updating victims and communities.

10. Case disposal. Disposal and/or retention of exhibits and other significant and relevant material, marking up of any case papers and crime recording systems

with outcomes; archiving relevant material; ensuring victims, witnesses and stakeholders are updated.

## 2.3 **Investigative Processes**

Important management processes that apply to phases of an investigation are:

- Enquiry management
- Actions (including initial fast-track actions)
- Investigative strategies and main lines of enquiry
- Information
- Resources
- Health and safety and risk assessments
- Communication
- Exhibits

## 2.4 **Enquiry Management**

Effective management refers to how investigations are run, organised and handled. Routinely applying and maintaining a good standard of methodical administration to enquiries provides the foundations for efficiency and effectiveness across all assigned investigations.

Most crime investigations do not merit the use of a Major Incident Room (MIR) unless it is a major or serious crime, though similar processes and principles can be adopted. It is helpful to know and learn what these processes and administrative procedures are.

### 2.4.1 **Major Incident Room and HOLMES**

Serious, series and complex crimes are managed through an MIR using a computerised database and action management system known as HOLMES (Home Office Large Major Enquiry System). There are nationally recognised and pre-scribed procedures and processes to determine how such enquiry systems are managed (see *Major Incident Room Standardised Administrative Procedures Guidance Manual* or 'MIRSAP'). These are well established and have been in existence for some considerable time (since circa 1981).

An MIR is the administration centre of an investigation. It is where the enquiry is controlled and managed, allowing information to be carefully scrutinised, prioritised and 'actioned' to the benefit of the investigation. Designated and titled roles such as Receiver, Statement Reader, Action Alloca-tor, Disclosure Officer, Indexers etc are included. Most UK detectives at some stage in their careers are likely to become involved in an enquiry that is run on HOLMES. Further information can be obtained from ACPO's *Major Incident Room Standardised Administrative Procedures Guidance Manual* (ACPO/Centrex, 2005) or Cook and Tattersall's *Blackstone's Senior Investigating Officers' Handbook* (2nd edn, OUP, 2010).

A scaled-down non-computerised version (sometimes referred to as a 'paper system') can be an extremely efficient way of managing an investigation. This allows enquiry details and information to be transferred later onto a com-puterised database (ie back-record converted) if necessary (eg if a victim of an assault later dies from their injuries or the case becomes part of a complex or larger linked series). It also allows detectives to gain familiarity with these proc-esses and administration systems.

Being familiar with MIR terms and abbreviations and using them regularly is recommended good practice (see box on p 25).

## 2.5 **Actions**

Actions are described as 'any activity which, if pursued is likely to establish significant facts, preserve material, or

| | |
|---|---|
| TIE | Trace/Interview/Eliminate |
| TI | trace/interview |
| TST | take statement |
| TFS | take further statement |
| RI | re-interview |
| OBT | obtain |
| ENQ | make enquiries |
| NOMINAL | person or individual (allocated number eg N14) |
| UF | unidentified female |
| UM | unidentified male |
| UU | unidentified unknown |
| UV | unidentified vehicle |
| PDF | personal descriptive form |
| M | message |
| A | action |
| HP | high priority |
| MP | medium priority |
| LP | low priority |

lead to the resolution of the investigation' (NCPE, *Practice Advice on Core Investigative Doctrine* (ACPO, 2005), p 77). Literally the term 'action' means doing something or performing an activity and is widely used in major crime investigations.

Actions can be used as early as the initial response phase, such as 'fast track' actions, which as the name suggests have a high priority. These could include seizing a CCTV recording before it is recorded over or sealing off and protecting an area which might be deemed a crime scene.

'Actions' are a set of instructions or directions, usually on a document or computer screen, that require something to be done. They are produced and recorded in a standard format and numbered sequentially. Pre-printed versions (or forms) can be used which serve as a method of logging, allocating, prioritising, recording, checking and generally managing all enquiry tasks and enquiries.

Details on 'Actions' include a sequential number (eg A8, A13 etc), instructions on what task (action) is required (eg TST from witness N9 Collins), who it has been allocated to, time and date allocated, source/origin of the enquiry and outcome. Once completed, supervisors and/or lead investigators check the contents to decide whether the task has been completed satisfactorily or whether further enquiries are required before it is recorded as being completed.

Actions have to be monitored and regularly reviewed and can be prioritised by markings with abbreviations such as HP, MP or LP (see earlier list). A simple check can then be made on what tasks have been designated the most/least important, where an enquiry is up to, what needs to be been done or what remains outstanding. Using, marking and prioritising actions helps record decisions and manage priorities more effectively.

A list, table or matrix of actions containing each number, a brief resumé, whether allocated or unallocated and who to, and current status (ie resulted or completed) can be a useful aid.

## 2.6 **Investigative Strategies and Main Lines of Enquiry**

Investigative strategies are used to progress an investigation. They are largely generic in nature and used in the context of a list (or menu) of possible options. Headings represent grouped activities that are likely to establish facts, find and preserve evidence and progress the investigation (see the checklist in this section). Their purpose is to represent a broad heading for actions that produce tactical activities relating to each particular strategy.

Before selecting which to use, there are considerations of proportionality, necessity, relevance, feasibility, cost and resources to take account of. Some strategies are resource intensive and costly (eg covert surveillance) and would be unjustifiable for use on minor or less serious crimes. Force policies and priorities influence which are feasible.

Investigative strategies differ from main lines of enquiry (MLOE) as the latter are more specific to key facts of an investigation, eg T/I witness X who may have seen offender leaving crime scene (1). Enquiries such as tracing and interviewing a salient witness, pursuing significant information, arresting a named suspect, fast tracking certain forensic exhibits etc are other examples. Main lines of enquiry are priorities aimed at particular evidence-gathering opportunities and can be applicable at any time during the course of an investigation.

---

**KEY POINTS**

- Investigative strategies need objectives, eg Communications Data Strategy:

  Objective: establish who the victim has been in contact with, who their associates are and what useful data can be extracted using available techniques and resources to assist the investigation.

- When determining MLOE, investigators are free to use any available information and material (ie intelligence) and not just what is admissible in evidence.

---

Prioritised MLOE aimed at gathering particular types of evidence come from a relatively small list of sources namely:

- victims/witnesses
- suspects (eg admissions or implicating others)
- forensic or fingerprint evidence (including specialists)
- searches
- passive or communications data
- circumstantial evidence
- financial sources

Invariably there are changes in priorities as some become less relevant and others more so. Effective control of an investigation can be maintained by (re)producing a MLOE list which should represent the salient information and material available and be regularly reviewed and updated.

**Checklist—Core investigative strategies[1]**

- Crime scene management
- Searches (ie physical and forensic)
- Tracing victims
- Tracing witnesses
- Identifying suspects
- Conducting house–to-house (H-2-H) enquiries
- Intelligence and analytical products
- Passive data (eg CCTV, ANPR etc)
- Communications data (eg mobile phone analysis, email and social media)
- Hi tech examination (computers and media storage devices)
- Victim information ('victimology')
- Victim's family/relatives and community liaison
- Forensic and fingerprints
- Internal and external communication (eg media appeals)
- Use of TIEs (Trace, Interview and Eliminate)
- Financial investigation
- External specialists and experts (eg NCA Crime Operational Support team)
- Proactive overt and covert policing methods

## 2.7 **Information**

Reliable information is the lifeblood of any investigation. The one 'golden nugget' that solves a case and saves hours of time and effort often comes from early contact with the investigating officer/team. Therefore an effective method of receiving, capturing, collecting, recording and dealing

---

[1] Investigative strategies are covered in Chapter 7.

with information is vital. Valuable time is lost if information gets overlooked, ignored or misdirected, and willing sources of information and potential witnesses can get frustrated or discouraged from assisting or recontacting.

Internal communications and message processing systems must be capable of receiving, identifying and notifying the lead case officer to pass on important messages or information. Investigators are advised to ensure a reliable channel of communication exists for when they are on or off duty (eg having a nominated deputy who is aware of the case and can receive information and instigate appropriate action).

HOLMES message recording forms are an instantly recognisable green, self-carbonating document (known as an MIR/6) and include all the details of the information, the originator, time and date received, and what is to be done with it. They are sequentially numbered, usually initially handwritten and given a priority marking, eg high or low priority, and are a good method of recording information as opposed to using ad hoc pieces of paper, emails or scribbled notes. It is useful to have a ready supply of these forms available and use them on a regular basis, as they are the correct prescribed national message recording method; their use will make any enquiry administration system appear far more professional and organised.

---

**KEY POINT**

A public contact number for the investigation team or officer (other than a general non-emergency police number such as '101') may be distributed while conducting enquiries, during media appeals, making H-2-H visits etc and circulated internally to colleagues and staff. Arrangements must be in place to receive calls and/or check automated or electronic message systems, emails or mailboxes, particularly during periods of absence, leave, courses etc. Investigators need to be assured that messages and information will be forwarded to them without delay. Consideration may be needed for interpretation facilities for callers who may not understand or speak English.

---

## 2.8 **Resources**

Investigators should identify what resources are required and use them to good advantage, ie manage them properly. Resources need to be proportionate to the level and type of offence under investigation, and much depends on whether they are necessary, justifiable and available, together with time and cost implications. Local policies, budgetary systems, authorisation and procurement regimes will probably influence such a decision.

---

### KEY POINT—TYPES OF RESOURCES

1. **Human**—officers, Police Community Support Officers (PCSOs) and police staff, Crime Scene Investigators (CSIs), fingerprint experts, hi-tech and Communications Data Investigator (CDI) specialists, forensic providers, specialist interviewers, witness liaison, media liaison, search teams, proactive (eg covert) assets, financial experts, community groups and outside experts and agencies (eg NCA)

2. **Financial**—local budget holders or special funding bids out of central funds, overtime, expenses and travel, forensic costs, authorisation for expert costs

3. **Physical**—office or desk space, vehicles, interview facilities, exhibit documentation and storage, computer access and printers, photocopiers, scanners

4. **Communications**—telephones, radios, hotline number and recorded message facilities, media publicity, inter/intranet access, bluetooth messaging, twitter/facebook accounts, useful contacts and conduits (eg Europol)

5. **Intelligence**—local and national intelligence systems, crime management systems, open source access, covert assets (eg surveillance and covert human intelligence source (CHIS))

6. **Specialist**—National Crime Agency (NCA) Crime Operational Support Team (COS), Serious Crime Analysis Section (SCAS), National Injuries Database, external specialists and experts, interpreters, witness intermediaries

---

Local volume crime investigation protocols may ensure certain resources are dispatched as a matter of policy. Tactical tasking and coordinating processes and systems also determine what can or cannot be deployed and are guided and influenced by local and national policing priorities and objectives, including the National Intelligence Model. Early anticipation and planning in order to make any necessary 'bids' or applications may hold the key to effective resource and asset procurement.

Extra staff, including experts and those brought in to assist, need to be briefed and directed as to what is required of them. Added considerations are any added budgetary requirements and constraints (eg overtime and expense claims), plus logistical and technical requirements, transport needs and access plus health and safety.

Good practice is to try and obtain or request any necessary resources as early as possible. This is to ensure evidence and information is quickly captured and secured. Added staffing levels can be reassessed and reduced later when initial priorities may not be as time critical. It is worth staying aware of what resources (eg specialists and useful units) are available in advance, particularly when performing 'cover rota' duties.

With competing demands, investigators must prioritise the needs of an investigation in line with available resources. Resources are always finite and operational decisions have to be balanced against (non-)availability, duly noting requests and refusals. Time management is a key skill, along with getting the most out of what is available. When staff are willing, eager and enthusiastic, success, even with few numbers, is far more likely.

## 2.8.1 Factors affecting resourcing

The type and category of crime under investigation will affect what resources are potentially available. There are some other factors to consider:

## 2 Investigation Management

- Seriousness of case (extent of victim harm or financial loss)
- Volume of work (eg number of victims, suspects and crime scenes)
- Solvability factors (eg forensic, witnesses, suspects or passive data potential)
- Complexity (organised crime, specialist area, linked crime, series crime etc)
- Levels of community and media interest, including public expectation
- Political considerations (eg status of suspect or local/national political priorities)
- Economic constraints
- Legalities
- Other events occurring at same time (competing demands)
- Organisational priorities and objectives
- (Un)convincing business case bid or request

### 2.8.2 Specialist support options

Some of the most common of these resources are:

- Forensic service providers
- Crime scene examiners
- Imaging and photography experts
- Fingerprint experts
- Specialist search teams (eg Police Search Teams (PST) and Police Search Advisors (PolSA) units)
- Criminal intelligence hubs/units
- Specialist investigative interviewers (eg achieving best evidence (ABE) trained)
- H-2-H teams
- Communications data specialists
- Hi-tech crime experts (eg specialist computer examiners)
- Financial investigators
- Trained Family Liaison Officers (FLOs)
- Covert operational support teams
- NCA Crime Operational Support (COS) Team and Serious Crime Analysis Section (SCAS)

---

**KEY POINT**

The NCA COS can be contacted via the Specialist Operations Centre on the national number **0845 000 5463**. The National Experts Database, witness intermediaries and other useful assets are also available through the same gateway.

---

## 2.9 **Health and Safety and Risk Assessments**

The Health and Safety at Work Act 1974 and Police (Health and Safety) Act 1997 state that due regard must be paid to the nature of activities and undertakings in order, so far as is reasonably practicable, to provide a safe and healthy working environment. The aim must be to prevent injuries and danger. As some areas of crime investigation are susceptible to the risk of harm, activities must be properly assessed so appropriate arrangements to manage and control any risks are in place.

Everyone involved in crime investigation must ensure risks are recognised and managed by adhering to safety principles, such as wearing protective clothing, ensuring any equipment is properly used and that adequate welfare principles are adopted. Any work activities posing significant risks to health and safety are to be identified and suitable recorded risk assessments undertaken.

There is a general requirement to conduct risk assessments under the Management of Health and Safety at Work Regulations 1999. The purpose is to identify measures necessary to comply with relevant statutory duties, and take steps to introduce control measures to manage risk. Risk assessments and control measures are generally generic, specific or dynamic:

1. Generic—produced for a variety of activities (eg executing search warrants) by identifying significant hazards that may be encountered and introducing suitable control measures aimed at reducing risks.

---

2. Specific—a systematic and detailed examination of a particular activity (eg arresting a suspect who has a police national computer (PNC) warning marker and intelligence for firearms and violence).

3. Dynamic—operational risk assessments sometimes need to change at a moment's notice and there may need to be spontaneous decisions made about health and safety for self or for others.

---

**KEY POINTS**

- Risk assessments help identify control measures and may involve a combination of all three types of risk, ie generic, specific, and dynamic.
- Control measures are introduced to lower and counterbalance the degree of risk. For example, if a requirement to enter and search a loft of a house is a 'medium risk', a specific control measure may stipulate that only officers trained in ladder safety and searching in confined spaces, with the correct protective clothing and equipment, are to be used. This would then lower the risk from 'medium' to 'low'.

---

## 2.9.1 Risk and control strategy models

Once a risk is identified a control strategy is required. Models exist to facilitate this, such as the risk assessment scoring matrix that measures probability versus impact. This uses the principle that the greatest risk is caused by a situation where the probability and impact scores are high. It follows that risks that are both low in impact and low in probability are not worthy of great concern. There are four strategies that can be adopted in relation to risks that need controlling, these are contained within the acronym **RARA**:

| | |
|---|---|
| **R** | Remove |
| **A** | Avoid |
| **R** | Reduce |
| **A** | Accept |

Changing tactics to achieve the same objectives will afford a means of removing, avoiding or reducing risks. Alternatively the risks can be deemed to be so negligible that they can be accepted.

## 2.9.2  Risk assessment scoring matrix

The matrix that follows shows how the top column (impact) can be multiplied by the left-hand column (probability) to produce a risk assessment score factor. For example, if it is 'highly probable' (5) that when going to arrest a suspect there will be strong resistance and violence used to obstruct or effect an escape, and if this occurs the impact will be very serious (4), the assessment score can be calculated as 20 (ie 5 × 4). However, the score can be reduced by introducing effective control measures, such as using a team of specially trained officers to conduct the arrest, who carry protective equipment, and staging the operation in the early hours of the morning by unannounced forced entry to the premises to add an element of surprise. In these circumstances the risk assessment score can be re-calculated, as it is now unlikely (2) that the arrest will be resisted, which produces a far more acceptable score of 8 (ie 2 × 4).[2]

| Impact<br>Probability | Catastrophic<br>(5) | Very<br>Serious (4) | Serious<br>(3) | Moderate<br>(2) | Minimal<br>(1) |
|---|---|---|---|---|---|
| Highly<br>Probable (5) | High (25) | High (20) | High (15) | Moderate<br>(10) | Low (5) |
| Probable (4) | High (20) | High (16) | High (12) | Moderate<br>(8) | Low (4) |
| Possible (3) | High (15) | High (12) | Moderate<br>(9) | Moderate<br>(6) | Low (3) |
| Unlikely (2) | Moderate<br>(10) | Moderate<br>(8) | Moderate<br>(6) | Low (4) | Low (2) |
| Very Unlikely (1) | Low (5) | Low (4) | Low (3) | Low (2) | Negligible (1) |

[2] There is further information about risk assessment and management available from the Health and Safety Executive (HSE) at <http://www.hse.gov.uk/>.

## 2.10 Communication

Communication can be separated into two types, internal and external. Internal communication refers to tactics and methods used to communicate, liaise, disseminate, brief and alert those within the police family. This might include conducting briefings and debriefings, circulating stolen property details or suspect descriptions, requesting information about sightings of vehicles, persons, suspects or victims, or writing updates or situation reports on the case under investigation.

External communication involves utilising outlets that are available within the mass media and public arena, such as television, radio the press and the internet. Also included would be poster campaigns, leaflet drops and use of social networking sites and websites, eg twitter, for distributing appeals and information.

### 2.10.1 Briefings and Debriefings

#### 2.10.1.1 Briefings

The term 'briefing' refers to when those involved in an investigation hold a structured meeting and discussion to cover all the important points in an investigation. There are other uses of this term, one of which relates to occasions when teams are 'briefed' before conducting or mounting a pre-planned operation. These types of briefing are slightly different, though no less important.

Briefings play a key role and it is extremely difficult to manage or control a team investigation without them. They are a means by which information is disseminated and shared, ideas, tactics and hypotheses are exchanged, progress is discussed, tasks are allocated, updates are provided and feedback is gained. Matters of interest and developments are discussed and pertinent issues raised. Briefings are a good tool for providing the vital communications link between colleagues, specialists, supervisors and managers.

It is important that briefings are controlled and structured. Whilst valuing contributions from those present who are adding value, individuals should not be allowed to unnecessarily dominate the session nor deviate from the main topic(s). Briefings are a means of motivating, as well as discussing the case, and provide a good opportunity for collective discussions and use of the 5WH (Who, What, Where, Why, When and How?) to identify information known and any gaps.

### 2.10.1.2 Debriefings

Debriefings are primarily used post initial response phase by assembling all those who were involved to share and gather information (also known as 'hot debriefs'). This includes analysing any proactive phase such as making arrests or conducting searches. The process involves discussing a chronological breakdown of events as they occurred, identifying who did what, where, when, why and how (5WH). They are an early opportunity to capture important information or evidence after an incident response. Everyone who was involved should be encouraged to attend and participate. Debriefings contribute to the production of urgent actions and lines of enquiry, the gathering of intelligence and identification of information gaps.

---

**KEY POINTS**

1. So-called 'hot debriefs' form a useful conduit for information in the early stages when staff need to impart knowledge or information following 'golden hour(s)' tasks.
2. At briefings and debriefings remember the important **A B C** rule (**A**ssume nothing, **B**elieve nothing, **C**heck/challenge everything). See Chapter 3.
3. Briefings and debriefings require some degree of structure and control to ensure the most is gained out of them.
4. Any notes or records taken should be retained for disclosure purposes.

---

## 2.11 **Exhibits**

This topic is covered more fully in Chapter 5 and refers to the collection, processing and management of forensic material such as biological, physical, documentary, electronic and digital material aimed at providing evidence for the investigation. The accurate and professional storage and handling of all exhibits must be maintained so integrity and total faith in related processes can be proved beyond all reasonable doubt to the satisfaction of inquisitorial examination.

### References

T Cook and A Tattersall, *Blackstone's Senior Investigating Officers' Handbook* (2nd edn, OUP, 2010)

*Major Incident Room Standardised Administrative Procedures Guidance Manual* (ACPO/Centrex, 2005)

# Chapter 3
# Investigative Decision Making

## 3.1 Introduction

Making good decisions and sound judgments are core skills and essential attributes of an investigator. Hasty and bold decisions are sometimes necessary when time is critical, whereas routine decisions are a little easier, simply because they require less effort. Tougher more complex decisions, however, demand more skill and effort (similar to tackling a complicated piece of arithmetic).

Decisions should be made methodically and justifiably for colleagues, supervisors, courts, internal/external review mechanisms and for victims of crime, their family, friends and communities. Failure to make good decisions leads not only to failed investigations but potential miscarriages of justice.

This chapter is dedicated to outlining some processes and approaches to decision making and problem solving and applying what is known as the 'investigative mindset'. The content should help demystify the complexities of good decision making and help crime investigators consider and apply a more logical approach to their thought processes. To begin with there are some fundamental principles to outline.

## 3.2 Creating 'Slow Time'

A phrase often used by experienced and senior detectives describes how they like to *slow things down* when making decisions, particularly at incidents that are frantic with activity. This involves taking control and remaining cool, calm and detached. It avoids the pitfall of allowing judgments to become clouded by making rash decisions and not thinking things through carefully. It takes nothing away from occasions when it is important to make bold decisions because of time criticality, such as arresting a suspect who is making good their escape.

## 3.3 The 'ABC' Rule

Decision making relies upon good information which must be carefully scrutinised, reviewed and assessed. It involves remaining sceptical and testing the accuracy, reliability and relevance of material relied upon. This rule is known as the 'ABC' principle (cited in *Practice Advice on Core Investigative Doctrine* (2nd edn, ACPO/NPIA, 2012), p 88).

> **A—Assume nothing**
> **B—Believe nothing**
> **C—Challenge (& check) everything**

Nothing should be taken for granted nor accepted at 'face value'. It is a mistake to assume things are what they seem. Investigators must try to seek corroboration, recheck, review and confirm facts, information and material. Applying scepticism is the best approach before placing too much reliance on information. Good investigators are confident and wise enough to remain sceptical and challenge/check through good probing questions.

**KEY POINT**

Every account should be checked for inconsistency or conflict with other material. Investigators can be misled if they have not paid

> sufficient attention to detail. Prima facie assumptions should not be made and material should never be accepted without questioning. Investigators should constantly search for corroboration.
> *Practice Advice on Core Investigative Doctrine* (2nd edn, ACPO/NPIA, 2012), p 88.

An example might be when information is received from an intelligence source that has not been properly evaluated or graded. In these circumstances it is wise to check the accuracy and provenance of the information and reliability of the source prior to making decisions based upon the information. This is where the **ABC** process applies, not making assumptions on accuracy until checks are made.

## 3.4  **The Investigative Mindset**

The ABC rule links into what is termed the 'investigative mindset' (*Practice Advice on Core Investigative Doctrine* (2nd edn, ACPO/NPIA, 2012)). This is a pragmatic mantra which effectively means keeping an open mind and remaining receptive to alternative suggestions; looking for other explanations and not becoming too focused on one or two theories or hypotheses. This is the appliance of an investigative mindset. It is aimed at allowing a more logical and methodical approach to good decision making.

---

**KEY POINT—INVESTIGATIVE MINDSET**

**The investigative mindset, can be broken down into the five following principles, these being:**
1. Understanding the source of material
2. Planning and preparation
3. Examination
4. Recording and collation
5. Evaluation

---

---

**KEY POINTS**

Good decision making comes from:
- slowing things down, taking control and being cool, calm and detached
- applying methodical thought processes
- not being indecisive when time is critical
- applying an investigative mindset

---

## 3.5 Problem Solving and the National Decision Model

Decision making involves an element of problem solving. Detective work requires a sequential and logical approach and there are some useful techniques aimed at simplifying the process. The aim is to incorporate a methodical collection and analysis of information and alternative solutions into a process that will help in the making of well-informed decisions. A less scientific approach is to jump to conclusions too quickly without proper thought and consideration. Good problem-solving skills are an important part of decision making and will produce different options, leading to a more informed, rational choice and decision.

There are different varieties of problem-solving models, though most contain a similar structure. One recommended model contains a simple step-by-step process (also cited in J Adair, *The Best of Adair on Leadership and Management'* (Thorogood, 2008)). It involves choosing a course of action or decision only after collecting sufficient information, then analysing the pros and cons of alternative solutions before making a choice.

A good problem-solving model for investigators is shown in Figure 3.1.

---

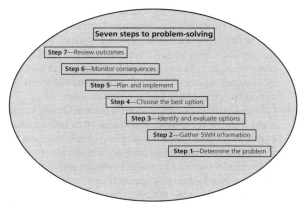

Figure 3.1  Seven steps to problem solving

An example of applying the model in a case of making an arrest is given here:

(1) Problem—X is suspected of a criminal offence and the objective is to make an arrest.
(2) 5WH information (Who? What? Where? When? Why? How?)—What is the type and nature of the offence? What is the evidence and justification for the arrest? What powers, policies and legislation apply? What is the suspect's last known address? What is known about their current whereabouts? When were they last seen? What previous convictions and warning markers are there (eg violent, uses weapons, drug abuser etc)? What existing curfews or bail conditions are in place? Who or what else (eg criminal associates, young children, elderly residents, dangerous pets, weapons or firearms) reside with them? What sort of property is it? How many entrances/exits are there? Where is the address and what other police activity has taken place there (eg searches or arrests)? Why is it believed they will be at this address? What are the known movements and times that they are likely to be present? What is the reliability of the information relied upon?

(3) Options and alternatives—Make the arrest early in the morning; conduct surveillance to confirm they are at the address; or arrest at another venue (eg place frequented); or wait until an intelligence source can place them at a location or address (eg covert human intelligence source (CHIS)); or arrange for the arrest by appointment through a legal representative.

(4) Chosen option—Decision: Arrest at current known home address in the early morning. Reason: this will increase likelihood of their presence and use an element of surprise to control risk, maximise evidence collection opportunities, ie forensic and physical evidence, and search of premises. Not to arrest by appointment, as it is believed the suspect could abscond once they learn they are being sought by the police and may also destroy evidence or interfere with witnesses. No suitable intelligence sources or surveillance resources are available.

(5) Plan and implementation—Arrest will take place (time and date) with operational report/order containing precise details of the arrest strategy, method, resources etc.

(6) Monitoring—Tactical monitoring will be dynamic (ie during the arrest phase) by lead investigator, arrest supervisor and communications/radio operator.

(7) Review—Debrief of arrest and search phase will take place at (ie time, date and location) and lead investigator will collate all relevant information and evidence, learning points, good and bad practice, what didn't work, what needs to change etc. What might be done differently next time?

---

**KEY POINT**

Crime investigators are accountable for their decisions and must be prepared to provide some rationale for what they did and why. Therefore any key decisions and their rationale should be properly recorded.

---

### 3.5.1  Evaluating options and alternatives (SWOT analysis)

The 'investigative mindset' rule applies when considering alternative solutions and options for making key decisions. The more alternatives considered, the greater the chance of selecting the best option or solution. One method of analysing the pros and cons or advantages and disadvantages of options is to examine their strengths, weaknesses, opportunities and threats (SWOT analysis); for example, looking at what threats there are (such as time, resources and cost implications) against what opportunities the option can provide, and so on.

### 3.5.2  'Do nothing', 'defer' or 'monitor' options

Sometimes a decision maker has to consider whether any action is necessary. It may, for example, be that cost outweighs gain. Therefore there may be an option to 'do nothing' (ie take no further action), 'defer' (put off until later) or 'monitor' (eg wait and see). In the arrest example given in the previous section, the suspect may be in prison or critically ill in hospital. This may provide an option to 'defer' an arrest until it becomes feasible—a decision that can be monitored and remain under review.

---

**KEY POINT**

A decision to 'do nothing' or 'defer' a decision must be justifiable. Not making a decision is a decision itself, which should be for the right reasons, properly recorded and communicated clearly where necessary to supervisors, colleagues and maybe even victims.

---

### 3.5.3  National Decision Model

The Association of Chief Police Officers (ACPO) has approved the adoption of a single National Decision Model (NDM) for the Police Service. The ACPO Ethics Portfolio and the National Risk Coordination Group developed this to provide a simple, logical and evidence-based approach to making policing decisions.

Adopting the NDM was part of a concerted drive to ensure a greater focus on delivering the mission of policing, acting in accordance with police values, enhancing the use of discretion, reducing risk aversion and supporting the appropriate allocation of limited policing resources.

Understanding the NDM will help investigators develop an appreciation of the professional judgment necessary to make effective decisions. The NDM is intended to be suitable for all decisions and can be applied to spontaneous incidents or pre-planned operations by an individual or teams of people, and to both operational and non-operational situations.

The pentagon at the centre of the NDM encompasses the Statement of Mission and Values (ACPO, July 2011) for the

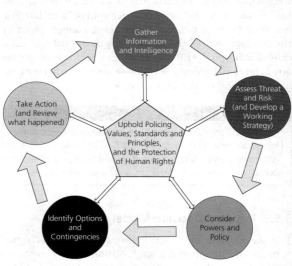

Source: *The National Decision Model* (ACPO, 2011)

Police Service: the corners of the pentagon connect to and support the five stages of the decision-making process. One step logically follows another, but the model allows for continual re-assessment of a situation and the return to former steps when necessary. The pentagon at the centre of the NDM is a reminder to keep the police mission and values at the heart of the decision-making process.

---

**Central Pentagon: VALUES: Statement of Mission and Values**

Throughout the situation, you should ask yourself:

- Is what I'm considering consistent with the Statement of Mission and Values?
  (You are wanting to ensure that decisions reflect an understanding of the police duty to act with integrity, be willing to take risks and protect the human rights of all)
- What would the Police Service expect of me in this situation?
- What would any victim(s), the affected community and the wider public expect of me in this situation?

**Stage 1: INFORMATION: Gather Information and Intelligence**

During this stage the decision maker defines the situation (ie, defines what is happening or has happened) and clarifies matters relating to any initial information and intelligence.

- What is happening?
- What do I know so far?
- What further information (or intelligence) do I want/need?

**Stage 2: ASSESSMENT: Assess Threat and Risk and Develop a Working Strategy**

This stage involves assessing the situation, including any specific threat, the risk of harm and the potential for benefits.

- Do I need to take action immediately?
- Do I need to seek more information?

---

- What could go wrong? (and what could go well?)
- How probable is the risk of harm?
- How serious would it be?
- Is that level of risk acceptable?
- Is this a situation for the police alone to deal with?
- Am I the appropriate person to deal with this?

Develop a **working strategy** to guide subsequent stages by asking yourself:

- What am I trying to achieve? (Amongst other things consider discrimination, good relations and equal opportunities)

### Stage 3: POWERS AND POLICY: Consider Policy and Powers

This stage involves considering what powers, policies and legislation might be applicable in this particular situation.

- What police powers might be required?
- Is there any national guidance covering this type of situation?
- Do any local organisational policies or guidelines apply?
- What legislation might apply?

**As long as there is a good rationale for doing so, it may be reasonable to act outside policy.**

### Stage 4: OPTIONS: Identify Options and Contingencies

This stage involves considering the different ways to make a particular decision (or resolve a situation) with the least risk of harm.

#### Options

- What options are open to me? (Consider the immediacy of any threat; the limits of information to hand; the amount of time available; available resources and support; your own knowledge, experience and skills; the impact of potential actions on the situation and the public)

If you have to account for your decision, will you be able to say it was:

- Proportionate, legitimate, necessary and ethical?
- Reasonable in the circumstances facing you at the time?

**Contingencies**
- What will I do if things do not happen as I anticipate?

**Stage 5: ACTION and REVIEW: Take Action and Review What Happened**

This stage requires decision makers to make and implement appropriate decisions. It also requires decision makers, once an incident is over, to review what happened.

**Action**
Respond:

- Implement the option you have selected;
- Does anyone else need to know what you have decided?

Record:
- If you think it appropriate, record what you did and why.

Monitor:

- What happened as a result of your decision?
- Was it what you wanted or expected to happen?

**If the incident is continuing**, go through the NDM again as necessary.

**Review**
**If the incident is over**, review your decisions, using the NDM

- What lessons can you take from how things turned out?
- What might you do differently next time?

## 3.6 The '5WH' Method

Good problem solving and decision making rely upon having sufficient accurate information and material upon which to base a decision. A decision is only a decision if there are choices, and asking the right questions is the best way to get the right answers. The more accurate the information, the greater the chance of making a correct decision. This is because more information provides a greater number of options and alternatives, resulting in 'informed decision making'. Senior Investigating Officers (SIOs) make a habit of recording all their decisions in policy files (also known as decision logs), alongside what information is known and available at the time. This is so they can explain, if necessary, why they chose a particular option and what information it was based upon.

Also known as the 6Ws or the 5W&H, the 5WH method is a highly effective tool. It will help stimulate thought processes, generate information and structure pertinent questions. It also provides a means of meeting the requirements of step (2) of the problem-solving model (as outlined earlier). The 5WH method stands for six strong, leading interrogative pronouns (which can be used in any particular order):

> WHO?
> WHAT?
> WHERE?
> WHEN?
> WHY ?
> HOW?

For example:

1. Who is the victim? (victimology)
2. What happened? (incident details)
3. Where did the incident take place? (geographical details)
4. When did it take place? (temporal detail—time and date)
5. Why did it happen? (reason and motive)
6. How did it happen? (method/modus operandi)

The primary 'Wh' prompts supplementary ones to produce a quick, simple, easy-to-apply method that can be adapted to fit most circumstances. The following table provides an example:

| Primary questions | Supplementary questions |
| --- | --- |
| Who is the victim? | Why was the victim targeted?<br>How was the victim(s) selected?<br>What type of victim was targeted (ie characteristics?)<br>Were or are they a repeat victim?<br>What risks are there of repeat victimisation?<br>What 'victimology' information is available<br>Who are their family, relatives and close friends?<br>Where is the victim?<br>What has the victim said happened?<br>How is the victim's welfare being managed?<br>What injuries have been received?<br>What did the victim do after the offence?<br>Who else has the victim spoken to since the offence?<br>What protection measures for the victim are required? |
| Where did the crime take place? | What has been done to preserve and protect the crime scene?<br>Who is at the scene?<br>Who has control of the scene?<br>What has been done to avoid contamination?<br>What is known about the location?<br>Why was the location chosen?<br>Was it a repeat location?<br>What does geographic spread suggest?<br>How was the location chosen?<br>How did offenders get to/from the crime scene?<br>What type of property has been targeted?<br>What is the link between the location, the victim and the offender?<br>What/who else is in the locality that could be linked?<br>What are the situational/economic/environmental factors?<br>How many crime scenes are there?<br>Have they been sequentially numbered?<br>What has been done at/with the crime scene(s)? |
| What searches have taken place? | What type of searches and where?<br>Who by and how?<br>What equipment or resources were used?<br>What has been found? Where is it/they now?<br>What records of searches have been made?<br>How long did the searches take?<br>What H-2-H enquiries have been made?<br>What CCTV has been recovered or is available? |

| Primary questions | Supplementary questions |
|---|---|
| When did the offence take place? | What is significant about the time and date?<br>Was this a core operating time?<br>How have the time and date been confirmed?<br>What else was taking place at the same time?<br>What peak times, days, seasons or cyclical links are there?<br>What are the frequency and intervals between offences?<br>Has there been any increase in these types of offences? |
| When was the crime discovered? | Who discovered it and how?<br>Why was the crime discovered?<br>Who was it reported to and by and how?<br>What actions did the person reporting the crime take? |
| How was the crime reported? | Who reported the crime?<br>When was the crime reported?<br>Where was the crime reported?<br>Why was the crime reported?<br>What was said by the person reporting the crime? |
| What exactly happened? | What crime has been committed?<br>What is currently known?<br>What information gaps are there?<br>What are the likely hypotheses?<br>What category of crime has taken place?<br>Who is known to carry out this type of crime?<br>What has been done to verify information?<br>What other incident(s) may be linked to the crime?<br>How many other similar crimes have there been?<br>What risks are there further offences might occur?<br>What information has been given out? |
| What has been stolen? | What is the description and value?<br>How much property has been stolen?<br>Where might it be traded or disposed of?<br>How could it be identified again?<br>What is the rarity of the item(s)?<br>What type of offender would steal it/them?<br>What does it indicate re choice of victim or location?<br>Are there any links to legitimate markets?<br>Is there a relationship with other criminality?<br>Who are the handlers/buyers of such property?<br>What quantities are being stolen elsewhere?<br>What things were not stolen and why?<br>Where was it recovered? (if applicable) |

| Primary questions | Supplementary questions |
|---|---|
| How did the crime happen? | What was the precise modus operandi (MO)? |
| | Was any weapon, tool or implement used? |
| | Was any trace or forensic evidence left behind? |
| | What transport might have been required/used? |
| | What is unique about the crime? |
| | What are associated traits and methods? |
| | What knowledge/skills were required by the offender? |
| | Have specific methods been used to evade capture? |
| Who are the witness(es) | Where are they now? |
| | What information have they provided? |
| | What has been done with them? |
| | What is their reliability, credibility or vulnerability? |
| | What current intelligence is available? |
| | Why and how did they witness the crime? |
| | What is the relationship between victim, offender and witness? |
| | Who are the witnesses' associates? |
| | What is their status (eg significant, vulnerable etc)? |
| | Who else have they spoken to about the crime? |
| | What is the relationship to victim/offender/location? |
| Who are the offender(s)? | What has been done to trace/arrest the offender(s)? |
| | What is known about the offender(s)? |
| | How many offenders were involved? |
| | What can the offender's behaviour tell us? |
| | What is the profile of the offender(s)? |
| | What is the description of offender(s)? |
| | How were/can the offenders (be) identified? |
| | Who are the key suspects? |
| | What intelligence is suggesting possible offenders? |
| | Who has previously carried out this type of offence? |
| | Who has recently been released from prison? |
| | Where is the offender(s) now? |
| What are the main lines of enquiry? | What is the outcome of any enquiries completed? |
| | Who has conducted them? |
| | Where and how have the results been recorded? |
| | What are the supporting investigative strategies? |
| | What are the likely solvability factors? |

| Primary questions | Supplementary questions |
| --- | --- |
| Why was the crime committed? | What was the motive? |
| | How committed—spontaneous or pre-planned? |
| | Was there any involvement of alcohol/drugs? |
| | Was it due to jealousy, revenge, financial gain? |
| | Was it part of a series? |
| | Was it sexually or racially motivated? |
| | Was it gang or OCG related? |
| What specialist resources are required? | What are they? |
| | What and whose authority is required? |
| | Where can they be obtained from? |
| | How can they be obtained? |
| | How much will they cost? |
| | Who will brief and manage them? |
| | What is required of them? |
| | Where and whom should they report to? |
| What forensic and fingerprint evidence is there? | What type of forensic examination is required? |
| | What type of evidence is it? |
| | How has it been preserved? |
| | What arrangements have been made to examine it? |
| | Who has been asked to examine it? |
| What exhibits are there? | What exhibits have been recovered? |
| | What has been done with the exhibits? |
| | Where are they stored? |
| | How have they been labelled and packaged? |
| | What is the strategy for examination? |
| | What needs to be fast tracked? |

The same process can be used for other purposes. For example, when reviewing information and actions taken by others, the questions can be used to obtain (or provide) a structured briefing of the circumstances. It can also be used as a template to brief and debrief others and to avoid missing vital information through disjointed delivery, as each relevant 'topic' can be covered one at a time.

## 3.6.1 Information gaps

Not all 5WH questions are answerable immediately and some may highlight missing knowledge and information. By using a table or matrix these gaps are easier to identify and log. A gap analysis can be done by organising not only what information is known, but also what is not known; an added third column can prompt suggestions as to where the missing information can be obtained. For example:

| 5WH question | What is known? | What is not known? | Where can it be obtained from? |
|---|---|---|---|
| Who is the victim? | 24-year-old male victim assaulted in the high street receiving wounds and bruising to head and body. | 1. Motive.<br>2. Victim movements prior to attack.<br>3. Has he been attacked previously?<br>4. Are any other attacks likely?<br>5. Details of victim's family and associates<br>6. Previous incidents or convictions<br>7. Identity of offender(s). | 1. Check victim's account, previous convictions, profile lifestyle and intelligence.<br>2. Re-interview victim and check witness accounts, CCTV, phone usage, timeline.<br>3. Check local hospitals, crime recording systems, family and associates.<br>4. Risk assessment and crime pattern analysis.<br>5. Victim interview and associates and intelligence records.<br>6. PNC/PND data, incident logs, local intelligence and partner agencies.<br>7. Investigation plan. |

## 3.6.2 The 'What?' question

One of the first 5WH questions is 'What happened?' It is important to retain an investigative mindset and not become overly influenced by initial contact and evaluation details (which might already have their own interpretation) or scene assessment, initial accounts, information and statements. See the section on hypotheses building at section 3.7

## 3.6.3 The 'Where?' question

The location where an offender commits a crime (ie the main crime scene) and surrounding geography can reveal information about them and their relationship to the victim. The Routine Activity Theory (RAT) developed by Lawrence Cohen and Marcus Felson (LE Cohen and M Felson, 'Social Change and Crime Rate Trends: A Routine Activity Approach' (1979) 44 *American Sociological Review*, 588–608) was based on the premise that offenders tend to commit crimes in areas they are familiar with, and in which they have had the opportunity to do so without someone or something being able to prevent them.

Examining the spatial and geographic characteristics of the surrounding crime scene environment, eg the local neighbourhood, usually provides a good 'feel' for the crime under investigation. This is the reason why personally visiting and assessing a crime scene is so important. It is recommended, however, that any visit (which may be further or supplementary to the initial visit) is made at the same time and day on which the offence occurred. This makes it more realistic and informative. For example, entering a crime scene that would have been dark at the relevant time should be done under the same conditions to gain an appreciation of what an offender, victim or witness would have experienced.

Two theoretical principles help in understanding the relevance of geography in decision making and crime investigation:

### 3.6.3.1 Rational Choice Theory

Rational Choice Theory is the theory that most offenders make a conscious decision to commit a crime by weighing up the pros and cons of what the rewards are against the chances of being caught. It means a decision to commit a crime is a rational and predictable one (see D Cornish and R Clarke, *Understanding Crime Displacement—an application of Rational Choice Theory* (cited in *Practice Advice on Analysis* (ACPO/NPIA, 2008) p 12). This is relevant because it relates to the geographic differences in opportunities for committing crime, ie some locations provide better opportunities than others, and this may be the reason why a location and victim have been chosen over others.

### 3.6.3.2 Problem Analysis Triangle

A further theoretical dimension to the importance of geographic information at crime scenes is the *Problem Analysis Triangle* (PAT). This states that for a crime to occur, an offender and suitable target must come together in a specific location without an effective deterrent (cited in *Practice Advice on Analysis* (ACPO/NPIA, 2008)). Therefore this association can be considered when making decisions as to who an offender might be in the context of their links to the victim and location.

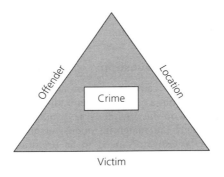

### 3.6.4 The 'When?' question

The timing (temporal) aspect of an offence is also significant. It links into important decisions around setting parameters for sightings and movements of potential suspects, elimination procedures and alibis, viewing times for passive data and CCTV, how and when proactive investigative strategies should occur (eg observations for an offender returning to commit more crimes) and ensuring resources are deployed at the most effective times and locations.

An accurate time must be established for when an offence occurred. When recording times and dates from victims and witnesses, they must be carefully checked and reviewed for accuracy. Corroboration should be sought using an accurate time source (eg via the BT speaking clock '123' service) and dates reliably confirmed. Cases can be lost by defendants being able to prove they were somewhere else when an offence is supposed to have been committed.

Prompts can prove useful for those unable to recall times and dates. Popular and reliable times of events can be used, such as TV programmes, sporting or national fixtures or events of note. These may need to be evidentially verified if timing becomes an issue later at court.

Investigators must also ensure they record their own times and dates accurately. For example, the time and date a decision was made, or when they arrived at a crime scene, or when they were told something. The possession and use of an accurate timepiece and calendar are important accessories to have readily available.

### 3.6.5 The 'Why?' question

Establishing what cause, reason or motive induced an offender to commit a crime is a useful line of enquiry as it may indicate who the offender(s) is. It may also assist in linking incidents and matching modus operandi.

However, investigators need to be mindful that if a motive is wrongly diagnosed and publicly stated it may in some cases unfairly demonise a victim and/or the community with which they are associated. For example, wrongly identifying the motive as hate crime or as a result of criminal revenge, or associating a victim with a particular activity (eg sex worker) or organised crime or gang. This could alienate investigators from important sources of information and discourage people from assisting.

### Checklist—Types of motives

- Gain (financial or otherwise)
- Revenge
- Personal cause
- Jealousy
- Criminal enterprise
- Gang-related (eg drugs, territory or power)
- Hate crime (racism, homophobia or other prejudice)
- Anger or loss of control (rejection, argument, drug or alcohol induced etc)
- Crime concealment or witness elimination purposes
- Sexual or violence gratification
- Power, control
- Thrill and excitement
- Mental illness/personality disorders (eg psychopath, narcissism, paranoid, schizoid)
- Political/religious/ritualistic causes
- Terrorism related
- To cover up or in the process of another crime (eg arson, burglary)
- Noble cause (eg mercy killing)

Motives can link into contributory causes of crime, such as drugs and alcohol. There is considerable evidence to suggest that violent offenders have often taken/consumed drugs and/or alcohol prior to committing a violent act, and this may feature as a line of defence. It is possible for victims to have taken them too, which may provide an indication as to what sort of activity they were involved in prior to a crime being committed. This can be useful information for building up an accurate picture on which to base a motive and understand the personality and habits of a victim or profile an offender. Violent offences such as a serious assault may also involve an element of victim precipitation, whereby the victim is the first to initiate violence towards the offender.

## 3.7 **Using Hypotheses**

An hypothesis, according to the *Oxford Dictionary of English* (2nd edn revised, OUP, 2005) is defined as 'a supposition or proposed explanation made on the basis of limited evidence as a starting point for further investigation'. In simple terms, this means 'playing the percentages' to come up with plausible explanations or theories about a crime which can then be graded and eliminated one by one until the most likely remains.

When posing 5WH questions (eg what happened?), the process of generating and building hypotheses is a useful investigative technique. It is also a means of populating step (3) of the problem-solving model (ie developing suggestions and options). Well-developed hypotheses are particularly useful when there isn't much information to go on, though a good hypothesis should make full use of all available information and material.

---

**KEY POINT**

Developing and applying hypotheses is a technique that establishes an explanation, theory or inference. E Adhami and DP Browne in 'Major Crime Enquiries: Improving Expert Support for Detectives' Police Research Group Special Interest Series, Paper 9 (Home Office, 1996) referred to these inferential processes as a series of 'if–then' rules (involving a sentence that begins 'If . . .' closely followed by 'then . . .').

---

Information relied upon for any hypothesis must be subject to the ABC rule. As an investigation ebbs and flows, more information becomes available and developing facts emerge; therefore all hypotheses should always remain **provisional**. This means they can be changed at any time and can and should remain under regular and dynamic review. Wherever possible it is worthwhile making a record of the information that was available at the precise time at which the hypothesis/hypotheses was/were made, which, as previously stated, is an important part in any recording process linked to decision making.

### 3.7.1 Heuristics and biases

When there is limited information about what happened, or who, when, where, why and how, experience, prior knowledge or memory are likely to be relied upon to help formulate hypotheses and apply intuitive decision making (or so-called 'gut feelings'). A problem arises, however, when this process becomes overly subjective and influenced by personal opinion and biases, rather than an objective assessment of facts.

Undoubtedly training, knowledge and experience enable bold decision making in *fast time or critical* situations that rely upon intuition, rather than deliberate slower reasoning or analysis. This allows the association of current circumstances with past examples in order to help in selecting appropriate and effective decision-making options and draw inferences that can, in some circumstances, prove very useful.

The theory of 'heuristics' refers to the use of experience-based knowledge (or 'working rules') for problem solving. As stated, this is when previous knowledge or experience is used to compare scenarios and draw similar conclusions (ie '. . . it looks like something I've dealt with or seen before so that is what it is'). However, this is not always totally reliable, as judgments can and do become unduly influenced by personal bias, such as perceptions of people, situations, locations or stereotypes. There may also be a lack of information or incorrect recall of the knowledge or experience being relied upon.

This may have an adverse impact on other important lines of enquiry if a preferred hypothesis based solely upon intuition is preferred at the expense of others. It may mean that decisions, evidence gathering and the selection of material are only geared towards supporting the chosen theory, rather than exploring other possible hypotheses. If the theory is thought to be correct, then investigators are more likely to believe unsound arguments that support it. This is known as 'verification' or 'confirmation bias'.

Wherever possible, the best option is to adopt a methodical and logical decision-making approach, as outlined in this chapter, together with an 'investigative mindset' that will help eliminate bias inherent in more intuitive approaches to decision making.

## 3.7.2 Rule of Occam's Razor

William of Occam (also spelt Ockham) was a fourteenth-century medieval logician, philosopher and Franciscan friar. Ockham was the village in the English county of Surrey where he was born. The rule of Occam's Razor, (sometimes expressed in Latin as *lex parsimoniae*, meaning the law of parsimony economy or succinctness) is a principle recommending that, from among competing hypotheses, the theory that makes the fewest complex assumptions is usually the correct one. In other words, when there are multiple competing theories, the simplest explanation is usually the most plausible.

Considering the majority of crime investigations are characterised by missing or ambiguous information, decision making can be quite complex, which can encourage complicated theories and hypotheses. Investigators can get easily drawn into developing *overly* complex theories and hypotheses, causing errors in decision making and judgment. Remembering to apply the principle of Occam's Razor should help minimise this danger.

### Checklist—Hypotheses generation

- The use of theories or hypotheses can be useful when there is limited information available
- Apply an investigative mindset and do not become overly reliant on intuition (ie keep an open mind)
- Ensure a thorough check of relevance and reliability of any material relied upon (wrong information = wrong conclusion)
- Identify what information gaps are linked to any hypothesis generated
- Hypotheses always remain provisional—keep them under constant review
- Whenever possible use colleagues and specialists (eg analyst or a Behavioural Investigative Adviser) to discuss and formulate ideas and hypotheses
- Rule of Occam's Razor—the simplest explanation is probably the right one

## 3.8 **Decision Recording**

Decision makers are accountable for their decisions and must be prepared to provide a rationale for what they do and why. In some circumstances the need to record decisions is prescribed by statute, required by organisational strategies, policies or local practices, or left to the decision maker's own discretion.

Whatever the circumstances, the police service recognises that it is impossible to record every single decision and that not all decisions need to be recorded. In most instances professional judgment should guide whether or not to record as well as the nature and extent of any explanation. The record should be proportionate to the seriousness of the situation or incident, particularly if this involves an element of risk.

Records and audit trails are necessary when noting justification for taking (or not taking) investigative decisions and actions. This safeguards valuable information and provides a record of the reasons (rationale) why certain decisions were made (or not made). In serious or complex crime investigations, this process is known as maintaining a policy file or decision log. Similar records can be kept on crime recording systems or in a day/enquiry book or note-keeping system.

There is a prescribed format for recording decisions that affect the course of an investigation. Timely and accurate records demonstrate good levels of transparency, accountability and integrity. They enable colleagues and supervisors to understand why a particular course of action was taken (or not) and enable the recalling of details and reasoning at a later stage (eg at court).

Key decisions should be recorded in a timely, permanent and legible format. In major enquiries self-carbonating books are used with sequentially numbered entries. All entries are signed and dated by the person making the decision and/or their nominee, and include details of the decision with the reason why it has been made (eg why a course of action has been taken or not taken).

Decision entries, like evidence in pocket notebooks, should ideally be recorded contemporaneously in a legible and durable format. In practice most investigators keep a 'daybook' specific to that enquiry in which to make notes, with an option to copy and transfer at a later stage details of decisions made. Entries must accurately reflect key decisions made, whether they are of a strategic or tactical nature over the course of an investigation. These include topics such as investigative actions, resource considerations and main lines of enquiry (search, forensic, suspect arrest, witness seeking etc).

Systematic recording of key decisions with supporting rationale based on information known at that time is an important skill to develop, practise and routinely use. This not only plays a key role in recording and explaining important decisions, but also serves as an aide-memoire when handing over cases to others and at times when decisions have to be accounted for. Good record keeping imposes self-discipline and aids structured and well-reasoned problem solving and decision making.

---

**KEY POINTS—DECISION RECORDING**

1. Three important elements of decision logs and entries are: (1) decision; (2) reasoning behind it; (3) information known, available and relied upon at the time the decision was made. All three should be linked together.

2. In cases where sensitive information is involved care must be taken where any related decision making is recorded. Cases that involve sensitive tactics necessitate record keeping with added confidentiality, including maintaining a separate 'sensitive policy file/decision log'.

---

Decision recording is best kept simple. The one adopted by most SIOs across the UK is known as the 'decision/reason' format and is as straightforward as it sounds. A decision is recorded in one paragraph and the reason or justification is placed directly alongside or below it in another. Two examples follow:

---

**Example 1**

*Decision: Request made for four additional staff to assist in conducting H-2-H enquiries in the immediate vicinity and line of sight and hearing of 86 Longfellow Crescent (scene of a burglary dwelling).*
*Reason: H-2-H in this vicinity is a fast track action as the scene of the burglary is overlooked by neighbours and there are insufficient resources to conduct the enquiries without undue delay.*

---

**Example 2**

*Decision: A male by the name of Ashley Simmons (date of birth 20.2.1986) has been declared a suspect for the burglary at 86 Longfellow Crescent and is to be arrested.*

---

> ***Reason:*** *His DNA and fingerprints have been found at the scene of the burglary and he has no legitimate access to the premises. Arrest is necessary to progress an effective investigation including the search of premises connected to Simmons, gather evidence and interview him under PACE.*

### KEY POINT

Part II of the Criminal Procedure and Investigations Act 1996 (CPIA) Code of Practice states:

> All investigators have a responsibility for carrying out the duties imposed on them under this code, including in particular recording information and retaining records of information and other material.

This includes keeping records of the conduct of the investigation.

## References

J Adair, *The Best of Adair on Leadership and Management* (Thorogood, 2008)

E Adhami and DP Browne, 'Major Crime Enquiries: Improving Expert Support for Detectives' Police Research Group Special Interest Series, Paper 9 (Home Office, 1996)

LE Cohen and M Felson, 'Social Change and Crime Rate Trends: A Routine Activity Approach' (1979) 44 *American Sociological Review*, 588–608

D Cornish and R Clarke, *Understanding Crime Displacement—an application of Rational Choice Theory* (cited in *Practice Advice on Analysis* (ACPO/NPIA, 2008) p 12)

*Oxford English Dictionary* (2nd edn revised, OUP, 2005)

*Practice Advice on Analysis* (ACPO/NPIA, 2008)

*Practice Advice on Core Investigative Doctrine* (2nd edn, ACPO/NPIA, 2012)

*Statement of Mission and Values* (ACPO, July 2011)

*The National Decision Model* (ACPO, July 2011)

# Chapter 4

# Initial Stages of an Investigation

## 4.1 Introduction

Key to most investigations is the early gathering and recording of accurate and detailed information, taking necessary action and securing evidence. Where possible this should begin from the first moment an initial call or report is received and continue on attendance and management of the crime scene(s).

Those connected with the initial stages must adopt the best and most professional approach. Initial assessments fed back to communications and control rooms can positively or negatively influence the way an incident is graded, categorised and dealt with in terms of seriousness, priority and resources. This period is often referred to as the 'golden hour(s)'.

This chapter contains useful checklists that serve as practical guides, aides-memoires, menus or prompts for the initial investigation and beyond. They are not exhaustive and it must be stated that over-reliance on fixed routines can sometimes be detrimental to the 'keeping an open mind' principle. Each case is unique and these are guidelines, not tramlines or tick boxes. Nevertheless it can be reassuring to have a bank of options and alternatives to refer to and stimulate thought processes and trigger investigative decisions.

For more serious crimes it is likely a senior investigator at some point assumes overall command and responsibility for directing and controlling the enquiry. However, it is the actions taken and tradecraft shown during the initial stages (ie before others become involved) that are often so critical to success. There is one point of focus in this chapter, the importance of establishing exactly what has already been done, by whom, and to what level and standard, to get things back on track if necessary. This is not possible without knowledge or an appreciation of what others have done, should have done or should be doing.

It is acknowledged some investigations are dealt with by not deploying officers and in some instances over a communications link (eg telephone or email) with no deployment at all. Others may fall outside an individual's level of responsibility or authority.

Investigators should understand the range of standard or generic responses and requirements for most types of crime, from volume and priority investigation to the more serious, such as violent assaults, sexually motivated attacks and high-risk missing persons. Knowledge, understanding and regular practice of correct processes ensure they are recollected more easily and personal learning and skills development routinely enhanced.

## 4.2 Teamwork

Crime investigation, particularly in the initial stages or 'golden hour(s)', requires dynamic *teamwork* as an essential ingredient for success. This is a combined effort between those who can use complementary skills and responsibilities to work towards a common goal. All members of the team contribute to the process of crime solving, whether it be the person who takes the initial report or the patrol officer who attends the scene. Each person and process connects in a chain that is as strong as its weakest link.

Crime investigators can make a good contribution towards creating a teamwork approach by coordinating all the work and activity. Various roles and resources in their team might include:

- Call-handler/taker/resource dispatcher
- Initial responders
- Additional resources (eg traffic officers, dog handlers, police search teams, intelligence officers, air support unit)
- Specialist resources (eg Crime Scene Investigator (CSI), forensic service providers, communications data expert etc)
- Other colleagues, crime investigators and units/departments
- Supervisors and line managers
- Internal police stakeholders (eg Neighbourhood Panels/ Community Policing Teams)
- Partner and external agencies and other interested parties (eg local authority)
- Crown Prosecution Service
- Coroner/coroner's officers/pathologists
- Victim support network
- Regional force resources

Momentum and progress needs to be consolidated and maintained to provide the foundations for a well-coordinated investigation. This requires a shared sense of purpose, positive, professional attitudes, and pooling of roles and skills.

Effective teams acknowledge that those around them have complementary skills. Effective cooperation and communication skills with the sharing of information and knowledge will help crime investigators bring it all together.

## 4.2.1 Working alongside other agencies

Emergency services and agencies often collaborate to form a team at various stages of an investigation. Working alongside the police might be paramedics, fire service, local authority, social care workers responsible for children and/ or adults, the National Crime Agency (NCA), the Independent Police Complaints Commission (IPCC), Victim Support, community workers, etc. Representatives of these agencies may have priorities other than crime investigation and their roles may complement or conflict with the needs of the investigation. In some circumstances they may also be the lead agency.

Joint working agreements (ie Service Level Agreements, multi- or interagency working) usually form part of the strategic objectives in most forces and are included in policy statements or policing plans. Protocols may stipulate matters such as primacy, roles and responsibilities, and information sharing, which need to be clearly understood to ensure an effective collaborative (team) response. There can be benefits and challenges to collaborative working, and professional territories and responsibilities need to be respected for a team to be effective.

## 4.3 **Golden Hour(s) Principle**

The 'golden hour(s)' principle comes from the medical world, where it is a basic rule in trauma cases that patients need to be managed expeditiously to avoid later complications. The same applies to the initial police response to a reported crime. There are clear benefits to a speedy and effective response, as prompt actions and decisions have far-reaching benefits, which is what the golden hour(s) principle refers to.

The golden hour(s) is a time when forensic evidence is freshest and easiest to detect (eg blood is still wet), memories are still sharp, witnesses are likely to be at their most cooperative, offenders are nervous and unguarded, with lies and alibis at their most vulnerable. This is why it is important to capitalise on all the available investigative opportunities during the golden hour(s).

The initial stage begins after the first report or contact to call management units, public enquiry desks, or via reports to officers or other staff or agencies. Correct incident categorisation and handling (be it a crime or not) will significantly help produce the best outcome. Many crimes can be quickly detected through prompt and decisive resource dispatch, locating and arresting offenders, obtaining witnesses, seizing CCTV footage, finding and preserving forensic evidence, etc.

## 4.4  **Detective Instinct**

Good awareness and instinct cannot be learnt solely from manuals, practical guides or in a classroom. They are qualities that are essential for those responding to reports of crime to ensure they notice important features or anything unusual or out of place. A savvy 'detective instinct' is and always has been something that can lead to taking quick and decisive action or finding the piece of evidence that solves the crime.

---

**KEY POINT—THE JDLR PRINCIPLE**

A simple principle to follow when responding to reported crimes and making initial enquiries is to use all the senses and instincts to identify anything that 'JUST DOESN'T LOOK RIGHT' (JDLR)—a self-explanatory principle.

---

## 4.5  **The 'Five Building Block' Principles**

The *Core Investigative Doctrine* (ACPO/Centrex, 2005) and the *Murder Investigation Manual* (ACPO/Centrex, 2006) describe the *Five Building Block Principles* which underpin the response phase and initial stages that apply to most investigations. Visually they have been made simple to remember (see the diagram that follows). Headings contained within the 'blocks' are self-explanatory and are all covered within this handbook, particularly when considering the initial actions (see the 'first responders—10 x golden hour actions' list later in this chapter).

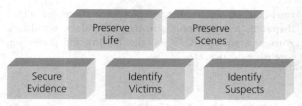

**Murder Investigation Manual** (ACPO/Centrex, 2006)

## 4.6 **Call Handling and Recording**

The 'call taker' is also a member of the investigation team who can immediately influence the initial stages of the enquiry in a positive way. Their role in obtaining, receiving and recording vital information, sometimes at the point of first delivery, is extremely important. This is when a crime or incident is likely be at its freshest, and recollections and emotions at their highest level, ie soon after they have occurred.

If a call or report is handled skilfully, important information can be obtained to launch and direct initial lines of enquiry. Depending on the circumstances, it is advisable to obtain a copy of any record or log made to review and scrutinise, so that vital information is not missed. For example, when a witness makes contact with the police, the log is likely to contain their first account of what they have seen or heard, so this record needs to be scrutinised very closely. Information contained in telephone calls and recordings sometimes gets omitted from incident logs or is not passed on, and there may be an interim recording of emergency calls made before they are switched through to the police, which is also worth obtaining and scrutinising.

Incident logs can include running commentaries about crime incidents and reveal useful information about the person(s) reporting, as well as being a contemporaneous record of the call takers actions and decisions, including resources dispatched, other agencies informed with names, contact details and times. This record is an essential source document from which to raise initial actions and begin an investigation or review enquiries initiated.

### 4.6.1 Role of call takers/call handlers

This role is now more proactive and investigative in nature. Call takers get inundated with vast numbers of routine calls and work in a high-pressure environment. By and large, they will differentiate those of a more urgent nature. Call handlers are not just a channel of communication; they are trained to offer guidance on some aspects of the investigation, such as crime scene preservation.

Call handlers are expected to adopt an investigative mindset, using open questions and the 5WH principles (Who, What, Where, When, Why and How). A call may be the only opportunity to elicit crucial information from a caller, who may also be a victim, witness or offender. Most callers have a wealth of information of benefit to the investigation and need to be asked relevant questions to extract it.

---

**KEY POINT**

The exact words spoken by a person reporting a crime or incident may prove vital to the investigation. For this reason the information given by the person making the report and any recording or logging mechanisms should be carefully checked. This includes details given to telephone exchange staff who transfer calls to the police and other emergency services.

---

## 4.7 Reports to Patrol Officers/Public Enquiry Facilities

Crimes may be reported to patrolling officers or at public enquiry desks. Similar principles that apply to call handlers will apply for extracting accurate details and information. Wherever possible witnesses should be encouraged to remain with an officer until the full extent of what they have seen, heard or know is obtained (or arrangements made for fuller interview).

If a person refuses to remain or to provide personal details (eg out of fear of intimidation or reluctance to 'get involved'), there is an option of recording information about them (eg age, height, ethnicity, accent, unusual features, clothing worn, who they are in company with, vehicles used, direction of travel etc). These details can later assist in establishing or confirming their identity and conducting follow-up enquiries.

Those reporting a crime could be involved in the crime themselves. If there are reasonable grounds to suspect their involvement, early consideration should be given to lawfully detaining them. It is not uncommon for offenders to speak to officers on cordons or to make reports at or near crime scenes, trying to look helpful, or they may return to crime scenes to observe what is taking place or offer themselves as witnesses. Sometimes they like to speak with journalists and reporters if present (eg Ian Huntley during the Soham murders investigation). This is why it is vital to record as much accurate detail as possible about and from them and for investigators to carefully debrief any officers and staff (and members of the public) who may have spoken with such persons.

## 4.8 **Initial Responders**

Not all the following procedures apply to every case, but crime investigators should fully understand and appreciate the need to check, review and confirm what necessary tasks have or have not been completed.

The important **ABC** principle applies (Assume nothing, Believe nothing, Challenge/check everything). Early mistakes and errors happen which must be identified and rectified quickly. There must be a clear audit trail of any remedial action taken to demonstrate the core values of transparency, professionalism and honesty of purpose and compliance with disclosure rules.

---

**KEY POINT**

When debriefing those involved in initial actions, it is best to encourage frankness and honesty about what has been done/not done. Mistakes cannot be rectified if they are withheld or unknown. Inevitably, some individuals may not comply with this rule, which is why it is important to **check**, **check**, and **recheck** all information provided.

---

There are different procedures for responding to different types of incidents. The five building blocks mentioned earlier contain useful headings (preserve life and scenes, secure evidence, identify witnesses and suspects) from which to produce a quick guide of ten basic golden hour actions for first attendees at more serious crime incidents.

**Checklist—First responders—10 × 'golden hour(s)' actions**

1. Victims—Search for, identify, support and attend to any victims or casualties (administer first aid where necessary, summon medical assistance if required and preserve life).
2. Conduct initial assessment—(use ABC principle) and provide a situation report using 5WH format (eg what happened? what resources are required? what officer/emergency services safety risks are there? where? who? when? why? how?).
3. Scenes—identify, secure and protect (ISP) crime scenes and any physical evidence (eg CCTV, weapons, mobile phones, clothing, blood marks, footprints, vehicles, escape routes).
4. Identify entry/exit route to scene with one point of entry and designated common approach path (CAP) and rendezvous point (RVP). Mark out and protect perimeter using barrier tape and cordons. Prevent unauthorised access and cross-contamination and commence incident scene log(s).

---

5. Identify persons reporting the crime and potential witnesses; separate and obtain first accounts. Ensure 'first descriptions' accurately recorded. Consider tactfully treating as crime scene (eg obtain outer clothing).

6. Identify suspects and consider early arrest. Identify likely escape route/direction of travel and means (eg public transport, car or on foot) and any flash (eg scent dog) searches. Check key locations and confirm identity of those found nearby. Treat suspects as crime scenes.

7. Make initial enquiries (eg house-to-house (H-2-H) type) and record all details, including who spoken to, vehicles present and anything that appears unusual at and around the scene. Include descriptions of people and clothing.

8. Intelligence. Seek and record all available and useful investigative information.

9. Victim's family/community—establish needs, concerns and expectations and keep informed.

10. Log details and times of all activities, actions taken, when, why, how, where and by whom.

Important decisions and procedures rely on the effectiveness and professionalism of first responders. They are expected to apply their knowledge and practical and investigative skills to gain maximum advantage for the investigation. Aspects that seem irrelevant in the initial stages often gain significance later. All actions and information must be recorded and, if relevant, are always potentially disclosable.

The circumstances and environment may be simple and straightforward; alternatively there could be challenges such as confrontational and difficult people to contend with in emotionally charged and volatile situations. Language and cultural barriers may present other difficulties, which may impact on responsibilities and investigative needs.

**KEY POINTS**

1. Initial responders and resource dispatchers should consider what/ where/how and when supporting resources can be put to best use, eg if suspects are making good their escape, covering possible exit routes instead of sending all resources to the scene.

2. 'Flash' or 'hasty' searches need to be systematic and methodical to swiftly identify and locate useful evidence, suspects or witnesses. Details should be recorded to assist fully managed (eg CSI and forensic) searches later.

3. Public areas and transport links such as taxi ranks, buses, tram and train stations may need to be checked for offenders or witnesses, including local hospitals in violence cases.

4. Scene preservation is important; so, too, is tracking offenders and pinpointing their direction of travel. Human scent dogs can prove useful but need to be deployed quickly.

## 4.8.1 Welfare considerations

The police and other agencies may have to deal with pressing emergencies at scenes, including spotting dangers and acting quickly. In extreme cases there may be a need to instinctively remove or avoid danger, to seize vital exhibits such as weapons or abandon or leave crime scenes because of imminent danger or the risks involved. Potential threats to members of the public and/or police officers may present no alternative.

In some inner-city areas there can be distrust of the police, bitter gang feuds, high incidence of drug/alcohol abuse, firearms usage, or hostile families and friends of victims. These added risks are the exception rather than the rule, but add complications and in some cases frustrate or impede initial investigative requirements.

The health and safety of victims, witnesses, the general public and responders is at all times of paramount importance and non-negotiable. For the avoidance of doubt, if there is a conflict of interest between public safety and an investigation, the former takes precedence.

## 4.9 **Preserving Crime Scenes**

One of the five building blocks is preserving crime scenes. This can be separated into three elements known as the 'ISP' principle:

> **I**—IDENTIFY
> **S**—SECURE
> **P**—PROTECT

All areas relating to a crime scene(s), once identified, need to be sealed and secured. A key task of initial responders is to prevent disturbance and stop unauthorised persons entering and/or disturbing and contaminating crime scenes. This includes supervisory staff, unless there is an urgent operational need. These three procedures are outlined below and more fully explained in Chapter 5.

1. **Identify.** Depending on the circumstances, there may be more than one crime scene and the initial response may only identify and deal with just one of a number. The identification of all other potential crime scenes can originate from information, observations or CCTV etc. If there is more than one scene, each should be sequentially numbered, eg Scene (S1), Scene (S2) and so on. A list of what may constitute a crime scene (such as a location, victim, escape route, vehicle(s) used, attack sites, suspects etc) is contained in Chapter 5.

2. **Secure.** There are a number of ways to secure crime scenes and much depends on the circumstances and environment. In serious or complex cases, cordons are used with high visibility tape to mark out the sterile area, and uniformed staff restricting and controlling access. Indoor scenes are generally easier to secure than outdoor locations, which need more resources to effectively keep sterile.

3. **Protect.** In addition to safety issues, officers should try to prevent any disturbance and interference from the

public, media, weather, animals etc. A common approach path (CAP) should be established for a single access and exit route, which needs to be the route least likely to have been used by the offender(s).

---

**KEY POINT**

An example of where there is more than one crime scene to iden-tify, secure and protect (ISP) is a violent or sustained attack in an apartment block. Separate scenes may be identified such as an apartment, elevator, landing, interior stairwell, lobby and/or adja-cent car park. Sufficient resources would be required to secure and protect these areas as quickly as possible to prevent contami-nation, eg from bona-fide visitors, residents or offenders.

---

Any item at a scene can be of evidential value and noth-ing should be touched or moved. If, however, something of a physical nature is in immediate danger of being lost, destroyed or contaminated, steps should be taken to protect or recover the item to preserve it. Removal should be conducted with minimum disturbance, care-fully recording the exact position and location of the exhibit. If possible it should be photographed in posi-tion (situ) first. This includes fragile material such as footprints, blood marks, footwear or tyre impressions in mud/soil which may be destroyed by the weather. Improvisation may be necessary to cover and protect items using available 'make-do' objects until the correct equipment arrives.

Once preserved and contained, nothing further need be done with a scene until a CSI arrives. Other pieces of evi-dence can be sought and collected including details such as eyewitness accounts, information offered, H-2-H and CCTV enquiries.

It is sometimes difficult to determine exact boundaries for scene cordons and preservation. If indoors, the task is much easier; outdoors, however, there are added complica-tions such as the weather, general public, vehicular traffic, terrain and location, etc. As a general rule it is preferable to make cordons as wide as possible, using natural boundaries, as they can always be reduced later. This is not possible the other way around.

### 4.9.1  Basic crime scene kits

Basic crime scene kits better equip staff to preserve evidence and minimise the chance of contamination. These should be carried by all operational personnel and as a minimum contain:

- cordon/barrier tape
- 2 × pairs of disposable overshoes
- 2 × pairs of disposable gloves
- major incident scene log forms
- exhibit bags and labels
- first-aid kit
- aide-memoire of actions

## 4.10  Emergency Responders

Ambulance crew, paramedics and fire crews attending scenes require debriefing soon afterwards as they have a habit of quickly redeploying. Often they arrive at scenes prior to police attendance, particularly if notified via their own communication systems. They create and keep their own records of attendance and involvement, including the circumstances of what they find and are told upon arrival. Sometimes they may obtain or hear accounts from victims, witnesses and even suspects. In some instances, therefore, consideration may need to be given to treating them as significant witnesses, depending on the extent of what they have seen or heard.

Emergency services personnel are not trained investigators and therefore must be carefully debriefed for relevant information. Details to obtain include how they gained entry to the scene (indoors or outdoors), where they have been and what they have touched or moved. They should be asked questions along the lines of: Who was present? What did they see? What did the victim say? What medical intervention was made and what items were left behind at the scene? (ie 5WH principles). In some circumstances they take their own photographs or recordings which could contain valuable information about who was around the scene (eg the fire service may take photographs to assist their own assessment and investigation into a fire, which could contain details of an arsonist, an associate or a significant witness). Some fire and ambulance service vehicles carry their own visual and audio recording equipment which investigators should make it a priority to obtain and examine.

---

### KEY POINTS

- Medical personnel (eg paramedics) always have primacy at scenes until victims have been attended to and treated (preservation of life is the first priority).
- Medical teams can unavoidably disturb and/or contaminate potential evidence. This should be considered when interpreting a crime scene. Using resuscitation devices such as defibrillator pads causes injuries or marks which, together with any discarded medical equipment, needs accounting for.
- Sensible judgment should apply when recovering trace evidence from 'emergency services' personnel, clothing, footwear or vehicles, eg ambulances. Local agreements usually provide guidance on what should/should not be retained or impounded for forensic examination. Usually samples can be taken without disrupting the ability of the emergency resources to continue providing a normal service. If ambulances and/or rapid response vehicles are located within a cordon, a path can be cleared for their release and tyre impressions or photographs taken prior to their release or at some later stage for elimination purposes. Normally if victims are placed within ambulances, the only items that should be considered seizing are blankets; it is not sensible to seize equipment needed for other patients, such as defibrillators. Investigators may need to discuss with the Crime Scene Manager (CSM) how best to deal with such circumstances.

---

## 4.11 **Crime Investigator Responsibilities**

Investigators should aim for early attendance at crime scenes to assist with the commencement or handover of an investigation. When dealing with certain types of enquiry or serious crime, it may be force policy to deploy a supervisor or senior detective to assume the role of Investigating Officer (IO) or Senior Investigating Officer (SIO) and take command. The initial investigator will be expected to have commenced preliminary investigations, obtained and reviewed all the pertinent information and begun a list of enquiries that have been or need to be conducted. A crime investigator is often the person initially in overall charge of the investigation.

Initial assessments should decide whether to hand over to a more senior supervisor and/or SIO. Until such time it must be clearly recognised that it is they (ie the crime investigator) who are in charge of the investigation. This sometimes occurs when a sudden death is reported with uncertainties about the circumstances (see Chapter 11) or in cases involving high-risk missing or vulnerable persons.

Appropriate administration and documentation should be used to begin a basic enquiry management system, including statement forms, personal descriptive forms, crime scene tape, exhibit management logs, forensic labels and bags, etc. These are the basis for implementing standardised administrative procedures.

The public often have different perceptions of plainclothes (non-uniform) investigators than uniformed staff. They can therefore take full advantage of rummaging around and engaging with members of the public (ie sources of information) who may otherwise be reluctant to speak or to be seen speaking with uniform police officers. Investigators should be skilled and adept at eliciting information from onlookers, 'working the crowd' or getting amongst bystanders and passers-by. Building rapport with those who may be useful as witnesses, sources of information and potential 'confidential sources', or informants (better known under the Regulation of Investigatory Powers Act 2000 (RIPA 2000) as covert human intelligence sources, or CHIS for short) is a core communication skill. Using intuition and insight like a sixth sense, gut feeling or hunch that says that something 'just doesn't look right' (JDLR principle) is another.

A comprehensive and useful checklist containing a top fifty bank of initial considerations for crime investigators is contained in the Appendix. If any of the bank of actions are completed or are in progress, a lead investigator's role is to not only confirm this but apply a 5WH-type review process. Reviewing, checking, making decisions, skilfully recording and directing indicate the necessary process of taking ownership of the investigation that has begun.

---

### KEY POINTS

- Investigators who are unable to attend a crime scene quickly need to confirm who at that time is in charge and make contact. Then begin the process of finding answers to the 5WH questions.
- Verbal instructions can get misinterpreted, so they need to be given or received as clearly as possible, then repeated back and noted.
- The process of reviewing and updating fast-track actions needs to commence quickly. High priority (HP) actions must be well founded, particularly if based upon uncorroborated information.
- Early assessments can trigger useful thoughts, eg what type or category of crime it is, what the motive might be, early investigative options, lines of enquiry, what resources may be required etc.
- Those nominated to protect crime scenes must be properly BRIEFED regarding any contamination issues, preventing unauthorised entry AND accurately recording details in scene logs. Staff must be reminded to look and appear professional and behave responsibly, ie not to look bored or disinterested.

---

### 4.11.1 Contact lists

One practical tip is to start and maintain a list and running log of important contact names and numbers rather than having to thumb through pages of notes to find details that have been written in amongst something else. A printed table attached to a clipboard or daybook is convenient and may be as simple as the one given here.

| Name | Role | Contact Number |
| --- | --- | --- |
| Julie Fletcher | Crime Scene Investigator | 07921 348762 |
| Dawn Pearson | Patrol Sergeant | 07770 723900 |
| Brendan O'Shea | Initial responder | Airwaves channel 34 |
| Jason McLintock | Initial responder/PCSO | Channel 34 |
| DC Javid Iqbal | Crime Investigator | 07834 259775 |

## 4.12 Attending Crime Scenes

Crime scenes yield lots of information and potential evidence. Hearing and reading about an incident and crime scene is not the same as being there, experiencing first hand and getting a *feel* for the environment, contours and layout of the location where the offence took place. This helps put everything into context and perspective and make sense of, for example, why a location or victim may have been chosen, eg ease of access or escape route.

Geographical (spatial) and time (temporal) detail for most crimes are always significant. Looking around a location (preferably on foot) and scanning the environment from a three dimensional (3D) perspective helps to develop knowledge about the crime and offender. It also relates to one of the primary 5WH questions, ie 'Where?'. Clues stem from probing this fundamental question and raise supplementary queries such as was it:

> Targeted victim?
> or
> Targeted location?
> or
> Opportunistic encounter?

Closely examining a scene and the surrounding location, geography and the social and demographic makeup of an area helps raise or answer 5WH questions. For example, who else may have been in the area or live nearby? What possible access and escape routes are there? Where are any buildings and places of interest? What are the distances between locations (if more than one crime scene or a series of offences) or the proximity of any key locations, events or hot spots? Where are locations where key nominals live, frequent or have been seen etc? A good map of the area helps greatly, together with someone with good local knowledge of the locality and community, and, if it is an older or historic offence, checking to see if the layout has changed (see also Chapter 3 and the *Routine Activity Theory*, *Rational Choice Theory* and the *Problem Analysis Triangle*).

## 4.13 **Victims and Witnesses**

Being a witness or victim of crime can be a distressing experience. Apart from physical trauma and injuries, there are potential emotional and psychological affects which may require support and welfare, either immediately or later. The effects of post-traumatic stress may not be initially obvious, but can occur in the most hardened of people. In the initial stages of an investigation, welfare needs have to be identified, addressed sensibly and, if necessary, some appropriate support arranged.

Help and support includes practical assistance, such as arranging new security locks, completing compensation forms or arranging counselling. In some forces this may be triggered automatically and form part of the reporting and response mechanism.

Some crimes may require more specialist kinds of support, eg sexual assault, hate crime, stalking, harassment and child abuse. Force policy may stipulate how, when, where and what support should be provided and it may be advisable to seek advice. Vulnerable or intimidated witnesses in particular require an enhanced level of support.

Some witnesses may be quite apprehensive about providing a testimony, attending court and giving evidence. In such cases support is likely to be required from one or other of the types of agencies available. Arranging support promptly (ie soon after the initial response) increases witness confidence and helps secure their cooperation.

Those who become affected through witnessing a crime, disorder or anti-social behaviour may be reluctant to engage with the police due to their perceived vulnerability. Specialist witness care and support units can be requested to offer moral and practical help. The range of available special measures may also need explaining, including how the judicial process works as part of the early witness encouragement and support process. As a general rule, the way in which people are first dealt with by the police influences their decision about assisting the investigation. First impressions always count.

## 4.13.1 Victims and Witnesses—Initial Actions

Victims and witnesses are invaluable assets who can provide evidence and fill information gaps. Steps must be taken to avoid them changing their intention to assist a police investigation or becoming discouraged by others. Witness testimony can also become contaminated and distorted if witnesses talk to or listen to others, watch or listen to news reports, or speak directly to the media. It is a golden hour(s) task to seek and obtain initial accounts while an incident is still fresh in their minds. More detailed considerations regarding witnesses are covered in Chapter 8.

### 4.13.1.1 Initial accounts

Initial accounts should be a focus of early investigative activity. It is not good practice to have different officers repeatedly asking the same witness for their account. Whereas if an officer obtains a witness account and records it, subsequent investigators can develop that information rather than asking a witness to repeat themselves all over again. To do otherwise may affect the integrity of the account provided and the entire interview and information collection process.

However, officers needn't be discouraged from seeking and obtaining *initial* accounts from victims and potential witnesses. There are guidelines in 'Achieving Best Evidence' on how and when certain categories of witnesses should be interviewed (eg visually recorded as vulnerable, intimidated or significant witnesses). This shouldn't detract from the importance of finding out what people have seen or heard, and without such information they cannot be classified. This information may be required to identify high-priority lines of enquiry, such as circulating the description of an offender or identifying a crime scene. If not obtained early, difficulty obtaining it later on may be encountered if there is a change of mind about cooperating with the police.

Initial accounts can and should be taken without prompting, editing or correction and be accurately recorded. Relevant open questions should be used to signpost a witness to the investigative areas of significance and an accurate written record of the information (including the questions that elicited it) made. The notes should be accompanied by accurate details for identifying the individuals and re-contacting them later. In certain circumstances it may be more appropriate (depending on the veracity of the evidence) to make arrangements for the witness to be hastily formally interviewed (ie visually recorded) by trained officers. Sometimes there may also be welfare implications when it is more suitable to take witnesses to a place of safety such as a police station to conduct the interview.

---

**KEY POINTS**

1. Details obtained from witnesses relayed to others must contain accurate information. These are recorded and if mistakes are made, particularly descriptions of offenders, they can undermine a prosecution case.
2. Some witnesses need lots of encouragement and support to provide evidence and their first impressions of how they are treated and dealt will have an influence on their willingness to cooperate.

---

Witnesses can also be crime scenes, particularly if they are victims or have come into contact with offenders. There may be potential for the cross-transfer of trace evidence such as fibres, DNA, fingerprints, or body fluids. Recovery may need tactful management so their cooperation is not adversely affected. Advice from a CSI about how to correctly seize any material should be obtained.

## 4.14  Arrest of Suspects

The arrest of an offender is a top priority when attending incidents, being mindful that suspects may still be present or could return. In order to reduce the risk of cross-contamination, wherever possible the arrest of a suspect should be conducted by an officer who has not been at the crime scene. However, the first officer(s) responding may be forced into taking spontaneous action. The lead investigator should take steps to reduce contamination and ensure every effort is made to reduce its possibility (eg using different custody suites or detention areas to other suspects in the same enquiry and using separate means of transportation).

Whenever there is an opportunity to be proactive and make an *early arrest* based on available information, then generally it should be made. The closer the detention to the time of the offence the more opportunity there is to prove culpability and recover evidence. Early arrest prevents offenders concocting alibis, intimidating witnesses, destroying or disposing of evidence and committing further offences. It also reassures the victim and/or the community, and limits the potential for 'taking the law into their own hands'.

---

**KEY POINTS—SUSPECTS**

1. What suspects say and how they behave during and immediately after arrest can provide compelling evidence. These details must be recorded as soon after the event as practicable and a suspect given an early opportunity to sign any notes. Not many offenders offer 'no comment' when arrested and what they do say must be noted and brought to the attention of the interviewing officers (and lead investigator).

2. Prompt action can lead to the identity and/or location of an offender. Initial police response should incorporate a search for suspects, such as the use of scent dogs. The checking of local hospitals in case offenders are injured is also worth considering.

---

### 4.14.1 Unsolicited comments

If early arrests are made, then as a general rule suspects should not be interviewed except at a police station (Police and Criminal Evidence Act 1984 (PACE) Code C 11.1). An interview is defined as the 'questioning of a person regarding his/her suspected involvement in a criminal offence'. If, however, a suspect becomes talkative and spontaneously speaks about the offence without prompting or insists on providing unsolicited comments, once the caution has been administered those comments should be carefully recorded. Voluntary comments or 'significant statements' may contain vital information or evidence about the offence under investigation. Denials also form part of the subsequent interview strategy when considered in the context of other evidence.

A *significant statement* includes anything which appears capable of being used in evidence against the suspect and in particular an admission of guilt (PACE Code C 11.4A). The term derives from Part III of the Criminal Justice and Public Order Act 1994:

> A significant statement or silence is one which appears capable of being used in evidence against the suspect in particular a direct admission of guilt or a failure or refusal to answer a question or to answer it satisfactorily which may give rise to an inference.

Suspects should be asked to sign an entry of any such statement after reading and agreeing it as an accurate and true record. Any refusal to sign should itself be recorded, together with the reasons, including any areas the suspect considers inaccurate. Significant statements should be incorporated into the subsequent interview plan to confirm and probe further during the interview under caution.

## 4.14.2 Identification of suspects by a witness

The principal methods used to identify suspects connected to a criminal investigation and the requirement to keep records are contained under PACE Code D (revised on 1 August 2004), sections 60(1)(a), 60A(1) and 66(1) Codes of Practice A–G effective from 1 January 2006.

> A record shall be made of the suspect's description as first given by a potential witness. This record must:
>
> (a) be made and kept in a form which enables details of that description to be accurately produced from it, in a legible form, which can be given to the suspect or the suspect's solicitor in accordance with this code; and

(b) unless otherwise specified be made before the witness takes part in any identification procedures under paragraphs 3.5–3.10, 3.21, or 3.23.

A copy of the record shall where practicable, be given to the suspect or their solicitor before any procedures under paragraphs 3.5–3.10, 3.21, or 3.23 are carried out.

## 4.14.3  Transporting suspects

Usually there are (force) guidelines on how to transport detainees to custody suites, but in exceptional cases they may have to travel in the rear of 'ordinary' police vehicles instead of custody vehicles. If so, this process needs managing carefully to:

(i) avoid any potential accusation of encouraging conversations about the offence during the journey (with the exceptions of unsolicited comments/significant statements and provisions for 'urgent interviews', any questions about the case should be saved for the formal interview when the suspect's rights under PACE can be assured and proper legal representation arranged);

(ii) avoid cross-contamination; and

(iii) ensure safety.

If there is more than one detainee, separate vehicles/vans should be used. Separate custody offices should also be used wherever possible to avoid cross-contamination or contact between them. A CSI/CSM may advise that covers are placed on the internal surfaces of vehicles being used to transport detainees and in custody areas to capture any forensic material that may drop off them and eliminate possible secondary transfer.

## 4.14.4  Treating suspects as crime scenes

Every suspect is a potential crime scene and source of evidence to prove or disprove their involvement in an offence. Depending on the offence, arrangements for the recovery of the suspect's clothing, footwear and other samples should be made quickly. Apart from samples such as fingerprints, DNA, and recovery of clothing and footwear, detained suspects can provide a wealth of forensic evidence and trace evidence from hair, blood, semen, paint, soil, gunshot residue, glass fragments, fibres, pollen, etc.

Sometimes it is necessary to obtain samples or seize clothing at the point of arrest rather than waiting until arrival at the custody office. Firearms discharge or explosives residue, dust and glass, for example, need to be recovered as quickly as possible, and, in some cases, the covering of exposed areas, such as the suspect's hands, upon arrest is good for maximising success. Advice should be taken on all forensic recovery issues and contamination avoidance from a CSI/CSM or forensic specialist.

Once arrested suspects can, if necessary, be medically examined by a Force Doctor/Medical Examiner (FME) for injuries, marks, bruising, tattoos or unusual features (eg for description purposes). These may help prove involvement in the offence (eg defensive scratch marks made by a victim). These should be photographed and mapped on a good drawing of the body. The doctor who performs the examination should be fully debriefed after the examination to establish what the suspect may have said to them.

### 4.14.5 Arrest contingency plans

The identity of a potential suspect may be known but their current whereabouts unknown, or an arrest for some reason cannot be immediate. If there is clear intention and investigative need to arrest the person(s) quickly, eg to protect the public or known individuals from serious harm, recover forensic evidence, prevent further offences being committed etc, details of the suspect and arrest requirement may need to be circulated.

It is often worthwhile having a pre-prepared contingency plan for if and when a suspect is arrested (including if they appear voluntarily), as this can occur when the lead investigator is unavailable or off duty. This plan needs to contain all necessary evidence, information and instructions for the arrest and detention of the suspect, for example details of the offence, what stolen property to search for, where to look, what forensic examination of the person is required, what to seize (eg vehicle, mobile phone, clothing), others they may be with who may also be implicated in the offence, details of any witness support once arrested, where all the case files and exhibits are stored (eg statements), how and when to contact the victim etc. The case officer may also wish to include their contact details and availability.

## 4.15  Initial House-to-House Enquiries

Conducting house-to-house (H-2-H) enquiries is a tactic used to identify suspects and witnesses, gather local information and intelligence, recover CCTV and provide community reassurance or crime prevention advice. In a high number of cases a victim is known to the offender, who often resides or has connections within a close proximity of the crime scene. It is entirely feasible, therefore, that a police enquirer may encounter, uncover and/or interview the offender during the course of their H-2-H visits.

This tactic can be used during the initial stages of an investigation and golden hour(s) period. It is then sometimes referred to as an 'information seek' or 'hasty' H-2-H, rather than a fully coordinated H-2-H strategy. Even if no specific parameters have been drawn up, it can still be utilised as an initial means of seeking information and identifying early lines of enquiry. Accurate records should always be kept of all places visited and persons spoken to, including negative responses.

During the initial stages, H-2-H enquiries should concentrate on any premises located *within line of sight and/or hearing* of the primary crime scene, or within any other known locations of interest, such as escape routes, or at any linked scenes, eg abandoned vehicles.[1]

## 4.16 **Operational Debriefings**

Debriefings are conducted to capture information regarding initial actions taken and information obtained by those involved in the initial response. The objective is to identify what action has been taken, by whom, its result or progress, and to capture all possible evidence and information that may assist the investigation. This could include, for example, details of potential witnesses, useful observations or comments from bystanders, information and opinions regarding possible suspects, suspicious circumstances that may be linked, any persons or vehicles of interest, and any possible intelligence.

A debriefing is a meeting aimed at clarifying the chronology of events and actions as they occurred, the people who did them, outcomes and learning points. Generally they should be conducted as soon after the event as possible when recollections are strongest and the enquiry is in progress. Debriefings contribute to identifying urgent actions and potential lines of enquiry, and in developing useful intelligence. So-called 'hot debriefs' form a major source of information to investigators.

Relevant documents, statements and exhibits should be handed over to the lead investigator at this meeting together with material gathered and recorded for the purposes of disclosure rules (Criminal Procedure and Investigations Act 1996 (CPIA)).[2]

---

[1] H-2-H enquiries are explained more fully in Chapter 6.
[2] Debriefings are also mentioned in Chapter 2, section 2.11.

---

**KEY POINT—RETENTION OF MATERIAL (CPIA)**

Section 5.1 of the CPIA Codes of Practice states:

> An investigator must retain material obtained in a criminal investigation which may be relevant to the investigation. This includes not only material coming into the possession of the investigator . . . but also material generated by him/her (such as interview records).

Section 2.1 of the same Codes of Practice provides a definition of 'relevant material':

> Material may be relevant to an investigation if it appears to an investigator, or to the officer in charge of an investigation, or to the disclosure officer, that it has some bearing on any offence under investigation or any person being investigated, or on the surrounding circumstances of the case, unless it is incapable of having any impact on the case.

## 4.17 **Major and Critical Incidents**

A crime may form part of a large incident or contain elements that put it into either one or both of two categories known as 'critical' or 'major' incidents. This terminology is widely used in the UK, not only by the police but also by other emergency services and some public bodies. Although it would be very unusual for anyone other than a person of senior rank to make a decision to declare a major or critical incident, crime investigators should be familiar with the terms and what impact they may have on an enquiry.

The basic principle is geared towards getting the response right at every level in order to prevent incidents escalating into critical incidents, or deteriorating if already identified as such. There is likely to be a force policy in existence explaining what is required should the need arise. Developing a proactive approach to victim support and community engagement following the discovery of certain types of crime will usually increase the public's trust and confidence in the police.

### 4.17.1 Major incidents

Early diagnosis of this category of incident will help to facilitate the deployment of sufficient resources. Typically, this category relates to major disasters, mass casualties or fatalities and matters of very large proportions. A 'major incident' may be declared by any of the emergency services that consider the criteria to have been satisfied. There will often be large-scale and combined resources mobilised, either deployed or on a standby basis.

Once a 'major incident' has been declared, all those initially responding should in principle apply the same emergency procedures. This means, in theory at least, that there is a consistent approach to the initial response not just from all the emergency services, eg fire and ambulance services, but any other relevant units and resources that become involved. It also means scene management and procedures are compatible, thus ensuring there is a clear approach to any incident so categorised.

The initial period of a major incident may be frantic, but in practice the police and other emergency services should quickly meet to discuss immediate priorities and implement an appropriate management or command structure as required for the incident. It is vitally important that crime investigators (moreover an appointed SIO/IO if the crime is of a serious nature) are involved in these meetings, discussions and decision-making processes to ensure the needs of the investigation are always considered, ensuring all evidence recovery opportunities remain of utmost importance.

**KEY POINT—DEFINITION OF 'MAJOR INCIDENT'**

The ACPO definition is:

Any emergency that requires the implementation of special arrangements by one or all of the emergency services and including local authorities, for any large-scale incident involving a large number of people and/or casualties, enquiries (media), resources.

## 4.17.2  Critical incidents

This term is used to describe any incident where police action may impact upon the confidence of victims, their relatives or the wider community. There are very few serious crimes, eg murder, that do not fall within the category of a 'critical incident'. Early recognition and declaration as such ensures that correct command and control procedures are quickly put into place. The term 'critical' may apply to a local area and/or the whole of a force or forces.

A key element of critical incident management is to give senior police management early notification of incidents that have escalated or have the potential to escalate into critical incidents. Good situational awareness should take into account the general feelings of vulnerability and insecurity and also the economic, political and social factors which impact on the community. Most forces have procedures to monitor and assess this, such as community impact assessments and the collection and analysis of community intelligence.

The decision to declare a critical incident can occur at any time during the various phases of an investigation. Identification may be as soon as the first telephone contact received by a call taker. It may also apply and be appropriate when an incident is being attended either by initial response officers or later by crime investigators. The process provides a means of focusing on all the 'critical' aspects of an incident and consequent decision making. For example, how family liaison support or community impact are to be addressed and managed effectively.

This special status has to be continuously monitored and it may be that as an investigation develops and more information becomes available, the decision to deem the incident 'critical' is reviewed. An example is when community confidence in the police response or the incident itself drops and becomes critical as the investigation develops. As a general rule, the case circumstances can become a 'critical incident' at any time, eg in the present, future or even past tense.

---

**KEY POINT—DEFINITION OF 'CRITICAL INCIDENT'**

The ACPO definition is:

> Any incident where the effectiveness of the police response is likely to have a significant impact on the confidence of the victim, their family, and/or the community.

---

## 4.18 Crimes involving Firearms

Crimes involving the use of firearms present different problems and challenges when, say, attending and dealing with crime scenes and the initial response.

It is likely that there is force policy, including a response plan, on how to deal with such incidents when they occur. Generally with any incident involving the criminal use of firearms, only trained and authorised armed officers in protected vehicles should initially attend the scene. This is potentially the time when the public, the police and other emergency services are at greatest risk. First officers attending must make an immediate assessment of the situation from the information to hand.

Officers who attend should apply basic firearm tactics, known as the Six Cs:

| | |
|---|---|
| **1. Confirm** | as far as possible the location of the suspect and that firearms are involved *without unnecessarily exposing oneself to danger*. |
| **2. Cover** | to be taken, if possible, behind substantial material. Brick walls are usually sufficient. Motor vehicle bodies or wooden fences *do not stop bullets*. |
| **3. Contact** | supervisors and convince them of the serious nature of the risk and call for suitable back-up. |
| **4. Civilians** | to be directed to a place of safety. |
| **5. Colleagues** | to be prevented from coming into possible danger areas. |
| **6. Contain** | the situation as far as practicable. Try to maintain observations on the suspect with an *emphasis on safety*. (See also *Manual of Guidance on Police Use of Firearms* (ACPO, 2006) and *Emergency Procedures Manual* (ACPO, 2002)). |

The operational response to a firearms incident may initially be one of neutralising the scene and ensuring it is safe to deploy other resources, including ambulance personnel. This may not necessarily aid the successful securing of a crime scene for evidential potential, but may be essential for safety reasons. It may still be possible to establish a rendezvous and forward control point, provided they are not so close as to be in danger from gunfire. Routes to and from the RVP must also be declared 'safe'.

The forensic recovery of firearms and ammunition, and the examination of scenes where firearms have been used, pose different requirements and procedures. The important points to stress for the initial considerations have already been covered in this section in terms of scene and exhibit preservation prior to a full and detailed examination and search, which are further discussed in Chapter 10.

## References

*Core Investigative Doctrine* (ACPO/Centrex, 2005)
*Emergency Procedures Manual* (ACPO, 2002)
*Manual of Guidance on Police Use of Firearms* (ACPO, 2006)
*Murder Investigation Manual* (ACPO/Centrex, 2006)

# Chapter 5

# Crime Scenes, Searches and Exhibits

## 5.1 **Introduction**

A crime scene is a key part of an investigation and the responsibility of the investigating officer in charge. Activity or actions undertaken with others at crime scenes influence the amount and quality of evidential material gathered. It is of paramount importance that crime investigators have a sound understanding of the roles, responsibilities and processes required.

Most material gathered generally involves some form of search, recovery and examination, but the resources applied to these processes will be dependent upon the nature of the incident and the policies and arrangements within a police force.

At crime scenes, investigators need to take charge, request and manage the resources required and available. At more serious and complex offences, a Senior Investigating Officer (SIO) takes overall command and control of the investigation, including crime scene decision making. However, a less senior crime investigator may have initial control in the early stages.

There is great potential for all sorts of information to be gathered from crime scenes, not just forensic material, and they are useful for:

- the identification of victims, suspects and witnesses;
- background information on victims, suspects and witnesses;
- evidential or intelligence material;

- establishing modus operandi;
- linking people to and from scenes;
- linking objects to and from scenes;
- corroboration of victim/witness/suspect accounts;
- linkage to other offences as part of a series.

## 5.2 **Locard's Principle of Exchange**

Locard's principle (Edmund Locard 1877–1966, frequently quoted French criminologist) states that 'every contact leaves a trace'. This means everyone who enters a crime scene both takes something away and leaves something behind. It is used as a method of linking scenes together and connecting a suspect to an offence.

Locard's principle is the basis on which forensic examination is based, because a transfer of materials occurs when two objects come into contact with each other. It is used in the investigation of crime to try and establish links between persons or objects. The types of material that can be transferred are infinite, but common types are:

- DNA from biological materials
- blood
- fibres
- glass
- soil
- hair
- pollen
- drugs
- paint
- firearms discharge residue

### 5.2.1 **Secondary transfer**

This refers to the process which might occur if a person who has trace evidence on them transfers it to a secondary place or person (an intermediary), for example, where a suspect has a victim's blood on their hands and physically connects with another person who transfers the blood onto something else. The location where the blood is located may be worth considering for examination and designation as a crime scene.

## 5.3 Identifying Crime Scene Types

It is relatively straightforward to identify and designate a primary location where an offence took place which could potentially yield vital material and evidence for the investigation. There may be opportunities to identify other potential crime scenes.

There are many types of crime scene and it is often the crime investigator who has the task of identifying them during an investigation. The sooner this is done the better the chances are for preserving and recovering evidence.

A location where an offence takes place is normally classified as the 'primary' crime scene, ie Scene (1), though there may be additional or 'satellite' scenes related to the incident.

---

**Checklist—Crime scene examples (eg places/people/items)**

- Location where offence took place
- Any vehicle(s) connected to the enquiry
- Location where an object may be suspected of being located
- Any victim (their body if deceased or body part)
- Place where victim last seen (eg if missing)
- Place where a victim has been deposited or moved from
- Any witness who has come into contact with a victim, offender or crime scene
- Suspects

---

- An attack site (not forming part of the 'primary' scene)
- Anywhere there is trace or physical evidence, eg footprints, fingerprints or blood
- Any articles connected to victim(s), witness(es) or offender(s)
- Premises or places connected to an offender or suspect
- Access or escape routes taken by an offender
- Place where a crime has been planned or has significant connection to the enquiry

**KEY POINT**

It is important that any crime scenes such as those contained within this checklist are identified as quickly as possible so they can be secured and preserved (ISP principle, see Chapter 4). This is to avoid contamination.

Crime scenes are always numbered sequentially, starting with the primary crime scene ie Scene (1), and continues, such as victim Scene (2), abandoned stolen vehicle Scene (3), suspect's address Scene (4) and so on. This is how they are referred to throughout the course of an investigation. It also makes it simpler to list what actions are required at each scene, eg when setting search or forensic strategies.

## 5.4 Health and Safety at Crime Scenes

It is the responsibility of all police personnel to ensure the health and safety of all persons present at crime scenes and also those who are likely to handle materials and items present.

There needs to be consideration of general hazards that are usually covered by generic operational risk assessments such as:

- slips
- trips
- falls

However, crime scenes can also contain specific hazards which require more dynamic and continuous risk assessment such as:

- biological (body) fluids or tissue
- chemicals
- toxins
- bites from insects and other animals
- dangerous and unsafe premises or terrain
- drugs, drugs paraphernalia and needles
- sharp items
- firearms, ammunition, component parts and explosives
- dangerous terrain and environments
- areas where there are dangers from water or ice
- difficult weather conditions
- hostile environments or areas
- unsafe buildings, gas, electric or other utilities

There should also be an awareness of the potential risks when items are disturbed or recovered at crime scenes, such as airborne infections. This should include the handling of exhibits, which, if potentially hazardous or dangerous, should be packaged and labelled in a manner that highlights the potential risks such as:

- 'biohazard' tape for items bearing bodily fluids
- health hazard labels for items such as powdered drug residue
- flammable labels for items such as solvent and accelerants
- sharps tubes for pointed and bladed instruments
- distinct exhibit labels indicating a firearm has been 'made safe'

There is potential for any variety of hazard to be present within any given crime scene and the following sections contain some of these, but it is by no means an exhaustive list.

## 5.4.1  **Blood-borne infections**

The risk of infection from body fluids can be high and protective clothing must be worn when handling materials contaminated with body fluids or tissue. Dried blood can be as hazardous as wet blood, and as blood dries small particles can become airborne and inhaled or ingested. Infection can cause medical and health problems from the following:

- Hepatitis B:
  - present in body fluids (blood, saliva, semen and vaginal fluid)
  - can be passed via open wounds
  - can be passed via needle stick injury
- Hepatitis C:
  - blood-borne viral infection
  - very rarely transmitted through other bodily fluids
  - transmitted when infected blood enters the bloodstream (usually through needle stick injuries)
- HIV:
  - spread through bodily fluids such as blood, semen, and vaginal fluids
  - can be spread via open wounds
  - can be passed via needle stick injury

## 5.4.2  **Wearing protective gloves**

The wearing of protective clothing assists in avoiding contamination by the mishandling of exhibits that are to be forensically examined. Protective gloves will protect both the material and the person when handling items of potential forensic value, provided there is an awareness of the need to change them when handling different/separate items. Items that carry body fluids, drugs, firearm or explosive residues due to the high transferability of such material and the sensitivity of the forensic processes may necessitate the wearing of two pairs of gloves (termed 'double gloving').

## 5.5  **Legal Powers**

Fortunately the public usually support the police at crime scenes and cooperate during any cordon exclusion area and scene examination. There are legal powers conferred under sections 8, 18 and 32 of the Police and Criminal Evidence Act 1984 (PACE) to secure premises for the purpose of a search. However, sometimes there are doubts about police powers in relation to seizing and controlling crime scenes, particularly where private property is concerned.

### 5.5.1  **Crime scenes**

*DPP v Morrison QBD*, 4.4.03; private property with public right of way—consent can be assumed in the first instance (*Telegraph*, 17.4.03; *The Times*, 21.4.03)

Confirmed that under common law police have power to erect a cordon in order to preserve the scene of a crime. The Divisional Court upheld this rule, given the importance of this function in investigating serious crime.

*Rice v Connolly* (1966) QB P414

Reaffirmed long-established principles that had not been challenged, confirming that police can take reasonable steps to keep the peace, prevent and detect crime, and bring offenders to justice. Within these principles, police can secure scenes for examination and therefore also arrest for obstructing a police officer in the execution of their duty any person who obstructed, hindered or frustrated such a process.

It follows that if any individual were to try and frustrate and obstruct the securing of a crime scene, they would commit an offence of obstructing a police officer in the execution of their duty. This would extend to any civilian police employee such as a crime scene investigator (CSI) who is regarded as an investigator for the purposes of the Criminal Procedure and Investigations Act 1996 (CPIA).

## 5.5.2 Seizing evidence

When not under the power of a magistrate's search warrant (section 8 of PACE which allows anything to be seized and retained for which the search is authorised), section 19 of PACE is relied upon for a power to seize evidential items which are **on premises**. This power extends to a constable or civilian designated an investigating officer (under section 38 of the Police Reform Act 2002, Schedule 4, Part 2, paragraph 19(a)) provided:

(a) they are on premises lawfully; and
(b) there are reasonable grounds for believing:
   (i) that the item seized is either (1) a thing which has been obtained in consequence of the commission of an offence (section 19(2)): eg stolen items or the proceeds of crime); or (2) that it is evidence in relation to an offence under investigation or any other offence (section 19(3)); and
   (ii) that it is necessary to seize it in order to prevent it being concealed, lost, damaged, altered, or destroyed (section 19(2)(b) and (3)(b)); and
(c) the item is not one for which there are reasonable grounds for believing it to be subject to legal privilege (as defined in section 10 (section 19(6)).

The term 'premises' for the purposes of this power under PACE is one that may be open to legal interpretation. However, the case of *Ghani v Jones* [1969] 3 All ER 1700 provides a ruling on the justification for taking articles where no one has been arrested or charged and is not restricted to being on 'premises'. This power should also extend to civilian investigating officers under Schedule 4 to the Police

Reform Act 2002. In summary, the ruling states there must be reasonable grounds for believing that:

(a) a serious crime has been committed;

(b) the article was either the fruit of the crime or the instrument by which it was committed or was material evidence to prove its commission;

(c) the person in possession of the article had committed the crime or was implicated in it; and

(d) the police must not keep the article or prevent its removal for any longer than is reasonably necessary to complete the investigation or preserve it for evidence; and

(e) the lawfulness of the conduct of the police must be judged at the time and not by what happens afterwards.

There may be occasions when this case ruling may be useful, for example when dealing with persons who are potential 'scenes' but not under arrest or on premises and items are required from them for examination, such as clothing, personal effects or mobile phones.

## 5.6  Role of Crime Scene Investigator, Crime Scene Manager, Exhibits Officer, Other Specialists and Experts

### 5.6.1  Crime Scene Investigator

The role title of this individual may differ from force to force and they could be known as Scenes of Crime Officer (SOCO), Crime Scene Examiner (CSE) and Volume Crime Scene Examiner (VCSE). For clarity they will be referred to as CSI.

In 1996 both the Association of Chief Police Officers (ACPO) and the Forensic Science Service recognised a key number of responsibilities for CSIs:

- Photography and videoing of crime scenes
- Location and recovery of potential physical evidence
- Location and recovery of finger and palm marks at crime scenes
- Packaging and storage of potential physical evidence
- Recording and sharing of intelligence on modus operandi
- Providing advice to investigators on scientific matters
- Preparation of statements and providing evidence at court

The main function of the CSI is to support investigators in their enquiries by the recovery and preservation of physical evidence. Additionally they should provide intelligence support regarding aspects of the crime scene, such as recurring footprints or glove marks at different scenes.

CSIs can be an invaluable asset not only in performing their core role of collecting fingerprints, forensic material and photographic evidence, but also in ensuring exhibits are correctly packaged, sealed and labelled. They should also be able to identify links between crime scenes and modus operandi.

### 5.6.2 Crime Scene Manager

The role of CSI has developed further in that on occasions they may perform the role of a Crime Scene Manager (CSM). When undertaking this role they may oversee the examination of a scene where multiple CSIs are in attendance. They will usually help prioritise and coordinate the examination strategy of a crime scene in consultation with the investigating officer.

### 5.6.3 Crime Scene Coordinator

A Crime Scene Coordinator (CSC) may be required if there are multiple crime scenes and they are needed to manage the scientific response to a serious crime on behalf of and in partnership with an SIO. They will be tasked with ensuring that sufficient trained staff are allocated and available, and to monitor all activity at crime scenes to prevent potential contamination by staff who have dealt with one scene being sent to another.

### 5.6.4 Exhibits Officer

The Exhibits Officer (EO) when appointed during an investigation has a pivotal role. They are responsible for the collation, recording, logging and safe storage of all exhibits gathered during the investigation. They take responsibility to ensure movements of all exhibits are accurately recorded, thus ensuring their continuity and integrity during the investigation.

This role should ideally be carried out by an experienced detective or investigator trained in aspects of exhibit handling, packaging, storage, documentation and, when required, the HOLMES Exhibit Management System.

The EO usually performs this role for the duration of the investigation, which may include case disposal when exhibits have to be disposed of or returned.

---

**KEY POINT**

The importance of maintaining the integrity of exhibits cannot be overstated. Even the strongest case can collapse if there is a breakdown in continuity of an exhibit, or if it has been handled inappropriately, labelled incorrectly or the packaging is damaged or has been tampered with. This is a core responsibility of an EO and/or crime investigator, if one has not been appointed separately.

---

### 5.6.5 Fingerprint Experts

Being able to identify a person from their fingerprints left at a crime scene is a fundamental requirement and process in any police investigation. Once fingerprints have been obtained from crime scenes and/or from exhibits by either

CSIs or forensic specialists, it is usual for a fingerprint bureau to undertake the comparison and identification of fingerprints through the use of their own experts. They use the national database (IDENT1) to compare marks from scenes against data held. The creation of a national database gives UK police power to identify people involved in cross-border crimes, and any prints submitted are automatically searched against unidentified marks. Fingerprint identification officers can give evidence to the courts and are deemed to be 'expert witnesses'.

### 5.6.6  Chemical Development Laboratory

The title of this support differs from force to force, dependent upon responsibilities, but they usually offer support in the chemical development of fingerprints that the CSI was unable to recover at a scene, document examination, searching of items for biological material or fibres utilising forensic light sources, the location and recovery of blood, firearm residue and controlled drugs.

### 5.6.7  Forensic scientist

The role of a forensic scientist is to examine and analyse materials submitted from crime scenes in an impartial and methodical manner for the purposes of providing potential evidence in criminal investigations. They are qualified in particular scientific disciplines, are afforded 'expert witness' status and can offer statements of opinion and interpretation of evidence. They can also offer expert support and advice for and at crime scenes.

Forensic scientists now come from a wide range of external forensic service providers. They usually analyse and examine items in a sterile laboratory, but can, in some instances, also attend crime scenes upon request. This can be a costly option and most forces have their own arrangements and processes for deploying scientists to scenes. It can be worth considering, as they may be able to offer additional specialist and expert advice and guidance that may not otherwise be available in force.

The duties of a forensic scientist can range from examining items for blood, body fluids, DNA, hair, accelerants, weapons, blood pattern analysis etc, to scientifically establishing links between materials on a suspect or item. They can help to identify and interpret a sequence of events and compare material gathered from different sources.

Some of the specialist disciplines available from a forensic service provider include:

- biology/DNA
- soil/pollen
- drugs and toxicology
- fibres
- glass
- footwear
- fire
- explosives
- firearms
- questioned documents
- crime scene attendance and interpretation

## 5.6.8 Other specialists and experts

There are many other experts and specialists, who, depending on the nature of the crime under investigation, may be able to assist at a crime scene. These include botanists and palynologists (study of plant spores and pollen), ballistics experts, entomologists (study of insects), forensic archaeologists, scene reproduction specialists etc. If there is a need for a specialism that is not usually provided by standard forensic providers, then an expert may have to be sourced externally. An important aspect is that there are added considerations to consider and extra financial implications for using their services, so it is always wise to seek advice before any external expert or specialist are asked to become involved in a case.

**KEY POINT**

The National Crime Agency (NCA) Specialist Operations Centre maintains a national 'expert advisers database'. It is always best practice to contact them for help and advice when considering employing the services of an external forensic specialist. They can be contacted on **0845 000 5463**.

## 5.7 **Crime Scene Preservation**

Actions taken at a crime scene must ensure investigators maximise any opportunities to gather material that may later prove vital to their investigation. Material gathered may later be used to identify suspects and witnesses, eliminate potential suspects and corroborate or refute allegations or versions of events as described by offenders, victims or witnesses. Not all material has to be used in court, but this does not mean it should not be collected.

**Definition—Material**

Taken from Criminal Procedure and Investigations Act 1996 Code of Practice under Part II of the Act:

Material is material of any kind, including information and objects, which is obtained in the course of a criminal investigation and which may be relevant to the investigation; Material may be relevant to the investigation if it appears to an investigator, or to the officer in charge of an investigation, or to the disclosure officer, that it has some bearing on any offence under investigation or any person being investigated, or on the surrounding circumstances of the case, unless it is incapable of having any impact on the case. Material can be used as evidence, intelligence or information or a combination of these.

It can be difficult at the outset of an investigation to identify what may become relevant and therefore investigators should err on the side of caution and recover all materials. The initial opportunity to recover these materials may also be the last. It is far better to collect something that is not important than to leave something behind that later becomes vital.

Investigators should always revert to the approach laid down in Chapter 4:

> **I—IDENTIFY**
> **S—SECURE**
> **P—PROTECT**

Crime investigators should be in close communication and liaison with the nominated CSI to ensure there is a clear understanding of what materials they are looking for, preserving and subsequently recovering to exploit evidential value.

Actions taken by responding officers can impact hugely on any subsequent forensic investigation. This is a time when destruction, contamination and transfer of material are most likely to occur. The initial attending officers have other things to consider when attending crime scenes as defined by the five buildings blocks and 'golden hour(s)' principles mentioned in Chapter 4. The first of those principles is the preservation of life, which means the responding officer's actions could be in conflict with the requirement for a forensic recovery of evidential material. However, once these tasks have been completed, the focus should return to identifying, securing and preserving (ISP) crime scenes until scientific support arrives.

Initial responding officers should always make a record of the actions they have taken at the scene, including any items they may have disturbed, and communicate this information to the CSI and the investigator. Failure to do so can lead to misinterpretation of a crime scene, causing difficulty to the enquiry. Investigators should proactively seek out and debrief the initial attending officers to obtain this information.

## 5.7.1  **Scene cordons**

Scene security cordons are a vital means of guarding crime scenes. They also protect the public, control sightseers and the media, prevent unauthorised access and interference (eg by offenders), facilitate the police and emergency services response, and preserve evidence and avoid contamination.

While it should always be a consideration to arrange scene security as quickly as possible, any action taken at a crime scene must be proportional to the matter under investigation. For example, offences of minor criminal damage would not justify road closures in order to set up cordons. Therefore the nature and seriousness of the matter under investigation must deem that cordons are justifiable and necessary before proceeding with scene security aided by cordons.

Cordon management begins with identifying the crime scene(s) and its size and parameters. In some cases the scene is patently obvious, such as a burglary at a house, but the extent of the scene may be larger than the premises and immediate vicinity, as investigators must consider access and exit routes used by offenders, victims and any witnesses. Parameters of the area to be cordoned must take account of these additional factors to enable a thorough and sterile examination.

It is helpful to obtain a good up-to-date map of the area so that cordoned off areas can be clearly marked out and used as an aid to brief the CSI and any other resources. This is also a useful piece of evidential material to prove that satisfactory arrangements were in place to eliminate any possibility of contamination.

## 5 Crime Scenes, Searches and Exhibits

Once a scene has been identified and parameters set, it needs securing before any search or forensic examination begins. This means preventing anyone other than *authorised personnel* from entering the cordoned area. This is usually achieved by the use of reflective barrier tape, signed police vehicles, police staff or the use of natural boundaries such as walls, fences, streams etc.

Indoor scenes are usually comparatively easier to secure by closing doors and placing officers at entry points—they are relatively self-contained—while outdoor scenes, particularly in rural settings, can add complications such as weather, traffic, people, elevated observation points etc. These tend to be more resource-intensive to ensure people are unable to cross cordon lines into the restricted zone.

### KEY POINTS

- The size of a cordon is important to protect and preserve evidence. A cordon that is too big can always be reduced, whereas a cordon that is too small cannot be enlarged. So as a precaution *always start big*.
- In firearm discharges, stray bullets can and do travel much further than a target or victim location. Therefore, proposed search areas for bullet heads may need to be significantly extended—a fact worth considering when setting cordon parameters.
- Cordons attract sightseers and onlookers, so those engaged in scene security duties need to be reminded what to say/not say if asked about the incident and investigation.

Only the person in charge of the investigation or CSI/CSM should permit access to a crime scene. This instruction needs clearly communicating to all those in attendance (including interfering and curious supervisors). There is little point in having a cordon in place if there are no clear rules about who can and cannot cross the barrier. Accurate records need to be kept about who goes in or out, which is dealt with in section 5.7.3.

## 5.7.2  Inner and outer cordons

In serious cases, two (and sometimes even three) cordons are required, which is standard practice at most murder or suspicious death scenes. Inner cordons are quite tight and set around the actual crime site, eg at the main attack site or where a victim was located. This is where the most thorough and painstaking forensic examinations are conducted and usually where screening such as tents and covers are erected.

Outer cordons are set within wider parameters to allow for physical searches, to protect the inner cordon and control overall access. The use of two cordons allows for greater control of the crime scene and for two types of search and recovery strategies, eg a more thorough and detailed search of the inner area and a more general search of the outer. Once these two cordons have been established, it will not be necessary for all officers and personnel to attend the inner cordon and therefore control of personnel can be maintained through rendezvous points located at the perimeter of the outer cordon.

## 5.7.3  Crime scene logs

Crime scene logs are a means of controlling and recording access to cordons. They are a record of everyone who enters and exits a crime scene, and not only prevent unauthorised access, but help preserve the integrity and sterility of a crime scene. They should be used at the earliest opportunity. Most forces have specially designed and printed books/forms for this purpose, which should be routinely carried by crime investigators in their 'grab and go' bags (see Chapter 1).

### Checklist—Crime scene logs

• Pre-printed books/forms should be used or, if necessary, neatly kept notes on blank paper or within a pocket/day notebook

- Scene logs become the exhibit of the person who starts them with all of those who subsequently take possession signing a continuity label
- Minimum details to be recorded are:
  - details of all those entering and leaving the scene
  - details of any protective clothing worn (eg over-shoes, protective gloves)
  - timings of entry and exit
  - purpose or role at the scene
  - full contact details
  - person's signature (in and out of the cordon)
  - location of scene cordons
  - weather conditions (and changes)
- Accurate content, eg spelling of names and times, is extremely important
- A separate log is required at each cordon, ie inner and outer
- Handover periods must be recorded on the log

## 5.7.4 Common approach paths

When using cordons it is necessary to designate a common approach path (CAP) to identify the best and only route in and out of a crime scene, eg for those who need to enter such as search and forensic teams. When required, a CAP should be established at the earliest opportunity and clearly marked out and used by **ALL** those going in and out of the crime scene. It should be one that is the least likely to have been used by the offender(s) or victims.

If preservation of life was a priority, the most direct route will have been used by initial responders to render first aid or check for life. Subsequent responders should also use the same route unless it is obvious the offenders have used it. All details of initial responders to an incident are required, and the CSI should be informed of the route they have used so their scene contamination and disturbance can be eliminated from that of the offenders.

---

**KEY POINTS**

- A common approach path (CAP) should be identified as the one *least likely to have been used by offenders or victims*
- It needs to be of sufficient size so that a CSI and their equipment can operate effectively
- At outdoor scenes, hard standing or compacted path areas are more suitable, as these can be searched and marked out far more easily than surfaces such as grassland

---

## 5.8 **Releasing a Crime Scene**

A crime scene should not be released until there has been sufficient time and opportunity to carry out all potential searches and examinations. This may have resourcing implications at some crime scenes and great consideration should be given to the relevant circumstances of each individual investigation.

If a scene is released too early, problems may arise if new information surfaces that requires additional considerations regarding searches and forensic examination. A primary crime scene should not be released until all initial high priority main lines of enquiry have been completed, such as suspect interviews (where the suspect has been arrested early in the enquiry) and interviews with significant witnesses. These interviews may produce new information that may need to be contextualised at the crime scene whilst it is still secure and preserved. Once a scene has been released, its sterility and integrity have been lost: so the rule to remember is *never release a scene too early.*

---

**KEY POINTS**

- Due to health and safety concerns some crime scenes may need extensive cleaning before they are released and re-opened to the public
- Always do one final check of a crime scene, preferably with a CSI, to ensure that every investigative opportunity has been considered and all potential evidence recovery has been completed

---

## 5.9 **Crime Scene Searches**

The primary objective for any crime scene search is to locate victims or suspects and to find and recover evidential material, information or items of intelligence. Planning and preparation for conducting searches is the best way to ensure success. However, in time-critical situations it may be necessary to conduct 'flash' or 'hasty' searches in the golden hour stages of fast-track actions. Looking for injured victims or escaping suspects are two clear examples.

Crime scene searches are not just limited to the recovery of forensic material such as blood, fingerprints and DNA, but also weapons, stolen property, discarded clothing or CCTV. The term 'search' can encompass different varieties and types of searches, and in order to specify which one, it must be prefixed with another word such as *'suspect'*, *'forensic'*, *'physical'*, *'premises'*, *' vehicle'* or *'missing person'*…search etc. A crime scene may require more than one type of search.

In some circumstances, one type of search may compromise another. For example, if both forensic and physical searching is required, which type of search should take precedence needs to be determined. In such circumstances, the forensic search usually takes priority, unless there are concerns around preservation of life or an immediate search for a victim or suspect is required.

Searches can be linked into other strategies, such as external communication and managing public reassurance. Conducting visible outdoor searching can provide visible reassurance to victims, families and communities, demonstrating that the police are conducting diligent enquiries. Images of these searches (eg line searches or underwater search units) are often used in the media, and care must be taken to control media access to ensure that they do not capture 'live' the recovery of any evidential finds. The potential for being photographed and recorded emphasises the importance for correct processes when recovering and handling material at a crime scene, as evidence of bad practice undermines a case.

**KEY POINTS**

1. The role of a search is to locate evidence, and the aim of a CSI or forensic specialist is to recover and examine anything found.
2. Searches benefit from meticulous planning, though 'flash' or 'hasty' searches for victims or suspects may be wholly justifiable and necessary if time critical.
3. Searches should be intelligence-led and based on facts that are available.
4. As with any investigative strategy, searches must have clear objectives (eg to locate X and Y).

## 5.9.1  Role of Police Search Advisers and Police Search Teams

Police Search Advisers (PolSAs) can be requested if the physical search is going to be complex or difficult, eg when searching large open spaces, difficult terrain, water, underground, premises, vehicles or vessels. A PolSA will:

- advise on most aspects of a search
- review any searches already conducted
- suggest parameters, methodology, techniques, search assets, health and safety aspects, logistical and technical constraints, and limitations of the search
- plan, direct, manage, implement and record the searches as required by the investigator
- advise on and obtain technical resources or specialists
- ensure that a search policy log and comprehensive records are maintained
- work in partnership with investigators to formulate strategies
- lead a Police Search Team (PST)

Investigators must ensure the PolSA is fully briefed with any relevant intelligence and information in relation to each search and is aware of the aims and objectives. Members of the search team need properly briefing on the matter under investigation, as it is not always possible to include an exhaustive list of things to look for. Investigators are more aware of the full facts and therefore able to spot items of interest, whereas search teams depend heavily on the quality of the briefing given to them. For this reason it may be useful for the lead investigator or someone with a good knowledge of the case to be present when the search takes place.

Where it is evident that a search will be protracted, complex or that a large area has to be searched, the PolSA may suggest a number of other agencies or specialists, eg blood/cadaver dogs, underwater search unit, air support unit, height access or confined space teams etc.

PolSAs and their search team are valuable assets and they shouldn't be left to work in total isolation from the lead investigator and enquiry team. They are very much part of the investigation team and where practicable should be invited to attend team briefings and given access to information and material they may need, including relevant developing intelligence about the case under investigation (see also 'Teamwork' in Chapter 4).

A PST works under the supervision of a PoLSA and comprises officers who are trained in specific search techniques used for searching for persons, vehicles, buildings, areas and routes and:

- are trained, equipped and resourced to provide an effective search response
- produce appropriate documentation relevant to the search
- provide high levels of assurance and raise the probability of achieving success
- work under the command and supervision of a PolSA
- have a heightened awareness of health and safety measures and dangerous materials

UK PSTs have established methods to search vehicles and vessels systematically, which may be considered to be over and above what would be conventionally conducted by a crime scene examiner. Vehicles and vessels contain many voids which criminals can exploit to conceal evidential

material. The search strategy would aim to move proportionality from a non-invasive search, perhaps utilising specialist detecting instruments (x-ray and police detector
dogs, like a drugs dog) to a more invasive search of voided
areas.

## 5.9.2  Premises searching

It is likely during most investigations that some form of
premises search will be required. These may or may not be a
crime scene per se, but should be treated as such until proven
otherwise. These searches may form part of crime scene
searches, general searches or part of an arrest phase or proactive strategy (eg search of a victim or suspect address).

Whatever type of premises search, the operation should
be carefully and methodically planned and executed. These
are big opportunities for an evidence harvest, and the more
thought and effort that goes into them, the more chance
there is of a successful outcome.

**Checklist—Premises searching**
- Careful planning and preparation are required
  beforehand
- Wherever possible make use of a PolSA and PST
- Consider what other specialists and resources may be
  required (eg scent dogs)
- Arrange availability and use of a CSI
- Nominate a dedicated investigator to manage each
  search
- Appoint an EO for the search
- Arrange the availability of image recording facilities
  (eg photography/video)
- Set clear objectives:
  - specific to offence/scene/offender/victim etc, includ-
    ing the potential for hidden places
  - state what is to be looked for

- o state what else to look for (eg lifestyle, association, fetishes, signs of attack site or disturbance, obvious added, new items or missing items, unknown keys)
- o what is to be seized/not seized, how, who by, why and when
- o target specific areas eg bathrooms and kitchens are used to clean away forensic evidence (search baths, sinks, washing machines, shower traps, toilet usage by offenders etc)
- o establish what other property is nearby to items seized to prove attribution (ie evidentially link items of value to a person)
- Cater for connected outbuildings, garages, sheds, gardens, roof spaces and vehicles
- Set criteria for specific recoveries:
  - o clear policy on what should/should not be seized and how (eg footwear to be checked against images of crime scene impressions)
  - o examination and recovery strategy (eg photograph item in position prior to recovery, stipulate what type of photography and whether to forensically recover for fingerprints or DNA)
- Produce a risk assessment
- Cater for dealing with persons (and animals/pets) that may be present
- Guard against cross-contamination and avoid same staff going to two different search locations

A search may allow for added tactical opportunities such as communicating with people who could be useful sources of information and/or witnesses (eg disproving alibis). Some may be innocent third parties who become unfortunately tied into and affected by a search, who, if dealt with tactfully and sensitively, could prove useful assets. Neighbours and people visiting the property at the time of the search may also be rich sources of information.

When items are recovered in areas such as bedrooms, it may be necessary to look for evidence to link a person to that room, eg evidence of their personal belongings being present. The closer these items are to the recovered item the better.

Premises searching must take cognisance of modern communications data technology that people now use and how best to find, identify and recover it. Smart phones and other devices such as wi-fi routers and games consoles, for example, are able to transmit via the internet. Data storage devices (eg flashdiscs) are becoming increasingly small and some are so very tiny (and easy to conceal) yet capable of storing vast quantities of information, photographs, contacts, recorded images etc.

Important finds, whatever their type, should be photographed before being recovered. This helps indicate exactly where they were recovered and what was around them or nearby at the time, what condition they were in etc. Photographs also allow investigators an opportunity to see exactly what an item looks like, which is more difficult once they are packaged and sent off to a laboratory.

### 5.9.3  Open area and water searches

These types of searches vary widely due to environmental factors and are more likely to be encountered in major and serious crime investigations.[1]

In a complex open area or water-based search it is essential the crime investigator, CSI and the PolSA visit the proposed search site together to consider, amongst other things:

- the extent of the area to be searched and environment involved (eg in a public park only the paths and tracks and areas in their vicinity potentially used by an offender

---

[1] More details can be found in T Cook and A Tattersall, *Blackstone's Senior Investigating Officers' Handbook* (2nd edn, OUP, 2010) Ch 5.

are searched for discarded items instead of the whole park);
- logistical and technical costs, resources and constraints;
- how the scene will be cordoned, contained and searched.

Whenever a water-based search is required, specialist advice should always be sought.

### 5.9.4 National Search Adviser

The National Search Adviser (NSA) is a resource provided by the Crime Operational Support team within the NCA. They have a remit for providing operational support to forces in relation to complex searches. This includes advice for:

- homicides, no-body murders, missing persons, abductions, and mass fatality disasters;
- locating human remains, concealed or otherwise;
- reviewing previous search activity or strategies on critical or cold cases;
- preparing and writing search strategies for SIOs and PolSAs.

The role includes acting as an independent adviser and facilitator to access specialists in relation to searches requiring geological (including geophysical, geochemical, hydrogeological, geomorphological), underwater and canine techniques. More information about the National Search Adviser can be obtained from the access number of 0845 000 5463.

---

#### Checklist—Searches general
- Plan each search methodically
- Determine power of entry or containment (PACE/warrant/common law)
- Ensure the search is intelligence-led (based on available information)

---

- Set clear objectives, eg what is to be recovered/not recovered
- Designate what areas are to be searched and by whom, how, why, when etc.
- Conduct a health and safety risk assessment (eg PPE—Personal Protective Equipment requirement)
- Plan for recovery of dangerous items (eg syringes, firearms, dangerous weapons, chemicals)
- Plan for areas and premises that need to be cleared for suspects or dangers prior to search
- Ensure there are suitable resources, equipment and experts
- Ensure and check appropriate records and documentation are completed
- Plan for how any media or visiting/watching public are to be managed
- Never lose sight of contamination and integrity issues
- Use a search as an opportunity to speak with those present for information
- Plan for vulnerable third parties who may be affected by the search
- Remain vigilant for any modern communications data devices or usage
- Have mechanism for reviewing/revising strategy in emerging information
- Remind staff to remember the JDLR principle!

## 5.10 **Exhibits Management**

### 5.10.1 **Preserving and recovery**

Whenever possible forensic exhibits should be left in position for a CSI or forensic specialist to recover or provide advice. However, if the material is at risk of being lost or damaged then steps should be taken to protect it; any steps taken must be done carefully and only when it is absolutely necessary.

## 5 Crime Scenes, Searches and Exhibits

The weather may be a factor at outside scenes, as rain, snow or wind may interfere with recoverable evidence. If it is not feasible to protect them, then any items should be immediately seized and exhibited, noting the original position. When covering items, care should be taken to ensure that any improvised cover does not come into contact with the item itself, thus adding further contamination. Items such as clothing or hats should be avoided, as there is a danger of contaminating the item with someone else's trace evidence, such as DNA.

Occasionally it may be deemed necessary to search a scene before it can be forensically examined. This should only be done after a risk assessment has been carried out that considers the benefits of a search against the risks of contamination or destruction of material.

### Checklist—Exhibit recovery

- Try to photograph items in position
- Record precisely and in detail the exact location items were located (and what was around them)
- Think contamination and always consider full forensic recovery
- Evidence that is fragile, could be easily lost or would only be available temporarily should be recovered first
- Fragile or sensitive exhibits should be stored and transported to prevent damage or degradation
- Exhibits should be placed in appropriate containers/bags and packaged/labelled correctly
- All those who handle an exhibit must sign the label
- Only one item per package/container
- Search documentation and witness statements must be completed
- ALWAYS ensure chain of continuity and custody of each item is adhered to

## 5.10.2 **Continuity and integrity**

An exhibit is a physical item that is recovered during the investigation of a crime. The process of demonstrating the continuity and integrity of the item begins the moment it is identified. Two key principles **MUST** be applied when dealing with items that are seized as potential evidence:

- continuity
- integrity

These principles are adhered to in order to prove there has been no mishandling or contamination of an evidential item, and to ensure no damage, loss or degradation of potential evidence occurs. The microscopic nature of some forensic material means it is easily transferrable and open to cross-transfer and contamination.

| KEY POINT—MEANING OF TERMS | |
|---|---|
| **Continuity:** | Continuous, complete and accurate record of all movements of evidential material from identification at a crime scene, recovery, transportation, examination, storage and any other investigative processes |
| **Integrity**: | Handling, packaging, and storage of evidential material that can demonstrate beyond all doubt there has been no interference, contamination, cross-transfer, tampering, destruction, or loss that could have occurred either intentionally or unintentionally |
| **Contamination**: | When something is added to an evidential sample from another, either accidentally or intentionally |
| **Cross-transfer**: | Process in which material from a location, person or item is transferred to another (eg when an officer who has been to a crime scene arrests a suspect and transfers material from the scene onto the suspect) |

### 5.10.3 Recovery and storage of exhibits

Recovered items need storing in a way that maximises the opportunity for the recovery of forensic evidence. It is always wise to seek advice about the correct packaging and storage of forensic exhibits to ensure that potential mistakes are eliminated. When storing materials that may be returned to their owners, they should be stored so they can be returned in the same condition as when they were seized. Extra consideration should be given when dealing with the return of contaminated items (eg bloodstained) to avoid health hazards or distress to the victims or others.

### 5.10.4 Exhibit labels

Exhibit labels must be attached to all exhibits and contain important information about how they have been handled. The labels contain standard fields that need to be completed. Details entered onto the labels need to be accurately recorded to avoid giving legal defence teams an opportunity to question the professionalism of the processes adopted during the handling and management of the item. Where there is a key exhibit in a court case, there could be attacks on the integrity of the exhibit or reliability of the police processes. Details included are:

- description of item:
  - key identifying features (note: avoid stating measurements or assertions such as a stain is 'blood'—use phrase such as 'apparent blood' or 'presumed blood')
- time and date:
  - precise time and date the exhibit was originally seized
- location:
  - must include sufficient details, such as precise location from where the item was seized, eg within boot of Ford Fiesta registered number AB12COP, or on third shelf next to a photograph of the victim on a display cabinet in right-hand corner of main lounge at 3 Henrietta Street, PE27 3RA

- person seizing:
  - include exhibit reference eg MH/1 (Michael Hill—1st exhibit)
  - signature and collar number of person finding
  - any persons subsequently handling must also sign continuity part of label

**KEY POINT**

A common mistake made with exhibit labels is when one of the continuity signatures is missing. This provides an opportunity for defence teams to place doubt over the integrity of a key evidential item and ultimately the professionalism of the investigation.

### 5.10.5 Sub-exhibiting

This occurs when an exhibit contains multiple items, such as a wallet and its contents. When initially recording the seizure of such an item, it should be described as 'wallet and contents'. There is no requirement to list individual items at this point. However, if items are removed from the wallet (MH/1), eg credit card, then it needs to be exhibited sequentially as MH/2—credit card taken from a wallet MH/1.

### 5.10.6 Principles for packaging exhibits

Exhibits must be packed and sealed at the time and location of seizure. Failure to do so will jeopardise forensic opportunities. By packaging and sealing at the time of seizure, the continuity and integrity of the exhibit is ensured. Advice should always be obtained from a CSI on the best methods of packaging exhibits.

### References

T Cook and A Tattersall, *Blackstone's Senior Investigating Officers' Handbook* (2nd edn, OUP, 2010)

# Chapter 6
# Forensic Investigation

## 6.1 Introduction

The term 'forensic' according to the *Oxford English Dictionary* (OUP, 2008) means 'relating to or denoting the application of scientific methods and techniques to the investigation of crime'. Forensic investigation provides opportunities to scientifically link suspects, victims, witnesses and locations. The results may corroborate or refute other material gathered during the investigation, including accounts from witnesses and suspects, and can be compelling evidence.

Whatever forensic tactics and techniques are employed will depend on the needs and specific circumstances of the investigation. Some of these can be used not only to implicate persons as being responsible for a crime, but also to eliminate them. Obtaining fingerprints or buccal swabs to eliminate against a crime scene stain or mark is something that may be included in a TIE strategy for example (see Chapter 7, section 7.2, Trace/Interview/Eliminate).

This highly specialised area involves scientific and other experts and this chapter merely seeks to provide crime investigators with an appreciation of the more common forensic techniques and opportunities that can be available to assist an investigation. It is always advisable to seek advice on any of the topics mentioned from a Crime Scene Investigator (CSI) or other relevant expert, as these techniques are constantly evolving and new ones being released. The most well-known and obvious of them all has been around a long time and is the first to be outlined.

## 6.2 **Fingerprints**

Fingerprints (including palm prints), due to their unique nature, are a widely accepted means of identification and broadly fall into three categories.

### 6.2.1 **Latent prints**

These marks are not easily visible to the naked eye and are developed by using powders or other chemical development techniques on clean, dry and smooth surfaces. The mark is then 'lifted' from the surface using low tack adhesive tape and secured to a clear acetate sheet.

### 6.2.2 **Visual marks**

These are marks deposited in another substance on a surface, eg visible marks in paint, blood, etc. They are photographed and it is good practice to recover and exhibit the item the mark was left on/in.

### 6.2.3 **Impressed marks**

These are three-dimensional marks found in soft materials such as putty, wax, etc. They are photographed and the item containing the mark should be recovered and exhibited if possible.

### 6.2.4 **IDENT1**

IDENT1 is the UK's central national database containing the fingerprints of all arrested persons and crime scene marks, it compares:

- crime-scene marks with other crime-scene marks to establish links
- fingerprints with crime-scene marks to identify links
- marks from detained persons with those already on record to establish identity

## 6.3 **Footwear**

Footwear impressions are present when someone walks into and out of a location. They are not always visible and specialist lighting techniques may be required to locate them. Footwear comparison focuses on sole patterns and their unique characteristics through wear or damage to provisionally link to scenes or suspects. A conclusive match between a suspect's footwear and any scene marks is possible if sufficient detail is present, However, wear and damage patterns can change with continued use, so comparison may only be valid for around a month following the offence, depending on how often the shoe has been worn. To be used in evidence, any links must be confirmed by a forensic scientist.

There are two types of footwear marks, namely:

- two-dimensional transfer marks, eg:
  o on hard surfaces such as tiles, glass, laminate flooring
  o substances transferred from the sole of the shoe to the surface leaving a two-dimensional impression, eg mud
- three-dimensional impressed marks, which are:
  o indentations on soft surfaces such as mud, snow and on some types of carpet

Apart from producing marks on surfaces, footwear may yield other forensic material to link to a scene, eg glass particles. Footwear impressions could also be found on a victim through force of impact from a stamp or kick.

It is important to remember that although forensic investigation may place the footwear mark at a location, the suspect must also be linked to the footwear for it to have evidential significance. In some circumstances, other forensic tests such as DNA will be required, or matching wear and tear of a shoe to a person's foot shape and walking style may be needed.

## 6.3.1 **National Footwear Reference Collection**

The National Footwear Reference Collection (NFRC) is provided free of charge to police forces and is a searchable library from which to identify different types of footwear from their sole patterns.

Identifying the make and model of footwear which made a mark provides valuable intelligence when planning and conducting searches, circulating information about the offence and pursuing other lines of enquiry.

Searching the NFRC may not provide a definitive answer when the mark for comparison is only partially complete.

## 6.3.2 **Seizing footwear**

The best method to seize footwear uses two sheets of paper. A person stands on one sheet and then steps onto the second sheet as they remove each shoe individually. This reduces the risk of collecting material from the floor.

Each shoe and the first sheet of paper are exhibited separately (one shoe per bag). If clothing is seized at the same time, the suspect should remain standing on the second sheet of paper until the process is complete. Gloves should always be worn when handling shoes due to potential risks from body fluids, glass shards etc.

Footwear impressions may be taken without consent from persons in custody if they have been arrested, charged or reported for a recordable offence and they have not had a footwear impression taken in the course of the investigation; or, if one has previously been obtained, it needs retaking because it is incomplete or it is of insufficient quality to allow satisfactory analysis, comparison or matching (Police and Criminal Evidence Act 1984 (PACE), section 61A[3]). This is a useful proactive technique to employ in custody units where footwear impressions are usually obtained by using a footwear recovery pad or a dedicated flatbed scanner.

## 6.4 **Clothing**

Recovering clothing and jewellery worn by a victim, suspect or witness at the time of the offence can provide various forensic opportunities, depending on the crime and its circumstances, eg contact blood staining, fibre transfer, analysis of the distribution of blood patterns, gun shot residue etc.

A point to remember is the forensic potential of areas of clothing, such as pockets, turn ups, seams and stitching, which have often been found to contain forensic material not readily visible, even after the garment has been washed.

The best way to seize clothing is:

- Stand the person on a sheet of paper
- Remove the outermost layers first as opposed to any 'top to bottom' sequence
- As each item is removed place it into a separate sack
- Note any areas of interest, such as rips, marks, potential blood stains, and record on the exhibit label
- Package items separately and seal them in the person's presence
- Complete an MG11 exhibiting the items and describing the process, including the method of packaging and continuity
- Unsealed packages, bags or sacks should not be left near to each other. CCTV from custody areas could be used by defence teams to challenge the integrity of any items seized

### KEY POINTS

- If clothing is to be placed immediately into exhibit bags, in some circumstances it may be worthwhile having it photographed beforehand. This will aid any identification process.
- If a suspect's belt is to be seized, where possible it is best not to remove it during the custody reception process in case material is trapped behind it which could be lost. In these circumstances officer safety, including potential concealed weapons, must be considered together with the safety of the detainee who must not be left alone until the recovery process above has been completed.

## 6.5 **Forensic Samples**

Forensic considerations following the arrest of a suspect will depend on the crime under investigation and what proof is being sought. This could be as straightforward as checking with fluorescent light for the presence of Smartwater (a water-based theft deterrent), to full forensic processing in serious offences. The potential forensic yield from the suspect and their clothing should form part of any planned arrest strategy, including cross-contamination prevention measures.

### 6.5.1 **Non-intimate samples**

A non-intimate sample is:

- a sample of hair (other than pubic hair), including hair plucked with a root or cut
- a sample taken from a nail or from under a nail
- a mouth swab
- a swab from any other part of the body apart from body orifices or intimate areas
- saliva
- skin impressions from non-intimate areas

---
**KEY POINTS**

- Non-intimate samples can be taken at a hospital or any other place where the person is detained
- Unlike intimate samples, a constable can use reasonable force if necessary if consent is withheld (PACE, section 63)
---

### 6.5.2 **Intimate samples**

An intimate sample is a:

- dental impression
- sample of blood, urine, pubic hair, semen or any other tissue or fluid

- swab taken from any part of the person's genitals, or from a body orifice other than the mouth

---

**KEY POINTS**

- Intimate samples require written consent from the detainee and authority from an inspector or above. They cannot be taken by force, but adverse inferences may be drawn in any subsequent proceedings if consent is refused without good cause (PACE, section 62(10)).
- With the exception of urine, all intimate samples must be obtained by a registered medical practitioner or health care professional.
- A dental impression must be taken by a registered dentist.

---

## 6.6 Fingernail Samples

Fingernail samples may contain skin tissue/DNA from a victim or suspect from a scratch during an attack. Forensic recovery is by using an approved kit and the following methodology, wearing gloves at all times.

### 6.6.1 Nail clippings

**Checklist—Nail clippings methodology**

1. Place sterile paper on a clean bench.
2. Place the suspect's hand over the paper and using the clippers provided, clip all the nails of one hand (some clippers retain the samples inside their body).
3. Return the clippers to the container they were supplied in and place into a tamper evident bag.
4. Fold the piece of paper inwards ensuring any deposited material is retained.
5. Place into the same bag as the clippers.

6. Seal and exhibit this bag then repeat the process for the other hand.
7. Store in a freezer.

## 6.6.2  Swabbing fingernails

**Checklist—Swabbing fingernails methodology**

1. Place the hand over a piece of sterile paper.
2. Open the ampoule of water supplied with the kit and drip 3 to 4 drops onto the swab (do not use water from any other source).
3. Replace the swab in its tube and seal as *control swab* (MH/1—control swab wetted).
4. Take a second swab and moisten with sterile water as above.
5. Run the tip of the swab under each nail rim, the surface of the nail and around the cuticle using the edge of the swab as well as the tip to maximise its available surface area.
6. Replace the swab into its tube and seal as *wet swab* (MH/2—Wet swab from right hand).
7. Take the third swab and, without wetting, run the tip of the swab under each nail rim, the surface of the nail and around the cuticle using the edge of the swab as well as the tip to maximise its available surface.
8. Replace the swab into its tube and seal as *dry swab* (MH/3—Dry swab from right hand).
9. Place all three sealed tubes into a tamper evident bag with the folded piece of sterile paper and exhibit as one item (MH/1—Wet and dry samples from .......).
10. Store in a freezer.

## 6.7 **DNA Samples**

DNA samples (buccal swabs) are usually taken from cells lining the inside of a person's mouth using an approved kit.

> ### Checklist—Buccal swabs
>
> 1. Ensure the person has not eaten or drunk for at least 20 minutes.
> 2. Ensure swabs and containers are fully sealed and undamaged.
> 3. Wear the disposable gloves provided and avoid coughing or talking over the samples.
> 4. Take one sample making at least six scrapes of the inside of the mouth.
> 5. Open a container and press down on the stem of the swab to eject the ridged swabbing tip into it.
> 6. Seal the top of the receptacle containing the swab and place into the bag provided.
> 7. Repeat this process for the second sample.
> 8. Seal the tamper evident bag in the presence of the donor.
> 9. Complete the DNA sample form with the appropriate kit (evidential/elimination etc).
> 10. Place the completed form along with the bag containing the two samples into the larger tamper evident bag, seal and store in a freezer.
> 11. Make an official notebook entry of the barcode and in the custody record if appropriate.

## 6.8 **Hair Samples**

Hair can contain evidence such as glass and body fluids, it can be used for DNA comparison with hair at a scene shed by an offender or pulled out during a struggle. Hair can also provide evidence of historical drug use and in some cases the racial origin of the donor.

There is always a risk of inadvertent secondary transfer of hair (and fibres), such as during transport in police vehicles. Records should be made of vehicles used to convey victims, witnesses and suspects, and cross-contamination prevention measures considered, such as using paper covers on vehicle seats, or putting suspects in protective forensic suits at the point of arrest.

Any hair sample should be no larger than necessary and the person should be given a choice where it is taken from. Forensic recovery is by using an approved kit.

### Checklist—Hair samples

1. Place sterile paper on a bench and ensure the suspect's head is over the paper.
2. Recover any visible evidence/foreign material using the tweezers provided or a gloved hand and place onto the paper.
3. Comb through the hair using the comb provided or the fingers of a gloved hand to loosen any particles.
4. Collect any material recovered onto the paper then fold inwards to retain it.
5. Place the paper, comb/scissors and tweezers into the same tamper evident bag and exhibit.
6. Exhibit the gloves worn separately.

Hair comparison:

1. Cut a minimum of 25 hairs, as close to the scalp as possible, from different parts of the head.
2. Do NOT use tweezers for comparison purposes as they may crush the recovered sample.
3. Store in a dry store.

## 6.9 **Deoxyribonucleic Acid (DNA)**

DNA is a complex molecule found in virtually every cell of the human body and in all living organisms. It carries genetic instructions in the form of a code (similar to a supermarket barcode), which can be used as a biological identification method. With the exception of identical siblings, each person's DNA is unique.

If saliva, blood, semen, skin or anything else containing cells is deposited by a person, it can be recovered and a DNA profile obtained to search on the National DNA Database (NDNAD) and potentially identify the donor. The significance of DNA cannot be overstated and is worthy of some further explanation of its investigative potential.

### 6.9.1 **Mixed DNA profiles**

If two people's combined DNA is recovered, ie mixed together from a location, a single profile can still be obtained. If the DNA of one of the people who has contributed to a mixed profile is known, it may be possible to remove it, leaving the DNA profile of the other person; for example, eliminating the DNA profile of a victim could identify a suspect. However, if neither person is known, it may be very difficult to separate the DNA of each person who has contributed to the mixed profile. Consequently there are strict rules about placing a DNA profile on the NDNAD when it has been obtained from a mixture.

### 6.9.2 **Incomplete DNA profiles**

DNA may decompose over time but the attrition rate is very difficult to predict. Sometimes relatively fresh samples degrade quickly and at other times complete DNA profiles can be obtained from relatively old samples.

An incomplete DNA profile can still be used to establish a potential link between an individual and a crime scene. The statistical probability of any match drops as the completeness of profile diminishes, but even very incomplete profiles can be used to conclusively eliminate a person from an investigation.

Summary of sample types and DNA potential recovery:

| Sample type | Source of DNA | Comments |
|---|---|---|
| Blood | White blood cells | Good source of DNA |
| Semen | Sperm cells<br>Non-sperm male cells | Good source of DNA<br>Good source of DNA |
| Hair with roots | Hair follicle cells | Good source of DNA |
| Skin/dandruff | Skin cells (dead) | Not a good source for routine analysis |
| Shed hair shafts (dead) | Adhering dead skin/follicle cells | Not a good source for routine analysis<br>Mitochondrial DNA (MtDNA) may be obtained |
| Sweat stains | Sloughed skin cells contained in fluid | Can be a good source |
| Vaginal fluids | Mainly fluid but may contain sloughed mucosal skin cells | Good source of DNA |
| Nasal secretions | Mainly fluid but may contain sloughed mucosal cells | Good source of DNA |
| Urine | Mainly fluid but may contain sloughed mucosal cells | Not routinely used as few cells generally present<br>Seek advice in serious cases |

### 6.9.3 Initial submission and analysis

Material bearing potential DNA is sent to a Forensic Service Provider (FSP) to extract and prepare a profile. The next stage depends on the objective to be achieved:

1. If the DNA profile is to be added to the NDNAD to identify the donor (eg from a discarded cigarette butt recovered from a scene), a simple one-page form GF111—Submission of Crime Stains (DNA) for the National Database is completed.

2. If the DNA profile is to be compared with another sample (eg a crime scene stain requiring comparison with samples taken from a suspect), the more detailed form MG21 is submitted.

### 6.9.4 Low Copy Number DNA

Low Copy Number DNA (LCN) (also known as Low Template DNA) is much more sensitive than standard techniques and is used when very few cells are available for analysis, or they are partly degraded. The sample is analysed first using the standard SGM+ technique and the results are amplified to provide sufficient material to obtain a DNA profile.

This process can produce a profile from extremely small samples, which means material previously analysed unsuccessfully using the standard process can be submitted for further testing. Due to its sensitivity, the risk of contamination and cross-transfer is high; however, results using LCN have the same discriminatory power as those produced by the standard process.

### 6.9.5 The National DNA Database

The National DNA Database (NDNAD) contains the DNA profiles of persons who have been arrested, cautioned, convicted and charged for recordable offences. It is one of the largest databases of its kind in the world, containing over 5 million profiles. Each time a new crime scene sample is received it is entered onto the database and regularly cross-checked against the profiles of individuals.

The originating police force is notified when a link is made between profiles, including the strength of the reported match. This is expressed in the numerical probability of a match belonging to someone other than the identified person, eg one in a billion.

## 6.9.6 **Police Elimination Database**

The Police Elimination Database (PED) contains the DNA profiles of police officers and operational staff and sits within the same framework but separate to the suspect/crime stain database. It can only be searched on the authority of an SIO and is restricted to officers and staff who attended the scene or had access to exhibits for elimination purposes only. There must be genuine grounds to suspect that contamination has taken place between the officer and the crime stain, and profiles on the PED cannot be speculatively searched against the NDNAD.

## 6.9.7 **Familial DNA searching**

Familial DNA searching (fDNA) is based on the principle that DNA is inherited with family members sharing certain characteristics. Children share half their DNA with their father and half with their mother; the extent to which siblings share their DNA varies, but tends be larger than with unrelated people.

Familial enquiries are expensive and can be resource-intensive so they are only used for the more serious offences. The written authorisation of an ACPO officer from the requesting force is required together with agreement from the NDNAD Strategy Board. Early liaison with the NCA Crime Operations Support Team is *mandatory* to advise on the complex issues surrounding potential filtering techniques.

A familial enquiry could be considered when a full DNA profile has been developed from a crime scene, and searched against the NDNAD with a negative result. A familial search of the NDNAD would produce two lists (parent/child and siblings) that could contain relatives of the unidentified person.

The search is likely to present hundreds of DNA profiles of potential family members of the offender for further research and enquiries. These are filtered further using further discriminating forensic techniques (Y-STR and MtDNA) and/or sophisticated calculations and analysis to prioritise the list based on a 'likelihood ratio' of success. The critical point to remember is that familial lists do not contain the offender (relatives are used to help identify them).

### 6.9.7.1 Y-STR

Males have an X and a Y chromosome (XY) whereas females are characterised by two X but no Y chromosomes (XX). The Y strand (hence Y-STR) is inherited unaltered from father to son and can be used as an additional filter during a familial DNA search.

### 6.9.7.2 Mitochondrial DNA

Mitochondrial DNA (MtDNA) is only passed onto children through their mothers, so although males have MtDNA, only females can pass it on to their children. If a female appears in the results of a familial search as a possible parent or sibling of the offender, for that to be true her MtDNA must match the crime scene stain.[1] If it does not, all her siblings and children are eliminated as possible offenders. Her father, however, is not eliminated.

## 6.10 Blood Pattern Analysis

Blood pattern analysis (BPA) is the expert interpretation of blood distribution, eg at an attack site. This can establish a sequence of events, assist to develop hypotheses, reconstruct events and refute or corroborate the accounts of victims, suspects and witnesses.

BPA determines how blood staining and splatter was caused on clothing, weapons and at the scene of the crime. It can also establish the approximate positions of assailants and victims in the sequence of events. This is a complex

---

[1] It is not always possible to obtain a Y-STR or MtDNA profile from a crime scene stain.

process with many variables and is only undertaken by a scientist (usually a biologist) who specialises in the analysis of bloodstains.

The scientist's knowledge of the physical properties of blood and how it reacts in certain circumstances is used to examine and interpret the blood staining according to size, shape, location and quantity, including:

- passive bloodstains
- projected bloodstains
- transfer/contact bloodstains
- 'velocity' impact blood stains
- low/medium/high velocity impact blood spatter

BPA may also indicate blood from different sources and determine what samples are taken for DNA profiling. It is also possible to assess the degree to which the assailant would themselves become bloodstained during the attack. Blood distribution may not be visible, so CSI's and forensic scientists can use chemical development processes to locate even minute traces.

## 6.11 **Tyre Marks**

Tyre marks are useful when a pattern for comparison is clearly visible, as skid and scuff marks with no apparent detail cannot be linked. The recovery techniques for tyre marks are:

- photographs to show their position within the crime scene
- close-up photographs to show detail
- recovery of the entire mark if left on a portable surface

Tyre impressions should be recovered by a CSI or a forensic vehicle examiner.

- Tyres must not be removed from a vehicle
- They must be photographed and then either:

- o the vehicle driven through a similar soft surface to recreate the mark or
- o the vehicle rolled along a roll of paper for at least one full revolution of the tyre

If the vehicle is driven through a similar soft surface, a cast is taken of the mark to compare with the scene. If sufficient detail is present, the brand of tyre that made the mark can potentially be identified. If a number of tyre marks have been left by the same vehicle, it is sometimes possible to calculate the width of the wheel base and use this information to establish the type of vehicle used.

When an examiner compares suspect tyres with marks at scenes, they seek to identify unique wear and damage, similar to the principles of footwear comparison.

## 6.12 Tool Marks

Any evidence of a 'tool' being used at a scene of a crime should be photographed and a cast is usually taken by a CSI for comparison with any tool/implement suspected of making the mark. This may link an offender to the scene by association. These marks normally fall into one of two categories.

### 6.12.1 Lever marks

These are created by tools like screwdrivers, crowbars, 'jemmys' etc used to force an entry. Any unique marks on the instrument caused by its manufacturing process, or by damage during use allow scientists to match a mark with the tool/implement that made it. Minute striations and imperfections in the mark have the most value, and ideally the item bearing the tool mark should be submitted for examination (eg window frame section). If this is not possible, a cast showing the fine detail is required.

When lever marks are present in painted areas, it is highly likely the tool will have picked up some paint onto the blade. A paint sample should therefore be obtained for comparison.

### 6.12.2 Cutting marks

Cutting marks are left when items such as padlocks and chains have been cut through using tools like wire cutters and bolt croppers. Such implements may also carry striation marks and imperfections which can be used for comparison between the cut item (padlock) and any tool recovered during the investigation.

## 6.13 Glass

When glass breaks it showers tiny microscopic particles (not just forwards, but also backwards) which can adhere to the clothing and hair of the person responsible for breaking it and anyone else in close proximity. This creates forensic opportunities if suspects are identified quickly enough, as glass fragments recovered from a person can be compared with fragments from the crime scene to establish a forensic link.

Different types of glass have different properties and react differently when broken. For example, glass used in bottles differs from laminated and toughened glass. Depending on the type of glass, options for forensic comparison include:

- physical fit—no two pieces of glass break in the same way so it may be possible to match pieces together to establish if they came from the same source (it is vital their packaging prevents damage during transit);
- Glass Refractive Index Measurement—this allows comparison between samples to identify if they came from the same source by examining their refractive index (several scene samples are needed as the refractive index can vary slightly from the same piece of glass);

- comparing the colour, thickness and density of the glass;
- comparing impurities present in the glass.

Any forensic material transferred to a suspect will gradually be lost over time (this is known as persistence). The rate of loss for glass fragments depends on their size and the nature of the retaining surface; closely woven fabrics are not likely to retain much glass, but wool or fleece material will retain much more. Washing and wearing the item accelerates loss, but if clothing is not worn or washed after contact the glass could remain on it indefinitely.

The type of clothing worn by a suspect and the time between the offence and its seizure therefore influences the likelihood of glass remaining in place and its forensic potential.

Glass fragments can be trapped in hair, upper clothing, lower clothing and the uppers and soles of shoes. This should be considered when clothing and samples are recovered from suspects and selected for forensic examination. Initial interviews prior to forensic submission should negate any plausible lie such as walking through already broken glass, as analysis may indicate how far the person was from the window when it was broken.

Samples of glass from broken windows should be taken from the actual window frame rather than being picked up from the ground to ensure its origin is not disputed.

## 6.14 Paint

Although paint is mass produced, its make up has wide variation due to the processes and raw materials used. Paint analysis can show transference between articles such as a crow bar and the point of entry in a burglary. Such transference can work both ways, with any paint already on a tool being transferred to the window frame while forcing entry.

The analysis of paint can show impact and force, eg when a person is struck by a vehicle. Any paint fragments embedded in clothing could have a distinctive appearance and provide evidence of impact, as opposed to light casual contact.

Paint samples analysed from scenes such as graffiti/hate crime may provide intelligence about the make and type of paint used. This could develop other lines of enquiry, such as identifying the location of sale, which in turn may lead to suspects. Any cans of spray paint recovered for comparison should be submitted as whole items to maintain the integrity of any sample taken from it later by a scientist.

### 6.14.1  Vehicle paint

Paint can be transferred when a vehicle collides with another vehicle or any other surface. The transferred samples may present themselves as smears, flakes or chips which can be analysed to establish any links.

Vehicles usually have four coats of paint, including pretreatment coating, primer, top coat and a clear coat. In some cases it may be possible for a scientist to determine the make, model and age of a vehicle from paint samples left at the scene of an incident.

### 6.14.2  Recovery of paint samples

Paint samples for forensic analysis should be recovered by a CSI using clean scalpels to scrape areas of paint down to the bare surface. When visible flakes are found at a scene or on clothing, they can be collected into paper envelopes and sealed in tamper evident bags.

## 6.15  **Soils**

Analysis of soil provides a forensic opportunity to link soils attached to surfaces (such as footwear or vehicles) to a location. The composition of soil differs between areas, including potentially even neighbouring gardens, depending on what is grown there or the type of any fertilisers used. Soil sample analysis includes:

- visual observation of colour and texture
- microscopic examination of the soil structure, which may reveal the presence of man-made, plant or animal material
- determining any minerals and rock fragments
- determining the size and distribution of soil particles

The significance of any evidence obtained depends on the number of common factors between the two samples. The more common points of comparison, the stronger the evidential link will be. However, any link will not be conclusive unless there is something unique about the samples that only exist at that location.

Botanical evidence, such as comparable pollen and plant spores from the same flowers and foliage can also be obtained from soil samples; this is sometimes a preferred option and involves the use of a palynologist.

## 6.16 **Fibres**

Fibres fall into two broad categories of natural (wool, silk, cotton) and man-made (nylon, polyester). Their analysis can potentially provide evidence of fibre type, colour, diameter, shape (cross-section), chemicals added during manufacture and comparison of dyes. Sometimes the origin of the fibre can be identified through pigments or dye contained in it.

Fibres may provide evidence of contact between people and surfaces, but the degree of any transfer depends on the nature of the item and the extent of the contact. Generally, closely woven material does not retain or shed fibres, whereas a fleecy type will.

As with glass, if the garment is washed or extensively worn after an incident the amount of available evidence will diminish, but if it is put to one side after the incident any fibres will be retained indefinitely.

The significance of fibre analysis depends on the circumstances of the offence and the number, combination and nature of the fibres recovered. The greater the number of comparable points, the higher the evidential value. Ideally fibres should be recovered by a CSI, but if this is not possible the same procedures as with recovering hair samples should be adopted.

## 6.17  **Firearms and Ballistic Material**

It is essential that every opportunity is taken to recover ballistic items (bullets, wadding and spent cartridges) from any incident where a firearm may have been discharged in suspicious or obviously criminal circumstances.

### 6.17.1  **Firearms recovery**

Any firearms found must be left in position to be made and certified safe by an Authorised Firearms Officer (AFO) or equivalent before any further action is taken. Weapons should always be treated as real and loaded until proven otherwise.

Once made safe, a CSI should undertake a forensic recovery for DNA and fingerprints, including taking photographs and noting the position of the safety catch or, in the case of a revolver, the position of the chamber and hammer.

Firearms should be secured in a protective box with a transparent window, which must be securely sealed and a 'made safe' certificate attached. Nothing should be pushed into the barrel of a firearm such as a pen or fingers; gloves must be worn during handling which should be retained, sealed and exhibited after the firearm has been securely sealed.

Wet firearms and components should be placed in boxes and sealed into paper evidence sacks. Plastic packaging

MUST NOT be used as this encourages rust which can change the striations and affect any test firing. This can also be detrimental to any subsequent court proceedings as, by the time of the hearing, the firearm may no longer be in the same condition as when it was recovered (eg no longer be capable of being fired).

Firearms and ammunition must not be stored, packaged or submitted for forensic analysis together. Care must be taken to ensure that the firearm and any related material is kept separate so that other exhibits, such as offender clothing, do not come into contact.

## 6.17.2 Ballistic examination

The ballistic examination of firearms can be split into three general areas which can provide a picture of what occurred, enabling accounts to be corroborated or refuted.

- Internal ballistics:
  - what happens inside the weapon
  - imperfections transferred from the barrel onto the bullet or wadding
  - establishing recoil and barrel pressures

- External ballistics:
  - behaviour of projectiles in flight after discharge and before impact;
  - trajectory, maximum range and momentum of the bullet determined by mathematical principles
  - aiding reconstruction of events such as position of victim(s) and offender when the weapon was fired, or the distance between firearm, offender and victim

- Terminal ballistics:
  - behaviour of the projectile on its target
  - penetration potential—ability to penetrate various materials;
  - wound ballistics—effect on living tissue

These examinations may also link ammunition to the firearm that discharged it and potentially forensically connect other incidents involving the same weapon.

### 6.17.3  Firearms discharge and explosive residue

Firearms discharge and explosive residue can be present on the hands, face, hair, clothing and jewellery of a person who has discharged a firearm or been in close proximity at the time. Places where a firearm or ammunition may have been stored, such as pockets and waistbands, should be checked for firearms discharge residue, as should places or items nearby to where a firearm may have been test fired.

Cross-contamination is a very real threat when dealing with microscopic nanogrammes of gunshot residue. For this reason, it may be necessary to use a specially prepared sterile custody escort vehicle and a custody suite (ie reception area and holding cell) that has been deep cleansed and can be proven to be free from discharge residue brought in from elsewhere (eg AFOs).

---

**Checklist—Collecting firearms/explosives residue**

1. Sampling kits MUST be sealed before use, NEVER use an unsealed kit
2. No one who has handled or been in the vicinity of firearms, ammunition or explosives within the previous seven days should recover samples or come into contact with them (eg AFOs)
3. Prevent secondary transfer through contact between the person taking the samples and any persons mentioned at 2
4. Do NOT use the kit if a regular user of firearms or explosives

---

5. Consider cross-contamination and transfer between multiple suspects and use multiple recovery officers at different locations
6. Thoroughly wash hands and forearms and wear a disposable overall before opening a kit
7. Only use the items from within the kit and make a note of the serial/batch number
8. Be aware that some cultures may forbid contact with alcohol (swabs)
9. Be aware some medicinal treatments (eg for angina) may contain nitro-glycerine

## 6.17.4 Using a firearms and explosive sampling kit

### Checklist—Sampling technique

1. Wear the gloves supplied with the kit.
2. Take one swab and rub it over the front and back of the gloves you are wearing and place the swab back into its tube—label this as control swab and seal in an exhibit bag.
3. Using a second swab, rub it over the face and neck of the suspect including the eyebrows (take care not to get solvent into the eyes). Replace the swab in its tube and seal in an exhibit bag.
4. Comb through the hair and any beard/moustache with the comb supplied with the kit. The comb has solvent material in it. If the suspect has no hair or it is difficult to comb, then run the comb across the head, ensuring that the solvent material makes contact. Place the comb back into the plastic bag it was supplied in and seal in the exhibit bag.
5. Using a clean swab, rub the front and back of the suspect's right hand—pay particular attention to the

web of the thumb, between the fingers and under any jewellery. Label as swab from right hand and seal in an exhibit bag.

6. Repeat 5 for the left hand.
7. Remove the nail scraper and gauze from its bag. Taking one finger at a time, hold the finger over the gauze and scrape the debris from the nail, wiping the scraper on the gauze after each nail. Replace the scraper and gauze into its bag and then seal in an exhibit bag.
8. Ensure each item is properly sealed before sealing the exhibits bag.
9. When sampling is complete, remove, bag and exhibit the gloves worn.

## 6.17.5 National Ballistics Intelligence Service

The National Ballistics Intelligence Service (NABIS) manages a national database of recovered firearms and ballistics material and provides a forensic capability to link offences where the same weapon or individuals are involved, including identifying persons concerned with importing, supplying, illegally adapting or converting firearms.

NABIS centres have facilities for test firing, analysing and linking firearms and ballistic material to items submitted from other incidents across the UK and are capable of linking bullets and cartridge cases to crime scenes and recovered weapons.

NABIS provides intelligence on submitted items, but does not develop this into evidence, which is delivered by forensic service providers. A firewall between intelligence and evidence is created with access to the NABIS database available to key staff in each police force. All recovered ballistic material should be submitted to NABIS for analysis via a force SPoC (single point of contact) as soon as practicable.

## 6.18 **Documents and Handwriting**

Documentary forensic evidence to assist investigations includes:

- handwriting and grammatical style analysis
- forged/altered document examination
- recovery of indented writing
- fingerprint recovery
- physical fit
- comparison of printed document to printer

### 6.18.1 **Handwriting analysis**

Forensic comparisons can be made between writing on a document (the questioned document) and samples obtained, eg from suspects. As writing and grammatical styles tend to be individual to the author and display their own character-istics, these comparisons may establish the 'author' of the writing, and/or whether a signature is forged or genuine. The same can be done with typed words and documents when checking for similar styles, punctuation, sentence length and grammar, etc. This could be useful when examining similarly produced documents that are found on a word processor, for example.

Comparison material can be written by the suspect on demand and under supervision ('on request' specimens), or be previous ordinary examples of their handwriting, such as letters, work documents, schoolwork correspondence etc (course of business writing).

The four general categories examined within handwrit-ing samples are:

- capitals—all the letters are written in upper case. An analyst will examine the number and direction of pen strokes used to construct the letters
- cursive—all the letters of a word are 'joined up'. This is the most common form of adult handwriting with vast variations in individual styles

- disconnected—a variation on cursive and includes breaks between some letters. These breaks vary from person to person
- signatures—highly stylised and often illegible. Signatures are often written in a completely different style to a person's general handwriting and are therefore difficult to link to normal handwriting

## 6.18.2 Forged handwriting

It is difficult for a person to consistently forge their handwriting; invariably they will write slower than usual to try and disguise their usual style, but they will often revert to normal, as letters are formed subconsciously. It is typical for a piece of forged handwriting to include lots of variations in the formation of letters and spacing etc.

When a case involves forged signatures, reference writing must be obtained from the loser/injured party. This allows the document examiner to exclude the account holder, and determine if the questioned signatures were made with any attempt at copying the genuine ones.

---

**Checklist—Handwriting samples from suspects**

- Should represent the suspect's usual handwriting
- Should contain sufficient writing to conduct an effective comparison
- Should be taken on a similar document to the questioned document eg a blank cheque template, another appropriate form or alternatively plain or lined paper
- If the questioned document is written in capital letters, the suspect's sample should be in capitals. The document examiner can only examine like for like, eg capitals v capitals or lower case v lower case. This should be specified in the request to the suspect
- Use the same sort of pen, preferably a well-used ballpoint

---

- Provide a suitable writing surface for the sample
- For signature comparison take at least 12 samples
- For cheque fraud take at least 12 signature simples and a further 6 handwriting samples
- Take samples at different times of the interview process
- Never show the suspect the original document (they may copy it)
- Dictate to the suspect what is to be written at a reasonable pace allowing a natural writing style to be used
- Don't help the suspect with spelling or the layout of specimens (spelling mistakes may be a common factor)
- The suspect should sign and date each sample as it is completed
- Each sample should be taken on a separate piece of paper and removed from sight when completed to prevent the suspect copying
- Sequentially number each sample with the time each was recorded
- Obtain course of business writing of the suspect if possible

Note: If in any doubt it is advisable to obtain advice from a forensic examiner before taking the samples.

### 6.18.3 Indented impressions

Indentations caused by the pressure of writing can travel through several sheets of paper; the most common technique used to reveal these is a simple non-destructive technique called Electrostat Document Apparatus (ESDA). This is not routinely undertaken and if being considered it should be recognised that treating a document with chemicals (Ninhydren) for fingerprint recovery first will render an ESDA test useless. Similarly, if the item to be examined has been subjected to wet conditions this can significantly reduce any indented impressions.

## 6.18.4  Printed documents

Document examiners may be able to establish if a document originated from a specific machine by comparing the printed item with defects produced by the machine. Some printers produce what is called a bitmap. This is not visible to the naked eye but can provide information about the type and model of machines involved in the production of the item.

### 6.18.4.1  Analysis of inks and paper/physical fit

Forensic examiners can compare inks on a document and compare different pieces of paper to determine if they are from the same source. They can also compare torn pieces of paper from a pad or a shredded document to determine the source through their physical fit.

---

**Checklist—Recovering/preserving documents**

- Always wear gloves
- If possible photograph or photocopy the original, depending on the requirements of the case
- To preserve for indented writing or footwear impressions, place the item into a box before placing it into a paper or plastic evidence bag
- NEVER lean on the document whilst completing exhibit labels
- Paper or plastic evidence bags are suitable if no indented impressions are required
- Store documentary exhibits in cool dry surroundings
- DO NOT stick, staple or clip anything to the exhibit
- Undertake chemical examinations last in any sequence of tests

---

## 6.19 **Drugs and Illegal Substances**

To list all drugs that are taken for illegal recreational purposes would not be beneficial, however some common drugs of abuse likely to be encountered include:

- Category A (eg most harmful):
  - cocaine
  - crack
  - morphine diacetate (heroin)
  - opium (opiod mixture)
  - Ecstasy
  - Lysergic Acid Diethylamide (LSD, acid)
  - Psilocybin mushrooms (magic mushrooms)
  - Methadone
  - Phencyclidine (Angel dust)

- Category B:
  - amphetamine (speed)
  - codeine
  - cannabis (weed, marijuana, hash, skunk) (reclassified from Class C to Class B in January 2009)
  - Methylphenidate
  - Ritalin (stimulant)
  - Pholcodine (opiod)
  - Methaqualone (Mandrake, Mandrax)

- Category C:
  - some other tranquilisers, stimulants and sedatives
  - anabolic steroids (for building muscle tissue)
  - Diazepam (Valium)
  - Temazepam (becomes class A when prepared for injection)
  - Flunitrazepam (Rohypnol)

## 6.19.1  **Types of drugs**

### 6.19.1.1  Heroin

Heroin is derived from morphine extracted from the opium formed in the unripe pods of certain poppies. It is typically brown in colour and contains between 4 and 21 per cent morphine. The process of manufacture involves the morphine reacting with acetic anhydride or acetyl chloride. This produces a powdered substance that is highly soluble in water, allowing it to be injected.

Before sale other substances are added or 'cut' into the heroin to increase the amount that is sold; these substances could include lactose, milk powders, sugars etc which therefore impact on the purity.

### 6.19.1.2  Cocaine

Cocaine is derived from the coca leaf; it is typically administered in powder form and can be sniffed, allowing it to be absorbed through the mucous membranes of the nose. Crack cocaine is manufactured by mixing cocaine with baking soda and water. This is then dried and broken into lumps known as rocks, which are normally smoked.

### 6.19.1.3  Amphetamine

Amphetamines provide stimulus to the user as they affect the nervous system, increasing alertness and activity. They are typically encountered in powder form and are most often inhaled by sniffing.

### 6.19.1.4  Club drugs

These are synthetically produced and include MDMA (Ecstasy), Gamma Hydroxyburate (GHB) and ketamine; they are typically found in tablet form.

### 6.19.1.5  Hallucinogens

LSD (lysergic acid diethylamide) is derived from certain types of grain fungus; a small amount causes auditory and visual hallucinations. It is typically taken by ingesting a small piece of impregnated blotting paper which has been soaked in a solvent containing dissolved LSD.

Psilocybin is similar to LSD but occurs naturally in a particular variety of mushroom known as 'Magic Mushrooms'.

### 6.19.1.6 Cannabis

Probably the most widely used drug in the world and now typically cultivated in the UK rather than imported. It comes in a variety of forms including:

- leaves/herbal
- Skunk (produced from specific varieties of the plant)
- resin
- cannabis oil

## 6.19.2 Cannabis cultivation

It is common for large houses or disused warehouses to be used for cannabis cultivation, enabling high yields of the drug. This sort of crime is now routinely linked to both national and international Organised Crime Groups (OCGs). Investigators should be mindful of the indicators for this type of activity when conducting enquiries and searches. The issues for investigation when dealing with these incidents include:

- identifying the premises and equipment
- establishing the actual and possible/potential yield from the amount of plants
- quality of the plants
- linking the scene to other cultivation operations or supplied drugs and OCG activity
- identifying all those involved in the cultivation chain of command
- added health and safety risks when conducting searches

The growth cycle of the cannabis plants is regulated by exposure to daylight, and in natural conditions it grows quicker in summer than in autumn. Indoor cultivation allows growers to reproduce the effects of daylight by using large, powerful lighting systems which allow the flowering to be regulated. By reducing the plants' life cycle, more crops can be grown in the same time period. Plants grown in this manner are cultivated in pots or by a method known as hydroponics, which doesn't use soil, and the plants are grown in circulating water (including added nutrients).

Although the method may vary from scene to scene, certain common factors may be present (this list is not exhaustive):

- lighting systems using high-powered lamps
- walls and windows painted white or coated with reflective coverings to maximise the lighting effects
- air circulation systems to prevent fungal growth
- seedling nursery area
- documentation detailing growing schedules
- water tanks, trays and pumps
- stocks of plant nutrients
- an electricity source (possibly abstracted)
- added security at the premises where it is being cultivated

OCGs are often linked with the large-scale cultivation of cannabis. In some cases entire premises, eg houses, are being obtained and occupied for this sole purpose.

### 6.19.2.1  Recovery of plants

Cannabis plant recovery depends on the scale and complexity of the cultivation operation and the evidence required for the charge in question. Guidance should be sought from FSPs regarding the volume of submission required for each specific case.

### 6.19.2.2  Packaging of samples

All plants and related vegetable matter should be packaged separately in paper evidence sacks (never plastic bags) and be submitted to the forensic laboratory as quickly as possible. Any cultivation equipment does not necessarily need to be submitted, but other opportunities for other forensic material such as DNA or fingerprints on these items should be considered.

The cultivation scene should be photographed by a CSI, including the use of a scale (ruler) to indicate the size of plants.

### 6.19.2.3 Health and safety at cultivation scenes

Premises used for cannabis cultivation are a hazardous environment with potential risks including:

- booby traps—check local intelligence systems to identify if this is a risk in the area
- electrical risks—installations at such scenes are often haphazard and poorly maintained with the mains supply bypassed—calling out the electrical supplier to ensure the safety of staff present should be considered
- trip hazards
- heat from large lamps capable of burning exposed skin
- chemicals present which may be corrosive
- the odour from the plants can become overwhelming; staff should wear disposable masks

Always wear disposable oversuits and gloves.

## 6.20 Illicit Laboratories

Much of the information regarding illicit laboratories is restricted, but can be accessed within forces. These laboratories may be involved in the manufacture of drugs or materials for use in terrorism offences. If an illicit laboratory is encountered while making unrelated enquiries, the following actions should be undertaken:

### Checklist—Illicit laboratories

- Due to the high risk (fire/explosion/chemical contamination) any personnel in the vicinity must retreat to a safe distance

- Mobile phones and radios should not be used in close proximity to the scene (inform the control room when a safe distance away)
- Do not switch any power supply on or off at the scene
- Do not touch or open any bottles or containers
- Keep the scene under observation from a safe distance
- Use cordons and scene logs to manage the scene
- Only those properly trained and equipped for searching in hazardous environments should re-enter the scene
- Check local force policy and arrangements for any multi-agency protocols (eg fire service)
- Be mindful these activities may be connected to terrorism or OCG activity

## 6.21 **Toxicology**

Forensic toxicology uses analytical chemistry, pharmacology and clinical chemistry to aid investigations into death, poisoning and drug use. Toxicology can be used in other types of cases, for example, when proving or disproving drug or alcohol usage by offenders, victims or even witnesses. Typical samples that may be examined include:

- urine
- blood
- hair
- saliva (oral fluid)
- other samples, such as organs, other bodily fluids or gastric contents obtained during an autopsy

A forensic toxicologist will consider their analysis in the context of the investigation, looking at issues such as physical symptoms and evidence collected at the scene (tablet containers, powders, trace residue). By considering these along with the submitted samples, they will determine which toxic substances are present, in what concentrations and their probable effect on the person concerned.

### 6.21.1 Forensic persistence

The following is a guide to forensic persistence when considering samples to be submitted for analysis:

- alcohol—up to 24 hours in urine
- drugs of abuse—up to 12 to 24 hours in urine, 48 hours in blood
- GHB—4 hours in blood, up to 6 to 12 hours in urine
- Rohypnol—18 hours in blood, 72 hours in urine

### References

*Oxford English Dictionary* (OUP, 2008)

# Chapter 7
# Core Investigative Strategies

## 7.1 Introduction

Core investigative strategies are methods and tactical options aimed at progressing an investigation. A strategy is a plan designed to achieve a long-term aim and the purpose of an investigative strategy is to:

- identify the most beneficial and appropriate tactics and lines of enquiry
- determine objectives for pursuing them
- identify investigative actions necessary to efficiently achieve those objectives, taking into account resources, priorities, justification and proportionality
- conduct the investigative actions to gather useful material and evidence or generate further lines of enquiry

Initial considerations should identify the primary objectives of the investigation with the main lines of enquiry and strategies needed to achieve them. These should not be treated as fixed plans applicable to all investigations; they should be selected as being the most suitable for that individual enquiry.

Consideration must be given to the legal and ethical aspects of any proposed action. Any investigative response should be justified and proportionate to the crime under investigation, with actions prioritised against available resources and driven by the investigation itself, not just adhering to a process of 'box ticking'.

Most of the strategies described in this chapter also feature in the *Core Investigative Doctrine* (2nd edn, ACPO/NPIA, 2012) and the *Murder Investigation Manual* (ACPO/Centrex,

2006) (MIM), but are suitable for most investigations and not just serious crime.

---

**Checklist—Investigative strategies**

- Suspect management*
- Witness trawls and management*
- TI/TIE enquiries
- Victims, family and community liaison
- H-2-H enquiries
- Forensic and general scene searching*
- Media and communications
- Intelligence
- Financial investigation
- Digital evidence (communications data and social media)
- Passive data generators
- Proactive enquiries*
- Covert enquiries*
- Specialist Operational Support and Crime Analysis Unit[1]

---

## 7.2 Trace/Interview/Eliminate (TIE)

The term 'TIE' is explained in detail within the MIM and Major Incident Room Standardised Administrative Procedures (MIR-SAP), and is a strategy which identifies groups of people likely to include an offender.[2] Subsequent enquiries into these groups can then eliminate those who cannot be the offender and implicate those who could be. This allows investigators to focus enquiries on those who are potentially implicated.

TIE strategies can be resource intensive and, if not carried out correctly, the process could wrongly eliminate an offender.

---

[1] Those marked * are covered in other chapters of this handbook.

[2] For a more detailed explanation of TIE strategy please consult the MIM or T Cook and A Tattersall, *Blackstone's Senior Investigating Officers' Handbook* (2nd edn, OUP, 2010), both of which provide greater detail of the strategy as used by SIOs in major crime investigations.

## 7.2.1 **Constructing TIE categories**

A TIE category is a group of people who share a common characteristic with the likely offender. The common characteristic will depend on the circumstances of the crime but could typically include:

- had access to the scene at the time of the offence
- lived in, or is associated with a certain geographical area
- associated, linked or related to the victim
- previous convictions for a similar offence (usually referred to as 'MO Subjects')
- physical characteristics similar to the offender (where a description is available)
- access to certain types of vehicle
- named as being of interest (eg via intelligence)
- registered sexual or dangerous offenders

This is not an exhaustive TIE category list, which could include anyone at the investigator's discretion. The more that is known about the circumstances of the crime, the greater the prospect of constructing an accurate TIE category.

## 7.2.2 **Populating TIE categories**

Once a decision has been reached on which groups are likely to include the offender, thought must be given to how many members of each group can be identified. Sometimes this is easily achieved with a certain degree of accuracy; for example, if the offence took place within a work place a check of company records identifying all employees would create a TIE category of 'those employed in the named premises'. On other occasions it is more difficult, for example those visiting a public place within the relevant time.

Useful ways of populating TIE categories are:

- using information generated by the investigation
- using official records (electoral rolls, membership lists, payrolls)

- police intelligence databases (eg PNC, PND, ViCLAS)
- public appeals and witness information
- 'snowballing'—interviewing members of a TIE category to identify other members of the group

### 7.2.3 Prioritising TIE categories

Populations of TIE categories can sometimes be large, making it difficult to complete enquiries on all the listed nominals. A decision then needs to be made on how to prioritise the list; one method is to apply further filters such as:

- geography (eg proximity to the scene)
- date of last conviction for MO subjects
- age (where age of the offender is unknown, priority can be given to those who fall in the most likely age range for that type of offender)
- gender

### 7.2.4 TIE elimination criteria

The purpose of the TIE process is to eliminate people from a category; therefore the criteria and level of elimination must be determined. This includes forensic or fingerprint evidence, description or independent witness/material to verify an alibi.

A person implicated in or eliminated from a TIE category is just that, and their implication/elimination should be tested vigorously against all available material and revisited when new information comes to light. They have NOT necessarily been implicated or eliminated from being the offender.

Members of TIE categories may also be potential witnesses, and this should be considered when conducting TIE enquiries.

As a result of TIE enquiries, a member of a category may be elevated to being a 'suspect' but only when there are compelling grounds or evidence for doing so, eg matching their DNA to the crime scene, or their alibi is proved to be false.

---

**KEY POINT—'PERSONS OF INTEREST'**

Some forces have replaced or supplemented the term TIE with POI (meaning 'persons of interest'). This terminology has crept into the police environment but has no place in a TIE strategy. A person is a TIE 'subject' or, if the circumstances change, a witness or a suspect. If the term 'person of interest' is used, an explanation must be recorded as to what precisely it refers to which may be required in court as to why a 'POI' has not been afforded recognised status, or given their lawful rights under PACE as a suspect.

---

### 7.2.4.1 Suspect parameters

These are the known characteristics of an offender and are used to implicate or eliminate persons from within a TIE category including:

- sex
- age
- physical characteristics
- fingerprints
- forensic comparison such as DNA, fibres, footwear or tyre marks
- ownership or use of vehicles (particular make or colour)
- ownership of or access to particular clothing

The value of these characteristics varies. Knowing only the sex of an offender has limited value; but DNA or fingerprint evidence is likely to eliminate all but the offender (unless there were multiple offenders and only one left trace evidence behind).

It is usually of value to set the elimination parameters a little wider than those suggested by the material gathered during the investigation. This allows for a degree of error in say, descriptions given by witnesses or victims.

### 7.2.4.2 Time (temporal) parameters

Time parameters are useful for eliminating subjects from a TIE category provided they are confirmed as accurate. When the exact time of an offence is unknown, the temporal parameters should be based on the earliest and latest times the offence could have been committed. This is often referred to as the *relevant time*.

### 7.2.4.3 HOLMES elimination criteria

There is a tried and trusted numerical coding system on the HOLMES database which electronically eliminates members from a TIE category. This coding system can be used when conducting TIE enquiries and is as follows:

1. Forensic elimination: eg DNA, footwear, fingerprints
2. Description (suspect parameters)
3. Independent witness (alibi)
4. Associate or relative (alibi)
5. Spouse or common law relationship (alibi)
6. Not eliminated

## 7.3 Victims, Family and Community Liaison

An important area of any investigation is liaising with the victim, family and community. This has become increasingly important due to changing attitudes towards policing methods following a number of high-profile cases. Policing is heavily dependent on the consent and trust of the public. Investigators rely on the cooperation of people to report crimes and incidents, provide evidence or information, assist in the identification of offenders, and act as a measure of local and national tensions resulting from criminal and policing activity.

Victims depend on the police to bring offenders to justice, and to help them by arranging appropriate support.

They may also have the added trauma of being a witness and providing evidence against defendants in court.

Having a point of contact for regular updates on the progress of the investigation is what victims need, in addition to a professional response and investigation of their crime. A poor service may have lasting negative affects when their assistance is required for something else at a later stage or another occasion.

Of increasing importance is investigators obtaining and sustaining high levels of trust and confidence in the police and the criminal justice system from victims, their relatives, close friends and local communities.

There are a number of agencies who also work to support victims of crime.

---

### Checklist—Victim support groups

| | |
|---|---|
| Victim Support | National charity which helps people affected by crime by providing free and confidential support <http://www.victimsupport.org.uk> |
| Suzy Lamplugh Trust | UK charity devoted to providing practical support and personal safety guidance <http://www.suzylamplugh.org.uk> |
| Refuge | Charity that provides temporary and emergency accommodation for women and children escaping from domestic violence <http://www.refuge.org.uk> |

---

| | |
|---|---|
| NSPCC | National Society for the Prevention of Cruelty to Children <http://www.nspcc.org.uk> |
| The Samaritans | Provide confidential emotional support for people who are experiencing feelings of distress or despair <http://www.samaritans.org.uk> |
| Criminal Justice System Online | Information about the Criminal Justice process for victims and witnesses <www.gov.uk/browse/justice> |
| Crown Prosecution Service | The CPS website contains useful information. <http://www.cps.gov.uk> |

## 7.3.1 Community impact and public reassurance

It is essential to take into account the impact investigations may have on a local community. Measures of success include:

- conviction of those guilty of crime
- confidence of the family of the victim in the investigation
- confidence and cooperation of communities in the investigation
- lowering of tensions within those connected to the investigation

Levels of community involvement vary from case to case. Most often this is confined to family members, close friends and relatives or specific members of a community. However, in larger investigations this may increase to the wider community.

In more serious cases the police may conduct a Community Impact Assessment (CIA), the purpose of which is to consider and manage the impact of the incident, particularly on minority or vulnerable communities by:

- enhancing investigative effectiveness
- protecting vulnerable individuals and groups
- promoting community confidence
- developing community intelligence

## 7.3.2 Family Liaison Officers

Deploying a Family Liaison Officer (FLO) is not restricted to homicide investigations, and an FLO strategy can be considered at the outset of any serious and complex investigation. When utilising FLOs, one of the main objectives is to maximise their investigative capability with the family whilst servicing their need for information and support.

Victims and/or their close family and friends are reliant on the officer in charge of the investigation (through the FLO) providing them with accurate and regular information. This is extremely important, otherwise they may listen to rumour and gossip which may not be accurate. It is extremely important that the information flow is controlled by the officer in charge and therefore constant communication between them and the FLO is required. The FLO should not disclose any information to the family that has not been previously agreed.

Advice and support from a local Family Liaison Coordinator (FLC) should be sought to ensure the most suitably trained FLO is appointed to the enquiry. The role is difficult and demanding and the FLO's position in any investigation should never be underestimated. They are not involved to solely comfort relatives of a victim; FLOs are investigators and for this reason should be PIP level 2 accredited.[3]

---

[3] The role of an FLO with a checklist is also referred to in Ch 9.

## 7.4 **House-to-House Enquiries**

On major crime investigations SIOs usually have the support of a house-to-house (H-2-H) coordinator who helps to produce a full structured H-2-H strategy utilising suitable resources. A set of national forms are used to document H-2-H enquiries when conducted in this structured manner (eg occupancy details form). These can be found within the publication *Practice Advice on House-to-House Enquiries* (ACPO/Centrex, 2006).

H-2-H enquiries are a very useful tactic to support investigations and do not need to be a resource-intensive activity. Single investigators can conduct effective enquiries using this technique. However H-2-H does require a methodical approach and when covering a large area it usually produces large volumes of material which need processing.

The main reasons for conducting H-2-H enquiries are to identify suspects, witnesses, gather evidence and seek information, to provide public reassurance and offer crime prevention advice. This section provides an overview of how to develop and implement a H-2-H strategy and further guidance is provided in the MIM and *Practice Advice on House to House Enquiries*.

### 7.4.1 **Developing a H-2-H strategy**

A successful H-2-H strategy requires a methodical approach with clear objectives and consideration of:

- identifying, determining and stipulating location parameters
- investigation of specific questions and subjects to be covered (ie questionnaires);
- documents to be completed (eg questionnaires, Personal Descriptive Forms (PDFs) and occupancy forms)
- timing of the enquiries
- identifying resources

- fast track (hasty) H-2-H enquiries
- a 'no reply' and/or 'not at home' policy for revisits (so no occupants are missed)

### 7.4.2 Identifying suspects

When a suspect is believed to live, work in or visit a particular area, H-2-H enquiries are used to try to establish the identity and description of all persons living, working in, visiting and connected to the premises targeted. Accounts should be obtained of all movements relevant to the investigation parameters and verified. H-2-H is the only sure method of achieving this objective and is a technique of particular importance on major crime enquiries when intelligence-led mass screening for DNA or fingerprints is being conducted or considered.

### 7.4.3 Identifying witnesses

Potentially H-2-H can identify witnesses to events (and sometimes additional victims) relevant to the investigation such as:

- events connected to an incident such as the encounter, attack or disposal site
- sightings or information about a victim or offender before or after the event
- sightings or information regarding relevant items or vehicles
- sightings or information about potential witnesses (including the identification of other previously reported unidentified nominals)

It is important to ensure that all relevant information is obtained during H-2-H enquiries, and using questionnaires incorporating the circumstances of the incident under investigation should be considered. Closed questions with 'yes' or 'no' answers should be avoided and open ones used instead, eg 'Do you own a white van?' answer 'No', but they might have access to someone else's!

The questionnaires can be in the following formats:

- standard H-2-H form
- bespoke (particular to that investigation) on any chosen documentation

Another form used to support H-2-H enquiries is the PDF (Personal Descriptive Form). This is comprehensive and requires attention to detail. Information sought should never be guessed at during completion as it is used for verification, cross referencing with other material and potentially identifying a victim, witness, offender or further lines of enquiry. It needs determining what type of occupants should be subjected to PDFs, eg all male occupants over the age of 8 years.

It is usual for both suspect and witness H-2-H enquiries to be conducted simultaneously, which assists with not alerting potential suspects who may live in the area.

H-2-H can also be used to reassure the public and provide crime prevention and personal safety advice during investigations. For this reason it can be worthwhile consulting with the neighbourhood policing team and/or community leaders to assist with this task.

External communications (eg media) and CCTV recovery strategies can be considered in conjunction with the H-2-H enquiries. This avoids duplication of effort and ensures any messages delivered by investigators during their enquiries are consistent with information released to the media.

## 7.4.4 Location parameters

To ensure effective H-2-H enquiries are conducted in the most relevant geographical locations, parameters should be determined and recorded. It is best to visit the scene and surrounding area to identify and set parameters rather than relying upon maps which may not contain all relevant detail of premises such as multi-occupancy buildings. Walking the area and making careful observations is best practice and will help to log all the streets and premises of interest, including those that are not easy to notice on street plans (eg Number 14A—the small flat around the back of a house).

When setting location parameters, it is useful to use natural boundaries to create zones. Such boundaries could be streets, paths, rivers, railway lines, major roads etc.

### 7.4.5 Fast track H-2-H

It is useful to conduct fast track H-2-H (often called 'flash' or 'hasty' H-2-H) at premises *within line of sight and/or hearing* of a particular location in the golden hour(s) period. This is always best supported by full H-2-H when resources allow. A good way to establish what could be accomplished during fast track H-2-H is to concentrate on areas where an offender may have been and consider the following (LEASH) locations:

> **L**—lain in wait
> **E**—egress routes
> **A**—access routes
> **S**—line of sight
> **H**—line of hearing

And LEAVERS for full H-2-H:

> **L**—last sighting of victim
> **E**—encounter site
> **A**—attack site
> **V**—victim frequented locations
> **E**—evidence and dump sites
> **R**—routes to and from any of the above
> **S**—sites and proximities to witnesses

A number of other support options can assist H-2-H enquiries including:

- interview advisors to formulate questionnaires
- geographical profilers to assist with determining location parameters
- community leaders regarding language and cultural issues

Leaflet drops and social media (eg use of Bluetooth technology) can also be an effective method of covering a large area to request public assistance. These leaflets must include contact details that will be answered should a member of the public respond to the request, and, depending on the demographics of the area, could be multilingual.

## 7.4.6 'No reply' policy

At some premises there will inevitably be no response, so a consistent policy needs to be decided upon to manage this problem. There are various options available, ranging from repeat visits (if so, how many and at what times and by whom?) or contact by other means such as telephone or leaflet drop/calling card. While there may be resource and time implications for making re-visits, this is always the best option as some residents need persuading to offer up important information or that they have seen something significant. Such information may prove vital to the enquiry.

---

**Checklist—H-2-H enquiries**

- When setting location parameters 'walk the route' to ensure all premises have been properly identified (eg to spot the small flat around the back)
- Questions should be worded carefully by avoiding closed questions eg 'Do you own a white van?' Answer:

---

'No' (but an occupant might use one belonging to someone else)
- If using a term such as 'suspicious' (eg Did you see anything suspicious/of interest?'), define what is meant by 'suspicious' or 'of interest'
- Avoid using two questions in the same sentence
- Ensure ALL occupants/visitors during relevant dates/times are accounted for
- Try and use correct documentation, eg questionnaire, PDF, house/premises occupancy
- Checks for passive data such as CCTV can be incorporated into H-2-H enquiries
- Have a 'no reply' policy (eg repeat calls, enquiries with neighbours, letterbox drop)

## 7.5 **Media and Communications**

The purpose of a communications strategy is to disseminate or receive information to assist the investigation. This can be done internally with colleagues or partners within the criminal justice system, or externally through the media or other outlets.

Advice should be sought internally and externally, especially when dealing with the media, community impact, equality, diversity or human rights issues. This ensures an appropriate level of information exchange is established.

Sources of advice may include:

- force press officers (or similar title, eg Media Liaison Officers (MLOs))
- community equality advisors
- crime reduction advisors
- local community leaders and councillors
- community groups or forums
- diversity support associations

- youth leaders and social service departments
- neighbourhood policing teams
- partner agencies

## 7.5.1 Internal communications

Investigators should look to utilise the following as internal communication:

- internal briefing tools
- operational briefings and debriefings[4]
- daily or extended briefing parades
- local, regional and national intelligence bulletins and publications
- digital briefing systems and email systems
- posters and notice boards
- individual briefings to:
  - senior officers
  - community officers
  - local intelligence
  - custody staff

This enables material and information to be requested and obtained about likely suspects, modus operandi, identification of vehicles, information about a victim, relevant intelligence etc.

The use of more formal briefings and debriefings supports this exchange of information and will be utilised on major and serious crime investigations. Such briefings may also benefit other investigations, depending on the size of the investigation team. Any briefings should be planned and structured to provide opportunities for the investigation team to contribute information and therefore obtain clear direction about the progress of the investigation.

If using more formal briefings investigators should consider:

- location
- notifications—who should attend

---

[4] Also discussed in Chapter 3.

- facilities and equipment
- record keeping and disclosure obligations under the Criminal Procedure and Investigations Act 1996 (CPIA)
- objectives
- structure (use of an agenda)
- removing distractions—mobile telephones etc

### 7.5.2 External communications

The use of the media in an investigation will be influenced by the enquiry itself. High-profile cases attract lots of media interest, but the media can be just as useful in volume crime investigations if managed correctly.

The following are reasons to utilise the media:

- identifying offenders
- locating suspects
- identifying victims
- appealing for witnesses
- identifying or locating property
- public reassurance

All media activity surrounding a case should be monitored and all material released to the media should be retained for disclosure purposes in accordance with CPIA.

### 7.5.3 Media holding statements

Releasing a holding statement can be considered early in the investigation to deal with incoming enquiries from the media. The information released should be limited to:

- confirmation the police are dealing with an incident
- location of the incident
- what the incident is being treated as
- appeals for information
- any reassurance messages
- contact details for the enquiry team/officer in charge

The media will invariably want more information following the issue of a holding statement. Consideration should then be given to what further information can be released and the timing to benefit and not prejudice the investigation. Another important consideration is the impact on the victim, their family or friends of any material released to the media. It is best practice to inform the victim of any releases prior to publication.

Consideration should also be given to mitigating the impact of the media making their own enquiries into the incident. This includes information readily available to them, such as victim information (including photographs) from social networking sites.

### 7.5.4 Identifying the offender

Tactics aimed at identifying offenders by publicising e-fits, CCTV imagery, photographs etc should always be cognisant of any identification issues to ensure compliance with the Police and Criminal Evidence Act 1984 (PACE) Code D.

Further guidance regarding the use of photographs and CCTV can be found in the *Facial Identification Guidance* (ACPO/NPIA, 2009).

### 7.5.5 Locating the suspect

If a suspect has been identified during the investigation but their location is unknown, a media appeal may be used to try and locate them. The integrity of the suspect's evidential identification must not be compromised by such an appeal and advice should be sought in advance from the CPS, the MLO and force solicitor.

### 7.5.6 Witness appeals

These appeals should be focused to ensure potential witnesses are identified by targeting areas and sections of the community most likely to have information to offer. These will include people who have witnessed the offence or another important event connected to it. Factors used to target witnesses could be their employment, residency, leisure activities etc.

### 7.5.7  Reassurance

The power of the media is very strong in the eyes of the public, especially at times of concern. A careful balance needs to be struck between reassurance and warning the public of potential future risks; especially when offenders are still at large following very serious assaults or sexual offences. The opportunity to offer general crime prevention advice as well as seeking information should be utilised.

### 7.5.8  Press conferences

Conducting media conferences should only be considered after consulting an MLO and should be fronted by more experienced investigators who have received media training.

### 7.5.9  Appeals for information

There are more opportunities now open to carry out appeals to the public such as:

- newspapers
- television and radio
- Crimestoppers and BBC Crimewatch
- posters and electronic display boards
- trade journals
- internet
- wi-fi hotspots
- hotlines
- sporting events

- using public figures
- social media outlets, Bluetooth, twitter and websites

The important thing when using any of the above as part of an investigation is to ensure there are sufficient resources to deal with any response, which could be significant.

## 7.6 **Intelligence**

For most volume crime investigations, the intelligence collection strategy may be set by the local tasking coordination process using the National Intelligence Model (NIM). This directs the sourcing and collection of all information relevant to the type of investigation. In major incidents and serious crime enquiries, consideration is given to forming a dedicated intelligence cell, specially set up to obtain and analyse information and intelligence to benefit that investigation.

Regardless of seriousness, most investigations require information to be generated to fill the intelligence and evidential gaps and help solve the case. Intelligence generated during an investigation may also benefit other investigations.

### 7.6.1 **Intelligence sources**

Many sources of information are freely available, including Open Source Research of the Internet (OSRI). Such sources are accessible to anyone via internet search engines, including law enforcement agencies. Generally no prior authorisation is required, but, depending on the circumstances (and potential breaches of privacy), prior authorisation under the Regulation of Investigatory Powers Act 2000 (RIPA 2000) could be required. As such, accessing such sources and deployment of resources depends on the complexity of the investigation and the necessity and proportionality of utilising the tactic.

## 7.6.2  Intelligence evaluation

All intelligence must be evaluated to check its reliability before being recorded in intelligence systems. It is important that personal feelings do not influence any evaluation, which should always be based on professional judgment and not exaggerated so that action is taken in respect of the information.

Investigators are responsible for evaluating any intelligence they submit, ensuring it is an accurate and unbiased evaluation based on their knowledge of the prevailing circumstances existing at the time. The 5 x 5 x 5 system should be used for evaluation and it should be remembered that intelligence is subject to the disclosure rules under CPIA.

## 7.6.3  Analytical support

A trained analyst usually assesses and interprets any collated intelligence during an investigation. They are able to identify information gaps, draw inferences and identify any material requiring further corroboration. This process assists with the development of an intelligence strategy and enables continual review of the progress of the investigation including:

- assessing the progress of lines of enquiry
- identifying new lines of enquiry
- identifying specific elements of an enquiry which would benefit from further development

## 7.6.4  Standard analytical products

To task an analyst effectively, a basic understanding of their techniques and the analytical products produced is required. These products depend on the initial tasking of the analyst and use standardised techniques described in the NIM including the following:

- Crime pattern analysis (CPA) to identify the nature and scale of an emerging or current issue such as:

- hotspot identification
- crime/incident trend identification
- crime/incident series identification
- Demographic/social trends analysis, which examines how demographic and social changes in an area or demographic group affect levels of crime/disorder
- Network analysis, which provides an understanding of the nature and significance of links between people, locations, telephones, finances etc
- Market profiles, which aim to identify the criminal market around a commodity or service. It can provide insight into the level of activity/availability/price
- Criminal business analysis profiles, which help:
  - develop an understanding of how a criminal activity or business operates
  - explain methods used and commodity flow
  - understand the business structure
  - explain roles and responsibilities
  - explain the business in the wider context of the market
- Risk analysis, which is an assessment of threat and risk with the impact and probability of something occurring
- Case/incident analysis, which examines an incident or series of incidents to support the investigation of serious crime and is often associated with major incidents
- Operational Intelligence Assessment (OIA), which is a method of ensuring the investigation remains focused on its original objectives. An OIA identifies if diversification from the agreed objective is occurring
- Results analysis, which evaluates the effectiveness of policing and partnership activity in relation to crime/disorder

### Checklist—Intelligence strategy

- Consider intelligence sources and dissemination (internal, Force Intelligence Bureau (FIB), other forces/agencies)

- Circulation bulletins
- Neighbourhood policing officers and community intelligence
- Analytical tools and products (eg CPA)
- Research suspects, their history and associates
- Research victims, their history, associations and life-styles (victimology)
- Research of locations including previous incidents
- Gain intelligence from briefings and debriefings
- Source Management Units eg use of CHIS
- Research intelligence systems and databases—PND/PNC/local intell systems/HOLMES/COMPACT/VISOR/NSPIS, custody records/QUEST
- Communications data and social media sites
- Covert tactics and resources are good sources of intelligence
- Information from other agencies

## 7.7 Financial Investigation

Financial investigation is not just directed at offences with obvious links to money and assets. Neither is it a tool just to recover criminal assets during investigations. Financial investigation can provide intelligence and evidence to exploit for all types of investigation.

Virtually everyone in the UK leaves some kind of financial footprint in their daily life which can be followed to:

- identify offences committed (including money laundering)
- locate and/or identify suspects, witnesses, victims, missing persons
- prove association with others and/or links to places and premises
- provide information around a person's location and movements
- establish use of services such as phones, transport and other amenities

- identify motives
- identify a person's lifestyle

Financial data may indicate motive, such as personal gain, debt or even financial stress-related domestic violence. Valuable lines of enquiry can be developed by identifying a credit card used to top up a mobile phone, or examining till receipts in retail premises, or use of ATMs (automatic telling machines) to see who was at or near a crime scene (as suspect or witness). A 'financial footprint' may put people in the same place together (ie victim, offender and location) plus any third parties who may be witnesses.

Searches of premises or vehicles should include checks for financial information that may help build a picture of a person's lifestyle or generate additional lines of enquiry (eg money suddenly going in or out of a bank account).

There is a vast amount of information available in the financial world, but investigators must have clear objectives when seeking it which are appropriate and beneficial to the enquiry. Vague and non-specific requests, such as 'obtain a financial profile', are not advisable.

Accredited Financial Investigators (AFI under the Proceeds of Crime Act 2002 (POCA 2002)) are permitted to make pre-order enquiries to financial institutions under the Tournier Rules (*Tournier v National Provincial and Union Bank of England* [1924] 1 KB 461). These permit disclosure of information to law enforcement agencies that would otherwise be a breach of contract between the institution and their customers. Financial data may therefore be disclosed in the following circumstances:

- to protect the public
- to protect the institution's own interests
- under compulsion by law
- with the consent of the owner

This material is gathered by AFIs and is supplied for intelligence purposes only; if it is to be adduced into the evidential chain (including questioning during interview) a production order is required, hence the term 'pre-order enquiries'.

## 7.8 **Digital Evidence, Communications Data and Social Media**

The technological advances in what is now a digital age provides many added investigative opportunities that were previously unavailable. Most people in their everyday lives leave some form of digital footprint which (in a similar way to financial data) can be used to:

- identify offences committed
- identify suspects, witnesses, victims, missing persons
- analyse what is being discussed about incidents and crimes
- prove association with others
- establish travel patterns and links to places and premises
- provide historical and live location data on a person's movements
- establish use of services and amenities
- identify motives including planning offences and researching defences
- obtain lifestyle intelligence and 'victimology'

This list is not exhaustive and it is routine to recover and analyse digital data from many everyday devices including:

- mobile phones (eg smart phones with applications that record location data)
- computers
- netbooks
- tablets
- online gaming devices, eg Playstation and X-Box
- wireless routers (that connect to and record connections to phones and computers)
- MiFi

- data storage devices (some of which are very tiny in size)
- satellite navigation systems
- internet-enabled televisions etc

Data that is likely to be recovered includes:

- internet history logs
- emails
- instant messaging logs
- media files
- text documents
- spreadsheets
- video/still images
- text messages
- location of use data

This list is not exhaustive and rapid technological advances inevitably mean a chapter such as this may soon be out of date. This type of digital information and evidence must be considered in most, if not EVERY investigation (eg during searching of persons, premises and vehicles). However, in all cases it is important to remember that digital evidence is subject to the same rules and laws that apply to documentary evidence. The onus is on the prosecution to show that the evidence produced is no more and no less than when it was first recovered.

Any digital evidence, communications data and social media strategy should be influenced by the four Principles of Digital Evidence contained in the *Good Practice Guide for Digital Evidence* (ACPO/NPIA, March 2012).

### Principle 1

No action taken by law enforcement agencies or their agents should change data held on a computer or storage media which may subsequently be relied upon in court.

### Principle 2

In circumstances where a person finds it necessary to access original data held on a computer or on a storage media, that person must be competent to do so and be able to give evidence explaining the relevance and the implications of their actions.

### Principle 3
An audit trail or other record of all processes applied to computer-based electronic evidence should be created and preserved. An independent third party should be able to examine those processes and achieve the same result.

### Principle 4
The person in charge of the investigation (the case officer) has overall responsibility for ensuring that the law and these principles are adhered to.

## 7.8.1  Digital evidence

Digital evidence is any probative information stored or transmitted in digital form that a party to a court case may use at trial. Before accepting digital evidence, the court will determine if it is relevant and authentic, whether it is hearsay, and if a copy is acceptable or if production of the original is required.

An effective digital evidence strategy should consider planning, capturing, analysing and presenting the material.

### 7.8.1.1  Plan

Planning is required to recover digital evidence from the most effective source that meets the needs of the investigation. Digital material is found in numerous locations including:

- locally on an end user—computer/mobile/smart phone/satnav etc
- public remote sources—websites for social networking/discussion forums etc
- private remote sources—Internet Service Provider (ISP) logs of users' activity/mobile phone company records etc
- 'in transit' material—voice calls, text messages, emails, internet chat

This information will often sit in more than one place, so planning should identify which location is the easiest to access. For example, if evidence is required of contact between two telephone numbers, it is easier to access the call data from the service provider than to forensically examine two telephones. When seeking 'in transit' evidence, the legal implications must be considered and the necessary RIPA authorisation obtained.

### 7.8.1.2 Capture

Capturing evidence refers to the actual 'on screen' capture of information, (eg a screenshot of an open website). The correct seizure measures should ensure any data seized is preserved to offer the best evidential opportunities and proportionality is addressed considering:

- whether the item is likely to contain evidence
- parameters for seizure based on the relevant time frame of the offence
- prioritising examinations based on the location of seizure, for example differentiating between phones found on a person and those found elsewhere, such as from a drawer, where different levels of examination may be appropriate
- evidence possibly stored online—devices in current use (actually connected to the internet) may be the best items to seize

### KEY POINT

Digital devices and media should not be seized just because they are present. Reasonable grounds and justification for seizure must exist. Records should be kept of all actions taken, including photographs/diagrams of equipment locations, any information provided by persons present and actions taken at the scene. Systems that are 'powered on' should be treated with special care; failure to do so may cause unwanted changes to the evidence.

## Checklist—Mobile phone seizure

- Consider forensic precautions/implications
- Record what is on the display
- If switched on, switch device off
- If switched off, do not switch it on
- Do not try to obtain the IMEI (International Mobile Station Equipment Identity)*#06#
- If practicable, obtain all passwords and PIN
- Seal the device in a 'Faraday bag'

## Checklist—Computer seizure

- Consider presence of legally privileged, special procedure or excluded material. If likely, seek CPS advice.
- Prevent any suspect and others from interfering with the equipment/evidence.
- If a device is believed to be involved in crime, take immediate steps to preserve the evidence by stopping anyone using it.
- If a computer is switched on, shut it down and prepare it for transportation.
- If computer is off, do not turn on.
- DO NOT search for evidence on computers, it may be overwritten or compromised.
- Photograph the computer and surrounding area as found prior to removal, including front and back plus any cables and connected devices.
- If something is displayed on the monitor, photograph the screen.
- If believed a document is currently open or a program running is likely to contain evidential data DO NOT power a computer down, DO NOT search the displayed material and contact an expert for advice.
- If encryption may be in use (eg a suspect has a high level of technical knowledge) obtain expert advice before powering down the computer.

- Unplug the power cord from back of the computer, not the wall. For laptops, remove the battery to prevent accidental start-up. Once this is done, remove the power lead; to prevent automated shutdown, do not close the laptop until the power is removed (pulling out the power lead could trigger a shutdown if a laptop is low on battery).
- Disconnect all cables and devices from the computer.
- Package components and transport and store them as fragile materials.
- Seize additional storage media.
- Keep all media, including the computer, away from magnets, radio transmitters and other potentially damaging elements.
- Collect instruction manuals, documentation notes and scrap paper found near the computer; these may contain passwords.
- If believed a computer is destroying evidence, immediately shut it down by pulling the power cord from its back (not the wall socket).

### 7.8.1.3 Analyse

Any communications data strategy links directly with a forensic strategy when decisions are required around the recovery of digital evidence and obtaining contact trace evidence (DNA/fingerprints) to link persons to the device.

An examination sequence should be planned which best supports the investigation by considering:

- the purpose of the examination
- the priorities of the investigation
- briefing the examiners with specific requirements
- initial triage/review of digital devices
- methods of reviewing large amounts of recovered data (including staff required)

Interpreting communications and digital data including its provenance and evidential value should be conducted by trained practitioners (CDI—communications data investigators) who can interpret and cross-reference it with other material to maximise the evidential value. For example, indecent images on a computer may require attribution to an individual; this could be supported by evidence of other recently opened files, search terms and log-on details used.

### 7.8.1.4  Present

Presenting digital evidence includes verbal dialogue between examiners and investigators to identify the best opportunities and relevant lines of enquiry to pursue, followed by statements or reports at the conclusion of the investigation/examination. Providing witness evidence in court may require analytical products to explain complex data to a jury. Digital forensic examiners should also indicate any limitations with the evidence they provide.

## 7.8.2  Social media

Social media such as Facebook, Twitter, You Tube etc, can assist an investigation with:

- searching for intelligence/information in a covert and overt manner
- witness trawls and appeals
- 'victomology'-type detail and association details
- providing reassurance messages to communities
- circulating crime prevention messages

### Checklist—Communications data

- Early engagement with the Force CDI-SPoC is most important. The CDI-SPoC can provide tactical advice and also prevent the loss of volatile data, such as voicemails, or freeze social media accounts.
- All devices a subject has or had access to should be identified and forensically examined at an early stage,

including mobile phones, tablets, computers, routers and gaming consoles, and should include the use of third-party applications and location-based services.

- Identify any usernames, passwords, email addresses or gamer tags which will identify data generated on devices that will assist the investigation.
- In the case of mobile devices such as smart phones, consider call data with cell locations, GPRS data, web logs (if applicable—currently Vodafone only), Wi-Fi access points and IMEI searches.
- For all devices consider third-party applications used by the subject, which will include email, gaming, VOIP technology (eg Skype), instant messaging, such as Blackberry Messenger (BBM) or Apple's iMessage facility.
- Confirm whether the subject uses social media such as Twitter, Facebook, Tumblr or LinkedIn. Identify whether the subject is a member of any special interest groups or forums. Enquiries via the Force CDI-SPoC will identify dates, times and IP (Internet Protocol) locations of most recent usage.
- Other enquiries such as H-2-H can be used as a means of establishing whether there are wireless routers that may connect to phones and computers nearby.

## 7.9 Passive Data Generators

The wide-ranging term 'passive data' covers all *automated* systems which gather and collate information, including automated:

- CCTV systems (not monitored)
- billing systems
- voice recording systems
- access/entry systems

- customer information, eg subscriber details, fuel and loyalty cards etc
- ANPR (Automatic Number Plate Recognition)
- satellite navigation systems
- speed camera systems
- images and data (eg captured on digital cameras and/or mobile smart phones and tablets)
- electronic (offender) tagging systems

These systems can generate large amounts of data which is periodically downloaded, archived or deleted. It is therefore important to recover any material while it is still available and, if it is to be used in evidence, demonstrate how the material was generated and prove its integrity and accuracy. The data generated can assist investigations with general or specific material.

### 7.9.1  General material

These include systems such as CCTV, ANPR etc, which can be used to locate, gather and view images to identify relevant people (witnesses or suspects) and vehicles.

### 7.9.2  Specific material

Specific materials are materials sought in relation to specific circumstances relevant to the investigation, such as:

- presence and activities of victims, witnesses, suspects or vehicles at particular locations and the times they were there
- relationships between individuals
- times of contact between individuals
- lifestyles of individuals
- routes taken and directions of travel

A Passive Data Strategy should consider the:

- objectives to be achieved
- what value the material will add to the investigation
- legalities of access (Data Protection Act, RIPA and PACE)

- proportionality of the request
- volume of data to be obtained
- use to be made of the material
- format of material produced
- length of time needed to find, collect and view
- resources required—human, technological, analytical and financial
- storage and preventing unauthorised access
- briefing regarding integrity and continuity of material

### 7.9.3 CCTV strategy

Recovery and analysis of CCTV is a routine line of enquiry in many investigations and should consider:

- setting parameters for premises and areas to be checked for CCTV systems, including private residences, public and business premises
- method of enquiry, eg a visual check or some form of H-2-H type enquiries to identify any hidden systems
- method of recovery, including making a record of times and dates on the recording system for accuracy against the speaking clock before removing the data
- enquiring if a maintenance policy exists for checking when the time was last reset
- noting camera angles, numbers, position, type of recording equipment (time-lapse or continuous), and locations captured in the image with the surrounding terrain to identify blind spots
- completing CCTV recovery forms and schedules, outlining precise locations and details of all systems and data recovered
- completing CCTV viewing records including the method and circumstances of any recognition made of people on the recording

---

**KEY POINTS**

- Not all CCTV is of reliable quality due to poor images or equipment. Dates and times and the integrity of captured material needs to be checked for accuracy before being relied upon. The ABC principle is applicable once more.
- Public appeals for private CCTV systems within a defined area can be made as part of a communication/media strategy, together with requests for personal recordings eg on mobile phones.
- Setting parameters and fast track actions for the early retrieval of CCTV are essential. Systems are generally used continuously and record over old material, sometimes in a 24-hour loop.
- If important CCTV cannot be recovered quickly enough, finding a way of recording it playing with another device (eg smart phone camera) as secondary evidence might be an option.

---

## 7.10 **Specialist Operational Support and Crime Analysis Unit**

National police resources supplied by Specialist Operational Support (SOS) and the Crime Analysis Unit (CAU) are now located within the National Crime Agency (NCA).

| **Specialist Operational Support (SOS)** | **Crime Analysis Unit (CAU)** |
|---|---|
| Specialist Operations Centre (SOC) | Serious Crime Analysis Section (SCAS) |
| Crime Operational Support (COS) | Missing Persons Bureau |
| National Injuries Database (NID) | CATCHEM |
| Central Witness Bureau (CWB) | |

These units and resources provide information, advice and specialist support to crime investigators and UK law enforcement agencies. Their core business is focused mainly around serious crimes, such as murder, rape, abduction, serious sexual offences or other crime-related critical incidents. Support is arranged through regionally based teams with extensive investigative experience, specialist skills, knowledge and expertise.

| | |
|---|---|
| Specialist Operations Centre | Single point of contact for police forces and key partners requesting advice and support in relation to specialist research, crime investigative and covert law enforcement advice and witness intermediaries. Also manages and provides a gateway to the Expert Advisor's Database. |
| Crime Operational Support | Focuses on sharing and dissemination of good practice, offering tactical and strategic investigative advice through deployable assets such as Regional SIO Advisers (RA) and Crime Investigative Support Officers (CISO). Subject matter experts and specialists, such as Behavioural Investigative Advisers, Forensic Clinical Psychologists, geographic profilers, and national advisers on topics such as search, investigative interviewing, family liaison and forensics can be made available to support investigations at no extra cost. |
| National Injuries Database (NID) | Unique national resource for police forces and forensic practitioners. Provides help and support to crime investigations on the causation of unknown injuries and wounds on victims, case examples of known weapon injuries, sourcing of forensic medical research and external experts, imaging of wounds, alternative light sourcing and body mapping. |
| Central Witness Bureau | Central services unit established to provide strategic and practical assistance to officers supporting protected witnesses. |
| Serious Crime Analysis Section (SCAS) | National unit for identifying any potential emergence of serial killers and rapists at an early stage in their offending. Collates detailed information relating to behaviours and features exhibited in the more serious of sexual offences. |
| Missing Persons Bureau (MPB) | Central hub for the exchange of information and provision of expertise on the subject of missing persons. Provides an holistic service for all missing person investigations, including children, supporting law enforcement and other agencies including specialist advice, national and international cross-matching of outstanding missing individuals, coordination of the UK child rescue alert system and specialist overseas services through Interpol and their international network. |

| | |
|---|---|
| CATCHEM | Centralised Analytical Team Collating Homicide Expertise and Management (CATCHEM). A database that holds details of all child murders/homicides committed in England, Wales and Scotland, from 1 January 1960 to the present date. This includes females under the age of 22 years and males under the age of 17 years at the time of death. It also includes details of long-term child missing persons, attempted murders and some cases of child abduction. The database utilises historical data to analyse current cases, and assists with statistical profiling of probable characteristics of an unknown offender, as well as comparative case analysis to identify potential links between offences. |

## References

T Cook and A Tattersall, *Blackstone's Senior Investigating Officers' Handbook* (2nd edn, OUP, 2010)

*Core Investigative Doctrine* (2nd edn, ACPO/NPIA, 2012)

*Facial Identification Guidance* (ACPO/NPIA, 2009)

*Good Practice Guide for Digital Evidence* (ACPO/NPIA, March 2012)

*Murder Investigation Manual* (ACPO/Centrex, 2006)

*Practice Advice on House-to-House Enquiries* (ACPO/Centrex, 2006)

# Chapter 8
# Managing Witnesses

## 8.1 Introduction

Section 63 of the Youth Justice and Criminal Evidence Act (YJCEA) 1999 and section 52 of the Domestic Violence, Crime and Victims Act 2004 define witnesses as 'any person called, or proposed to be called, to give evidence in the proceedings'.

This definition is not confined to eyewitnesses to the actual crime; it also includes those who can provide indirect or circumstantial evidence.

Gathering accurate and reliable information from victims and witnesses significantly influences the positive or negative outcome of an investigation. Properly conducted interviews provide focus to identify and support other lines of enquiry. Public confidence in the police and their investigative techniques is heavily influenced by witness contact. Having to repeat accounts several times by being passed from officer to officer and unnecessary delays in conducting the interview, often leave witnesses with a very negative perception.

## 8.2 Witness Identification

Identifying and locating witnesses is a main line of enquiry. Some are self-evident, such as those who remain at a scene and identify themselves to responding officers, or those who present themselves at cordons or who contact the police by some other means.

Other witnesses require some investigative activity to locate. This could be for any number of reasons, such as being unaware they are in possession of information relevant to the investigation, or being reluctant to engage in, or being hostile to the enquiry. Experience has shown that witnesses are more willing to cooperate whilst events are still fresh in their mind.

It is essential to identify and deal with witnesses before they are influenced by external factors, as their memory may become distorted by talking with others (including other witnesses) or following media reports.

Each case differs depending on the nature and geography of the area and the timing of the incident. Offences occurring at night time may be witnessed by people who are not present at other times and vice versa, eg taxi drivers, fast food vendors, delivery persons, night clubbers and night workers, shop and office workers etc.

The search for witnesses should not be confined to the scene of the event.

## 8.3 **Principles of Investigative Interviewing**

In 1992 the Home Office produced seven principles of investigative interviewing applicable to victims, witnesses and suspects. These were revised in 2007 and are reproduced below:

1. The aim of investigative interviewing is to obtain accurate and reliable accounts from victims, witnesses or suspects about matters under police investigation.
2. Investigators must act fairly when questioning victims, witnesses or suspects. Vulnerable people must be treated with particular consideration at all times.
3. Investigative interviewing should be approached with an investigative mindset. Accounts obtained from the

person being interviewed should always be tested against what the interviewer already knows or what can reasonably be established.

4. When conducting an interview investigators are free to ask a wide range of questions in order to obtain material which may assist an investigation.

5. Investigators should recognise the positive impact of an early admission in the context of the criminal justice system.

6. Investigators are not bound to accept the first answer given. Questioning is not unfair merely because it is persistent.

7. Even when the right of silence is exercised by a suspect, investigators have a responsibility to put questions to them.

## 8.4 'PEACE' and Achieving Best Evidence

PEACE remains the recognised framework for police interviews with victims, witnesses and suspects and is compatible with the phased approach described in Achieving Best Evidence (ABE) and illustrated in the following table.

| Achieving Best Evidence | PEACE |
| --- | --- |
| Planning and Preparation | **P**lanning and Preparation |
| Establishing Rapport | **E**ngage and Explain |
| Initiating and supporting a free narrative account. Questioning | **A**ccount, clarification and challenge. |
| Closing the interview | **C**losure |
| Evaluation | **E**valuation |

Extracted from the National Investigative Interviewing Strategy (NPIA/ACPO, 2009)

## 8.5 **Planning Witness Interviews**

Planning is essential to conducting an effective interview which meets the needs of the investigation, whilst supporting the witness to give their best evidence in court. Each interview is different; the planning requirements depend on the circumstances of the witness and/or the complexity of the interview, which must have specific aims and objectives to accomplish.

The first stage of planning is to assess the witness, including any initial account they have already provided. Depending on the circumstances, the witness may themselves be a 'scene' requiring forensic recovery avoiding cross-contamination (see Chapter 6). The timing of the formal interview may be influenced by any medical attention required or forensic examination/recovery which should be prioritised.

The perfect situation is for interviewers to have extensive information about the witness but minimal information about the event, apart from its nature, location, timeframe and how it was reported. In these circumstances the interviewer is unlikely to inadvertently influence the witness account. However, this is rarely possible due to interviewers also being engaged in other aspects of the investigation.

### KEY POINT—INTERVIEW ADVISERS

Utilising specialist interview advisers (PIP Level 2, previously known as Tier 5) is not confined to suspects. Advice is available on all aspects of witness interviews and should be sought as early as possible in investigations involving complex witness issues.

In all cases a written record of the planning process should be maintained and an interview plan produced containing clear aims and objectives.

The checklist below covers some generic planning considerations:

**Checklist—Initial considerations**

- Identify if the witness is significant, vulnerable or intimidated
- Assess the witness to identify and address any issues impacting on the interview, eg personal circumstances, age, gender, physical/mental disorder or learning disability, cultural/religious considerations, first language, injury, trauma, medication taken, any current or previous contact with the police or other agencies, any relationship or contact with the alleged offender
- Identify any consent issues that may impact on their participation in the interview
- Assess the extent of any reluctance or hostility
- Based on what is already known, assess what the witness is likely to have seen, heard or otherwise experienced concerning the matter under investigation
- Decide on the method of recording (video, audio or MG11 with no recording)
- Identify any special measures to be applied for
- Set specific achievable objectives for the interview and identify topics to support them
- Obtain appropriate advice if necessary
- Obtain the resources to conduct the interview
- Prepare an interview plan
- Conduct a risk assessment to establish the extent, if any, to which the witness may be at risk of intimidation and take action to mitigate

## 8.6 **Witness Assessment and Classification**

A witness should be 'classified' as early as possible to identify if they are 'significant', 'vulnerable' or 'intimidated'. This influences the method of recording and the presentation of their evidence in court, including any special measures applications required.

These classifications should not be applied too rigidly as some witnesses may cross over categories. Their circumstances could also change during the investigation, eg by becoming a victim of intimidation when none was present before or at the time of their interview.

---

### Definition—Significant witness (ineligible for 'special measures')

Significant witnesses (SWIT also referred to as 'key' witnesses) are those who:

- Have or claim to have witnessed, visually or otherwise, an indictable offence, part of such an offence or events closely connected with it (including any incriminating comments made by the suspected offender either before or after the offence) and/or
- Have a particular relationship to the victim or have a central position in an investigation into an indictable offence.[1]

---

Where practicable a SWIT should be interviewed on video (including DVD) unless they do not consent, in which case the interview should be audio recorded. If the witness does not consent to audio recording, a statement may be obtained directly. In each of these cases the reason for not consenting to video or audio recording should be included in the MG11.

With multiple witnesses, it may be necessary to limit the numbers who are video or audio recorded according to the resources available. A written record should be made of this decision with the selection criteria, eg the witnesses who are most evidentially valuable and factors such as their proximity and line of sight to the event, sobriety/intoxication at the time, availability and willingness to assist the enquiry.

---

[1] *Achieving Best Evidence in Criminal Proceedings, Guidance on interviewing victims and witnesses, and guidance on using special measures* (Ministry of Justice, 2011) (ABE) and the *Murder Investigation Manual* (ACPO/Centrex, 2006) (MIM).

There is no statutory provision for significant witness interviews to be played to the court as their evidence-in-chief by the prosecution. The *defence* may ask permission to play some or all of the recording to support their case, particularly if they intend to challenge the manner of questioning.

## 8.6.1 Consent

*The Code of Practice for the Victims of Crime* (Criminal Justice System, 2005) and the Witness Charter require witnesses to be given sufficient information to make an informed decision on whether to consent to the interview. This means explaining the purpose of the interview, including the witness potentially attending court.

---

**Definition—Vulnerable witness**

Vulnerable witnesses are:

- All child witnesses (under 18 years); and
- Any witness whose quality of evidence is likely to be diminished because they:
  - Are suffering from a mental disorder (as defined by the Mental Health Act 1983) or
  - Have a significant impairment of intelligence or social functioning, or
  - Have a physical disability or are suffering from a physical disorder.[2]

---

## 8.7 Child Witnesses

Before the implementation of the Coroners and Justice Act 2009, child witnesses were aged under 17 years and classified as being of two types:

---

[2] Section 16 YJCEA, amended by section 101 of the Coroners and Justice Act 2009.

(1) those in need of special protection concerning sexual or violent offences; and

(2) children giving evidence in all other types of case.

This distinction no longer applies, so all child witnesses are treated the same regardless of the offence.

The presumption is that child witnesses will give their evidence in chief by video recorded interview, and any further evidence by live TV link unless the court is satisfied this would not improve the quality of their evidence. However, with the agreement of the court, they may opt out of giving their evidence by video recorded interview or by live link or both. If they do this there is a presumption the child witness will give evidence from behind a screen, unless they also choose to opt out of this special measure and the court agrees.

Where a video recorded interview is made before a child witness's 18th birthday, they are still eligible for video recorded evidence in chief and live TV link after they turn eighteen.

---

**KEY POINTS—DECISION TO RECORD THE INTERVIEW**

- When deciding whether or not to allow a child witness to 'opt out', the court must be satisfied the quality of their evidence will not be diminished. This decision is taken on a case-by-case basis and does not mean the interview should not be visually recorded during the investigation stage.
- The staged process of explaining the opt-out process to the child or their carer where capacity is an issue is described in *Achieving Best Evidence* (Ministry of Justice, 2011 (paragraphs 2.29 to 2.39).

---

## 8.7.1 Fraser Guidelines

A child can consent in their own right provided they can understand the implications of the interview, including the use to which it is to be put, but the consent of a parent or guardian is required if they cannot understand. This follows Lord Fraser's judgment in the 1985 case of *Gillick v*

*West Norfolk and Wisbech AHA* (3 All ER 402) and is often referred to by the term 'Fraser' or 'Gillick' competent.

Informing the child's parents or guardian of the interview and consent are separate issues; however, except in exceptional circumstances, they should be informed even where the child has the capacity to consent to the interview themselves.

## 8.8 **Mental and/or Physical Disability**

Witnesses with a mental and/or physical disability are only eligible for special measures if the quality of their evidence is likely to be diminished by reason of their disorder or disability (section 16(1) YJCEA). This means the 'completeness, coherence and accuracy' of their evidence, and the witness's ability to provide answers which address the questions put to them that can be understood individually and collectively by others. A physical disability which does not affect the ability to communicate does not classify the witness as vulnerable.

## 8.9 **Identifying Vulnerability**

In principle everyone, whatever their age, is competent to give evidence, unless the court finds they are unable to understand the questions put to them, or they are unable to give answers which can be understood (section 53 YJCEA).

The court must consider the special measures that are available to assist the witness, so identifying an individual's abilities as well as disabilities is important during the planning phase of the interview.

Historically the police have found identifying vulnerability difficult, particularly when the indicators are not easily recognised, such as limited speech and understanding. Hidden factors to consider could include a witness's inability to read or write, responding inappropriately or inconsistently to questions, focusing on small points or the irrelevant rather than the important issues, a short attention span, being eager to please, becoming withdrawn or over exuberant.

Apart from visible behaviour, other indicators of vulnerability include;

- receiving Disability Living Allowance
- resident at a group/residential home or institution
- employed in a sheltered workplace
- attending a specialist day service
- possessing certain prescription medicine
- receiving support from a carer
- receiving support from a social worker or community psychiatric nurse

## 8.10  **Mental Capacity Act**

The Mental Capacity Act 2005 applies to anyone over 16 who lacks mental capacity, and a decision needs to be made concerning them. It establishes a principle that everyone is assumed to have capacity unless established otherwise, and provides an obligation on the police to try and communicate with people where mental capacity is an issue; including modifying the language used when providing information, enabling it to be understood.

Where mental capacity is an issue, the overriding principle is to act in the best interests of the individual, which may involve consulting widely with persons known to them and, in the interview context, may be relevant to witnesses over 16 where consent to a visually recorded interview is required.

---

### Definition—Intimidated witnesses

Intimidated witnesses are those whose quality of evidence is likely to be diminished by reason of fear or distress in relation to testifying in the case.[3]

---

[3] Section 17(4) YJCEA.

---

When deciding whether a witness is intimidated, the court considers the nature and alleged circumstances of the offence, the age of the witness and, where relevant:

- their social and cultural background and ethnic origins
- their domestic and employment circumstances
- any religious beliefs or political opinions
- any behaviour towards the witness by the accused, members of the accused's family or associates, or any other person who is likely to be either an accused person or a witness in the proceedings

**KEY POINTS**

- Intimidated witnesses are vulnerable due to their circumstances rather than their personal characteristics *(Speaking Up For Justice: Report of the Interdepartmental Working Group on the Treatment of Vulnerable or Intimidated Witnesses in the Criminal Justice System* (Home Office, 1998)), the Code of Practice for Victims of Crime indicates that the families of homicide victims fall into this category and are entitled to an enhanced service from the police
- The police have a responsibility to identify vulnerable and intimidated victims and ensure this information is passed to other organisations with responsibilities under the Code

## 8.11 Complainants in Cases of Sexual Assault

Complainants in cases of sexual assault automatically fall into the intimidated category. However, there is now a rebuttable presumption that video evidence in chief will maximise the quality of their evidence so they may opt out. This must be decided on a case-by-case basis and is the complainant's decision, provided they give their informed consent.

Opting out of video evidence in chief does not mean the interview should not be visually recorded; it means it is not played to the court as the complainant's statement and an MG11 witness statement is taken and used instead.

---

**KEY POINT**

Not all complainants need or want to use their visually recorded interview as their evidence in court. Some victims, on realising the defendant can see them on the live link screen, have preferred to give their evidence from behind a screen; others may prefer to see the alleged offender in court and give their evidence without screens. This is decided on a case-by-case basis.

---

## 8.12  Witnesses to Gun and Knife Offences

Witnesses to specified gun and knife crime also automatically fall into the intimidated category unless they opt out. The offences included in the definition of gun and knife crime are extensive and contained in the legislation concerning:

- murder and manslaughter
- Offences Against the Person Act 1861
- Prevention of Crime Act 1953
- Firearms Act 1968
- Criminal Justice Act 1988
- Violent Crime Reduction Act 2006

---

### Offence—Witness intimidation

Witness intimidation is an offence in its own right under section 51 of the Criminal Justice and Public Order Act 1994; it can be committed before the crime has been reported, during the investigation, or after the case has been heard at court.

---

## 8.13 **Special Measures**

A range of special measures are available under the YJCEA to help vulnerable and intimidated witnesses give their best evidence in court; they apply to prosecution and defence witnesses but not to defendants who give evidence.

Special measures are granted by the court if it is agreed any or a combination of them would improve the quality of the witness's evidence, including:

- screens to shield the witness from the defendant when giving evidence
- live TV link allowing the witness to give evidence from outside the court room
- giving evidence in private (limited to sexual offences and those involving intimidation by someone other than the accused)
- removal of wigs and gowns by judges and barristers in the Crown Court
- use of video recorded interviews (visually recorded statements) as evidence-in-chief

Vulnerable (not intimidated) witnesses are also eligible for:

- using an intermediary who specialises in helping those with communication difficulties
- special communication aids, eg an Alphabet Board

### 8.13.1 Early special measures meetings

Any of the special measures (or a combination of them) which would help a witness give their best evidence should be identified and communicated to the Crown Prosecution Service (CPS) as early as possible, either by recording on the case file (MG2) or through an early special measures discussion/meeting.

Unless it is impracticable to do so, a pre-interview early special measures meeting takes place where there is any doubt as to whether or not to video record the interview, where an intermediary or aids to communication are involved, or where there might be an issue regarding an interview supporter.

The police are responsible for calling early special measures meetings during the investigation where necessary and the CPS can call a meeting after reviewing the case file. In practice, these meetings are usually telephone discussions with decisions recorded on form MG2.

Special measures are not automatically granted and prosecutors must have sufficient information and evidence to support the application. Witnesses should not be promised or misled into believing that they are guaranteed to be granted any special measures.

### 8.13.2  Registered intermediaries

A registered intermediary is a communications specialist accredited by the Ministry of Justice. They can provide assistance when interviewing people with communications difficulties. This includes witnesses with learning disabilities and very young children.

The intermediary conducts a pre-interview assessment and provides advice on conducting the interview, including questioning techniques. During the interview, the intermediary is allowed to explain questions and answers so far as is necessary to enable them to be understood by the witness or the questioner, without changing the substance of the evidence.

Approval for the admission of evidence obtained through an intermediary is applied for retrospectively to the court, who may also appoint an intermediary to assist the witness in giving evidence.

Police forces have different internal processes for obtaining a registered intermediary and advice is available from the NCA Specialist Operations Centre.

### 8.13.3  Interview supporters

An interview supporter's role is to provide emotional support to the witness, not to facilitate communication. They are not appropriate adults who are no longer referred to in the Police and Criminal Evidence Act 1984 (PACE) regarding witness interviews.

The views of the witness should be sought before the interview on the identity of any interview supporter. They cannot be another witness or potential witness in the case, people allegedly involved in the offence in some way, interpreters or intermediaries.

It is not best practice (and rarely necessary) for an interview supporter to be present in the room with the witness during their video recorded interview. Depending on the witness's wishes, the supporter is usually located in another nearby room during the interview.

With the permission of the court, an interview supporter may now accompany the witness in the live TV link room while they give evidence.

## 8.14 Interpreters

When English is not a witness's first language it may be necessary to conduct the interview with an interpreter, depending on the wishes of the witness if they have sufficient understanding of English.

Interpreters should be briefed before the interview to explain the questioning techniques to be used and how they may impact on their interpretation, for example by not filling pauses when used deliberately to allow the witness to focus plus, accurately translating what has been said.

Questions should be directed to the witness for the interpreter to translate. A common mistake is interviewing the interpreter and not the witness.

## 8.15 Reluctant Witnesses

Reluctant witnesses are those who have the ability to provide testimony but are unwilling to do so. This could be due to fear of the offender, not trusting the police/criminal justice system, or their personal circumstances and the perceived consequences of giving evidence.

There is no single tactic to overcome reluctance. The first stage is to identify the reason(s) and mitigate them. Gaining the witness's trust is crucial, so the timing, location and method of any approach needs careful consideration to prevent the witness being compromised and caused difficulty.

Reasonable steps should be taken to address their concerns and, depending on the reasons for their reluctance, the witness could be categorised as intimidated and be eligible for special measures. Other options include additional security measures and referral to support from the Victim Support Service and Witness Care Units. No false promises should be made or pressure put on the witness to give evidence.

---

**Checklist—Security and protection measures**
- Providing a 'Homelink' alarm system
- Providing a portable personal attack alarm
- Upgrading security at the home address
- Installing temporary CCTV
- Entries on briefing and intelligence systems
- Critical Address Register entry to prioritise any police attendance
- Temporary relocation
- Using an agreed codeword when making contact

---

Where life-threatening intimidation is involved, if certain criteria are met full witness protection is a consideration. This has life-changing consequences for the witness and significant resource and financial implications. Witness protection is a protected tactic and any further advice should be sought from local or regional People Protection Units or SIOs.

## 8.15.1 Witness summonses

Paragraph 4 of Schedule 3 to the Crime and Disorder Act 1998 provides a power to bring a relevant witness before a magistrates' court, either by summons or warrant, to make a deposition before the court. This should only be considered in exceptional circumstances if:

1. A person is already charged with the offence in question.
2. The witness has provided information which is of value to the prosecution but has refused to provide a written statement.
3. The procedure would not place them at unacceptable risk if the evidence is produced, which cannot be mitigated by special measures (screens, anonymity).

## 8.15.2 Hostile witnesses

Hostile witnesses are people who are believed to have witnessed an offence, part of an offence or events closely connected with it, but who are opposed to the investigation process (ABE 2011, paragraph 2.144). This could be due to their lifestyle, their own criminality, a close relationship with the alleged offender and/or intending to appear as a defence witness.

Some hostile witnesses simply refuse to cooperate with the police, whilst others may provide false information intended to support an alleged offender's account.

Where a hostile witness consents to be interviewed, it should be visually recorded in accordance with the significant witness guidance; any refusal to visually or audio record the interview should be dealt with in the same manner.

### KEY POINT—NEGATIVE STATEMENTS

Where a hostile witness claims not to have any information to assist the investigation, every effort should be made to record this in a witness statement. These 'negative statements' are useful if the person intends to appear or later appears at court as a defence witness.

## 8.16 **Witness Anonymity**

Open justice is a fundamental principle enshrined in Article 6(1) of the European Convention on Human Rights (ECHR). This underpins the requirement for prosecution witnesses to be identifiable to the defendant and the open court, and to support the defence when presenting their case by cross-examining the witnesses.

Sometimes this principle acts as a barrier to successful prosecution, particularly in cases of homicide, organised crime, and gang and gun offences, where revealing the witness's identity would put them and their family/friends at risk of serious harm.

Potential witnesses also have rights under Article 2 of the EHCR (right to life) which the police have a positive obligation to protect.

### 8.16.1 **Investigation Anonymity Orders**

The Coroners and Justice Act 2003 (sections 74 to 83) created Investigation Anonymity Orders to reassure people with information in gang-related gun and knife murder that their identity will be protected throughout the investigation and permanently afterwards.

The qualifying criteria are:

- the offence must be murder or manslaughter
- the person likely to have committed the offence is aged between 11 and 30 years and
- is a member of a gang where the majority of its members are aged between 11 and 30 years
- the informant has reasonable grounds to fear intimidation or harm if identified
- the informant must have information that will assist the investigation and without an order would probably not provide the information

The application is made by a Superintendent on behalf of the Chief Officer of Police to a Justice of the Peace.

At the time of writing the Secretary of State is to review the use of Investigation Anonymity Orders.

---

**KEY POINT—ANONYMITY AT TRIAL**

A separate Witness Anonymity Order must be applied for if the investigation proceeds to trial.

---

### 8.16.2 Witness Anonymity Orders

An Investigation Anonymity Order does not guarantee the witness anonymity at trial, so a separate application must be made for a Witness Anonymity Order (sections 86 to 90 Coroners and Justice Act 2009).

An order made by the court requires appropriate specified measures be taken to ensure the identity of the witness is not disclosed in, or in connection with the proceedings. These include:

- their name and other identifying details being withheld and removed from any material disclosed to any party to the proceedings
- using a pseudonym
- the witness not being asked questions that might lead to their identification
- use of screens
- the witness's voice being modulated/distorted
- the order will not allow a witness to be screened so they cannot be seen by the judge or other members of the court (if any) or the jury (if there is one)

---

**KEY POINT—WITNESS ANONYMITY**

Witness anonymity including information security requires careful management to prevent compromise. Anonymous witness interviews must be meticulously planned and executed so engaging an interview adviser in the process is essential.

---

The Act and the Guidance apply to all witnesses, including undercover police officers and test purchase officers. Applications must be authorised by Heads of CPS Complex Casework Units or Heads of Division.

## 8.17 Interview Resources and Contingencies

The resources required for an interview will reflect the needs of the witness, such as the requirement for any interview supporter, interpreter or intermediary. Interviewers should always ensure they are properly equipped to conduct the interview as follows:

**Checklist—Equipment and resources**

- Interview suite
- Suitable location if the interview is not being conducted in a dedicated suite
- Recording equipment, including portable equipment and a background screen if required
- Aids to communication if required
- Interview plan
- Note-taking material
- Paper for the witness to produce a sketch or plan
- Exhibit labels
- Maps, plans or diagrams which may be required for the witness to mark locations of significance during the interview
- Exhibits or copy exhibits to be shown to the witness during the interview if required

### 8.17.1 Contingencies

Planning the response to possible contingencies may prevent a future legal challenge to the interview process.

Researching and evaluating the witness assists in identifying potential issues which can be anticipated and planned for, eg an assessment of their lifestyle may provide indicators of potential admissions to criminality.

### 8.17.1.1 Witness involvement in offences

Witnesses could admit criminal offences during the interview and this contingency should be planned for. Such admissions fall into two categories:

1. Admissions concerning or linked to the offence under investigation, eg assisting an offender.
2. Admissions to offences unconnected to the offence under investigation, eg a witness to a serious assault admitting taking drugs shortly before.

Admissions to other offences should take into account the seriousness of the crime under investigation, measured against the seriousness of the offence admitted by the witness.

Where the priority is to obtain evidence from the person as a witness, the interview can proceed (ABE 2011, paragraph 3.146). However, if during the interview it is considered the evidence of the witness as a suspect is highly relevant to a particular case, the interview should be terminated (taking care not to close it abruptly) and the witness told they may be interviewed later about the matter they have made incriminating admissions to.

Decisions on witness admissions to offences should be made by the officer in charge of the investigation in consultation with the CPS if necessary. Promises of immunity from prosecution should never be made or offered during the interview.

### 8.17.1.2 Witnesses who become suspects

Where there is no subjective reason to suspect a person is involved in the offence under investigation they should be treated as a witness or a TIE (see Chapter 7).

If, however, during interview a 'witness' admits involvement in the offence, they should be allowed to finish what they are saying but must not be asked any further questions. At this point any further questioning must be conducted under caution with access to legal advice.

The interview should be closed and the officer responsible for the investigation informed immediately to decide whether to caution and arrest the person whose status has now changed from witness to suspect due to self-incrimination.

### 8.17.1.3 Suspects who become witnesses

Not every person interviewed under caution for an offence is prosecuted; they may be eliminated and released, or disposed of by other means, such as cautioning.

Before a person who was previously a suspect is interviewed as a witness they must be released from any obligations as a suspect, meaning they must be unconditionally released. A person cannot be on bail to return to the police station and simultaneously be treated as a witness in the same case.

The interview recording(s) and associated material produced when the person was a suspect are unused material. The defence may compare any account given by the witness with their interview under caution, so it is important to identify and explain any omissions, anomalies or changes of information between the person's witness and suspect interviews.

A different situation arises when a suspect is charged with an offence connected to the crime under investigation but is willing to provide evidence against any accomplices or co-accused.

In these circumstances, the person responsible for the investigation must consult the CPS. An option (with CPS agreement) is for the person to enter an early guilty plea, be interviewed as a significant witness, then provide evidence before they are sentenced.

## 8.18 Serious Organised Crime and Police Act 2005

Sections 71 to 75 of the Serious Organised Crime and Police Act 2005 (SOCPA) provide opportunities for criminals (including convicted persons) to give evidence for the prosecution against accomplices in return for reductions in sentence and even immunity from prosecution.

The options in such circumstances are:

- granting conditional immunity from prosecution for assistance (section 71)
- providing a 'restricted use undertaking' for any information the individual provides for a prosecution or investigation (section 72)
- powers available to the court when sentencing persons who plead guilty to take account of their undertaking to assist an investigation or prosecution (section 73)
- powers for a person sentenced to be referred back to court for their sentence to be discounted when they assist an investigation or prosecution (section 74)
- when sentencing people under section 74, courts can exclude people from the court or impose reporting restrictions

This tactic is used for offenders who could provide evidence against the higher echelons of serious organised crime and terrorist groups. Interviews with these 'assisting offenders' is a highly specialised area involving high-level CPS authorisation, risk assessment, resource and cost implications and detailed planning.

## 8.19 Interview Objectives and Structure

Whatever recording medium is used (if any), and whatever the circumstances of the witness, it is essential to plan and structure the interview with clear objectives to achieve, supported by relevant and properly sequenced topics.

Common criticisms of visually recorded interviews are they are overly long, often contain confusing, repetitive and unnecessary detail, create ambiguity rather than clarity and can even undermine the witness due to the manner of questioning.

Review processes consistently identify the reason for these issues as failure to plan. It cannot be overemphasised that planning is not a luxury to sacrifice in the belief that it wastes time; effective planning actually saves time by producing more focused and timely interviews which meet the needs of the courts and the investigation.

Investigative interviews are not confined to the evidential account of the event experienced by the witness; they also support the investigation by obtaining information to identify and support lines of enquiry which themselves may not be relevant to the court. For this reason structure is important.

The structure of a witness interview is summarised in the table that follows.

| Phase 1 | Rapport |
|---|---|
| Phase 2 | Witness's free narrative account of the incident(s) |
| Phase 3 | a) Topic division and probing of the witness's account of the incident<br>b) Topic division and probing of case-specific information important to the investigation |
| Phase 4 | Closure |

Extracted from ABE 2011 (Figure 3.2, page 77)

It is beyond the scope of this chapter to describe in any great detail how to conduct the interview. Detailed guidance is contained in Chapter 3 of ABE 2011 and other approved professional practice.

The four-phased structure applies to all witness interviews, but a key point to highlight is the importance of getting to the purpose of the interview (eg the event) at the beginning in Phase 2. After covering any necessary rapport, Phase 2 of the interview deals with the witness's description of the incident by obtaining their uninterrupted account of the event.

This is followed by Phase 3(a) where the *account of the event* is divided into topics, then probed and expanded for further information. Phase 3 separates into areas of *general investigative practice* and *case-specific material* which reflect the differing needs of the court and the investigation.

Depending on the complexity of the interview, the circumstances of the witness and/or volume of material to be covered, it may be necessary to conduct a series of interviews with a distinct break between phases 3(a) and 3(b).

### 8.19.1 General investigative practice

General investigative practice applies to all witness interviews and includes subjects such as:

- points to prove the offence
- other people present at the time, including if they are known to the witness and their description (using the ADVOKATE mnemonic)[4]
- anything said by the witness to a third party after the incident, eg evidence of first complaint
- assessing any identification evidence provided by the witness using the ADVOKATE mnemonic

---

**A—A**mount of time the person/event was under observation by the witness.

**D—D**istance from the witness to the person/event.

**V—V**isibility—including lighting conditions at the time, does the witness wear spectacles and were they worn at the material time.

**O—O**bstructions—obscuring the witness's view.

---

[4] The ADVOKATE mnemonic is from *R v Turnbull and Camelo* (1976) 3 All ER 54.

> **K**—**K**nown or seen before—does the witness know or have they seen the person before and in what circumstances.
>
> **A**—**A**ny reason to remember—anything specific that made the person/incident memorable to the witness.
>
> **T**—**T**ime elapsed—how long since the witness last saw the person prior to the incident.
>
> **E**—**E**rrors—or discrepancies in the witness's description.

## 8.19.2 Case-specific material

Case-specific material is specific to the witness and differs from case to case and witness to witness; it links to the *investigative areas* or identified topics to be covered. This information may be revealed during the witness's free recall of the event or during questioning to expand it. However, if the material has not been mentioned by the witness and explored in these phases it should then be introduced by the interviewer.

Such material includes investigative areas such as:

- disposal of items used in the commission of the alleged offence if the witness has knowledge of this
- any *significant evidential inconsistencies* between the witness account and other material gathered during the investigation
- any *significant evidential omissions between* any account provided and other material gathered during the investigation
- whether any information omitted is important enough to warrant further investigation
- explaining any knowledge the witness may have of an alleged offender or victim, including any background/relationship history, places frequented, any events related to, or similar to the alleged offence
- background information that might enhance or detract from the witness's credibility, eg alcohol consumed or

drugs taken by the witness and their level of intoxication at the time of the event

- any information concerning the likelihood of witness intimidation (to avoid any confusion this should be covered later in the interview after the account of the event has been dealt with)

Case-specific topics should link the interview to other lines of enquiry, for example obtaining information relevant to the strategies for forensic evidence, identification, media, CCTV, search, passive data, victimology, intelligence and arrest.

---

**KEY POINT—SOCIAL NETWORKING**

The impact of social media is now being recognised in the criminal justice process. It is potentially a source of bad character on the witness depending on the issue in the case, for example Facebook pictures in 'gangster poses' or behaving inappropriately when drunk which could be used in court to undermine their credibility. This should be considered when researching a witness's credibility.

---

# 8.20 Post-interview Responsibilities

## 8.20.1 Evaluating the interview

The witness interview should be evaluated to establish:

- what any information provided says about the alleged event
- whether any new lines of enquiry have been identified
- whether any fast track actions/urgent lines of enquiry have been identified that need communicating immediately to the enquiry team
- any gaps or omissions in the witness's account when compared with other material available to the enquiry
- any inconsistencies in the witness's account when compared with other material already gathered and assessed

---

- any welfare issues requiring post-interview support for the witness (eg experiencing an unexpected traumatic reaction)

---

**KEY POINT—OBJECTIVITY**

Evaluating a witness interview should be an objective assessment of the information they have provided and not their behaviour whilst revealing it, which could be tainted by the interviewer's opinion on the veracity of the witness.

---

## 8.21 **Supplementary Interviews**

Effective planning should reduce the need to conduct further interviews with the witness. However, evaluation or developments in the investigation may necessitate a supplementary interview, such as:

- the witness indicates to a third party they have significant new information which they did not disclose during the initial interview but they now wish to tell the investigation team
- the initial interview identifies new lines of enquiry (or wider allegations) which cannot be satisfactorily explored in the time available
- when preparing their defence an accused raises matters not covered in the initial interview
- significant new information emerges from other witnesses or other sources

In such circumstances, a supplementary interview should be planned and recorded in the same medium as the original. Consideration should be given as to whether a supplementary interview is also in the best interests of the victim/witness and a record made of the decision.

Further evidential interviews should not be conducted to try and retrieve a situation where the witness's evidence has been compromised by use of inappropriate questioning techniques in a previous interview.

## 8.22 **Interview Products**

### 8.22.1 Significant witnesses

Apart from exceptional cases, the evidence of a 'significant witness' is adduced in a Criminal Justice Act 1967 witness statement (MG11) compiled by reviewing the recording as soon as possible after the interview. The witness does not need to be present at this point.

The witness is asked to read the statement, indicate any alterations or additions they consider necessary, and sign it, having agreed the statement's content.

There is no requirement to visually record the statement signing unless the witness reveals significant new or changed information whilst checking it. In this case, a supplementary visually recorded interview should be conducted to provenance and preserve the integrity of the additional or changed information.

The witness statement is submitted as evidence with the case papers, and the recordings with any notes and other material are unused material.

---

**KEY POINT**

In exceptional cases it may be appropriate to take a brief written statement from the witness introducing the recording, then produce a transcript of the interview instead of a section 9 CJA (Criminal Justice Act 1967) statement. In these rare circumstances, prior agreement from the CPS is essential.

---

### 8.22.2 **Statement chronology and content**

Generally, evidence written in a statement should be direct evidence reflecting the first-hand knowledge of what the witness saw, heard, felt or otherwise experienced, otherwise it is likely to be hearsay and inadmissible in court.

Hearsay is an extensive subject and the rules have never been absolute. If there is any doubt about the information's relevance or otherwise, particularly in complex cases, the hearsay should be included. It is then open to the CPS to either edit the hearsay or request a further statement to be obtained omitting it.

Written statements should adopt the following chronology:

1. Introduction
   • Set and describe the scene
2. Circumstances
   • Describe the incident/event in chronological order, explaining the physical and verbal actions of the persons present
   • Record the event first before moving on to background material
3. Descriptions
   • Description of offender(s) in as much detail as possible
   • Names or descriptions of relevant others at the scene
   • Use the ADVOKATE mnemonic
4. Objects
   • Detailed description of objects involved, eg any vehicle, weapon, stolen property (including where stolen from)
   • Identify any objects produced as exhibits with an exhibit number
   • Chronologically list any exhibits
5. Other issues
   • Information which links to the case-specific information if relevant, eg antecedents and victimology, personal relationships, movements etc

### 8.22.2.1  Victim personal statement

• If including a victim personal statement (VPS) about the impact of the offence on the victim, underline after the main body of the statement and record the VPS in the victim's own words, or consider recording in a separate statement.

### 8.22.2.2 General rules and practice

- If applicable, the opening paragraph explains the interview was visually (or audio) recorded
- The witness's own words should not be converted into police jargon
- Anything said by an accused should be recorded in direct speech (as far as the witness remembers it)
- Errors should be crossed out with a single line and initialled by the witness at the time the statement is made
- The address or telephone number of a witness should not be included in the body of the statement unless it is relevant to the enquiry, eg a burglary victim
- All surnames should be in capital letters
- If a witness is under 18 state their exact age
- Signatures are required on each page and the declaration on page one

### KEY POINTS

- Witness statements should represent the chronological order of the events which may not be in the same order that the witness revealed the information when interviewed. When preparing the statement, it is permissible to organise the information to structure the statement.
- The previous point should not be mistaken for permission to edit the witness's account. All information about the event must be included in the statement to prevent accusations of being selective.

## 8.22.3 Investigative summaries

Witnesses rarely provide all their information in a chronological order at the first time of asking. Some witnesses provide comprehensive information during the interview with key details revealed at different points in their account or during the questioning phase.

It could be essential for others involved in the investigation to have a clear understanding of the information provided by the witness, but it may be impractical for them to view the video recording. This often occurs during major investigations where decision makers are not directly involved with conducting the interview, but require the information before a witness statement is prepared.

Upon completion of an interview, the compiling of an accurate chronological 'investigative summary' of the information should be considered. This differs from a Record of Video Interview (ROVI) in that the chronology of the document reflects the alleged incident and not the order that the witness recalled the information during their interview. In other words, the information about the account and each relevant topic is all in one place within the document.

Chronological investigative summaries assist others, including the officer responsible for the investigation when making decisions about further lines of enquiry. They can also help the interviewers of any suspects with their interview plans and decisions concerning the content of pre-interview briefings with legal representatives.

Investigative summaries also inform any early special measures discussions with the CPS and any later special measures applications.

The preparation of a chronological investigative summary is described in further detail in ABE 2011 (page 87).

### 8.22.3.1  Record of Video Interview (ROVI)

A ROVI should be compiled in every case where a vulnerable or significant witness is interviewed and a visual recording made. As far as possible they should provide a chronological summary of the conduct of the interview (unlike an investigative summary which chronologically describes the event) and be as succinct as possible. A ROVI is different from any notes made during the interview.

### Checklist—ROVI content

- Identify that a rapport phase took place (more detail may be required concerning some vulnerable witness interviews)
- Identification issues, including descriptions and the ADVOKATE points
- Location of the event(s) witnessed
- Points to prove
- Time, frequency, dates, locations and those present when the offence occurred
- Injuries
- Threats and admissions made
- Key statements made by the witness, other witnesses, the suspect
- Anything negating a potential defence
- Any aggravating factors
- Any issues undermining the prosecution or assisting the defence case
- A short summary of a VPS if made on the same recording
- Background material of no apparent relevance should be summarised in general terms

### Checklist—ROVI completion

- ROVIs should always be recorded on a form MG15 and be typed if possible
- Include timings recorded in hours, minutes and seconds using the clock shown on the video and speakers
- Identify speakers against the relevant entry

### KEY POINTS—ROVI

Although prepared from the same interview:
- a ROVI is a chronological record of the interview
- an investigative summary is a chronological record of the event

---

A ROVI is different from a ROTI with a suspect and is not:

- a statement
- a transcript
- a replacement for the video or
- an exhibit
- a chronological investigative summary

---

## 8.23 Photographs, E-Fits and Identity Procedures

If a witness is to view photographs or an identification procedure, their witness statement containing the first description of the suspect should be recorded before the viewing.

Additionally, where a visually recorded interview has been conducted, the production of facial composites using E-Fit or other systems, or producing an artist's impression should also be visually recorded. This enables the court to hear the evidence from the witness in the same medium as their main evidence-in-chief and may reduce the need for them to give additional evidence by showing how the E-fit/ sketch was obtained.

Staff compiling images with witnesses using these procedures should be trained to the appropriate level to record the interview.

## 8.24 Refreshing the Memory of a Witness whose Evidence is Visually Recorded

Witnesses are entitled to see a copy of their statement before giving evidence and, unless it has been ruled inadmissible, a visually recorded interview may also be shown to the witness before the trial to refresh their memory.

How, when and where this viewing is done is decided on a case-by-case basis. The aim is to enable the witness to give their best evidence in court. It is a police responsibility to arrange for prosecution witnesses to view their video recorded interviews; the CPS should be consulted about where this should take place and who should be present.

Police forces have their own policies and procedures for facilitating the viewing. In some areas Witness Care Units or support staff are responsible and in others it is for the officer in charge of the investigation to organise.

In all cases, the purpose should be explained to the witness and their views sought; a record must be kept of anything said during the viewing. The timing should take account of the witness's needs, ability to concentrate and the date of the trial to maximise the benefit, eg it is generally bad practice to rush a viewing on the morning the witness is due to give evidence. However, if the witness is scheduled to give evidence that afternoon, a morning viewing may be beneficial.

Issues such as providing support to the witness while they refresh their memory and any implications of this at trial should be raised for a decision at the Plea and Case Management Hearing (PCMH).

## 8.25 Defence Witness Interviews

Accused persons in all Crown Court trials are required to submit a statement before the trial setting out the nature of their defence and the details of any alibi witnesses they intend to call. These are generally referred to as defence statements and are compiled by the legal representative and signed by the defendant; they are not section 9 CJA statements and should not be confused with such.

Since 1 May 2010 the accused is also required to provide details to the prosecution of anyone they intend to call as a defence witness at the trial (other than the defendant). This notification allows an opportunity for the police to interview them before the trial unless they have already obtained a statement from them during the investigation.

The defence witness must be asked whether they consent to be interviewed and informed:

- the interview is requested following their identification by the accused as a proposed witness either for an alibi or as a defence witness
- they are not obliged to attend the proposed interview
- they are entitled to be accompanied by a solicitor (at their own expense)
- a record will be made of the interview and they will be supplied with a copy

If the witness consents to the interview they must be asked:

- whether they wish to have a solicitor present
- whether they consent to a solicitor attending the interview as an observer on behalf of the accused
- whether they consent to a copy of the record of interview being sent to the accused
- even if they do not consent, the disclosure obligations under the Criminal Procedure and Investigations Act 1996 (CPIA) may nevertheless require the prosecution to disclose the record of interview to the accused (and any co-accused)

The accused or their legal representative should be informed before the interview that:

- an interview has been requested with the witness
- whether the witness consented to the interview or not
- if the witness consented, whether they also consented to a solicitor attending the interview as an observer on behalf of the accused
- if the accused is not legally represented and if the witness consents to a solicitor attending the interview as an observer on their behalf, the accused must be offered the opportunity to appoint a solicitor to attend before the interview is held

- a reasonable date, time and venue for the interview must be nominated (with notification of any changes)
- with consent of the witness, the accused's solicitor must be given reasonable notice of the arrangements and be invited to observe the interview

Conducting the interview:

- An accurate record must be made, whether the interview takes place at a police station or elsewhere
- The record must, where practicable, be a visual recording with sound, or audio recording, or a section 9 CJA statement (MG11)
- Any witness statement must be completed during the interview and timed and signed by the maker
- A copy of the MG11 and recording (if made) must be served on the witness, and, if the witness consents, provided to the accused or the accused's solicitor

---

**KEY POINT**

- A defence witness is not under any legal obligation to be interviewed, or make a statement to the police. If they refuse, an official note book entry should be completed and an MG11 produced by the officer describing the full circumstances.
- Provided the accused's solicitor was given reasonable notice of the interview taking place, the fact that they are not present does not prevent the interview being conducted.
- If the witness withdraws consent to the accused's solicitor being present, the interview may continue without them.
- If the witness intends to appoint a solicitor for the interview, they must be permitted to attend.
- The MG11 must be completed whilst the interview is in progress; this means it is not prepared later by reviewing the recording, as with a significant witness interview.
- The interview will always be unused material and will need listing and describing on the MG6C.

---

## 8.26 **Witness Charter**

The Witness Charter (Criminal Justice System, 2009) applies to all witnesses regardless of whether they are a victim. It sets out what help can be expected from the police by witnesses to a crime or incident and the standards of service from other criminal justice agencies and lawyers if the witness is asked to give evidence for the prosecution or the defence in criminal proceedings.

The Charter outlines 34 standards on the level of service a witness should expect at every stage in the criminal justice process and intends to ensure every witness receives a level of service that meets their individual needs.

### References

Achieving Best Evidence in Criminal Proceedings, Guidance on interviewing victims and witnesses, and guidance on using special measures (Ministry of Justice, 2011)

*Murder Investigation Manual* (ACPO/Centrex, 2006)

National Investigative Interviewing Strategy 2009 (NPIA/ACPO, 2009)

*Speaking Up For Justice: Report of the Interdepartmental Working Group on the Treatment of Vulnerable or Intimidated Witnesses in the Criminal Justice System* (Home Office, 1998)

The Code of Practice for the Victims of Crime (Criminal Justice System, 2005)

The Witness Charter (Criminal Justice System, 2009)

# Chapter 9
# Managing Suspects

## 9.1 Introduction

Having identified that a crime has been committed, the next objective is usually to identify the offender(s). Suspects can emerge from any of the 'golden hour' actions and main lines of enquiry described in previous chapters. Managing suspects requires management of risk and community impact and exploitation of evidence-gathering opportunities available, from arrest and forensic recovery through to detention management and interviewing.

Generally, suspect status should only be declared when:

- tangible evidence exists to directly link a person to involvement in the offence, eg physical/forensic evidence, eyewitness testimony, CCTV or
- circumstantial evidence exists of sufficient strength to provide reasonable objective grounds for suspicion based on known facts or information (as opposed to merely a hunch) or
- there is a strong intelligence case supported by properly graded and evaluated material (ie using the 5 x 5 x 5 system)

Nominating a 'suspect' is a significant phase in an investigation and needs careful consideration, with the rationale and justification being recorded, usually in a policy file/decision log.

The term 'suspect' implies there are reasonable grounds to suspect a person's involvement in an offence. It affords them protection and rights under the Police and Criminal Evidence

Act 1984 (PACE), including legal advice and being cautioned before questioning. It is important not only to declare suspect status when appropriate (as there needs to be justification for doing so), but also in some circumstances to justify why a person is not a nominated suspect to defend possible accusations of deliberately circumventing their legal rights.

---

**KEY POINT**

The term 'suspect' should not be confused with the term 'subject' which is often used during investigations. The two terms can become confused not only in police circles, but also by the media and sometimes even lawyers, so any misunderstandings need to be corrected quickly.

---

## 9.2 **Powers of Arrest**

The amendments to PACE by the Serious Organised Crime and Police Act 2005 (SOCPA) mean arrests can be made for any offence provided certain conditions apply. For an arrest to be lawful the arresting officer must have:

(1) reasonable grounds to *suspect* an offence has been committed, and the person committed it, or they were in the act of committing, or were about to commit the offence; AND

(2) reasonable grounds to *believe* arrest is necessary for one or more of the specified reasons (known as the necessity test) to:
   a. ascertain the person's name
   b. ascertain the person's address
   c. prevent the person causing physical harm to themselves or suffering physical injury
   d. prevent loss of or damage to property
   e. prevent an offence against public decency
   f. prevent an unlawful obstruction of the highway
   g. protect a child or vulnerable person

    h. prevent any prosecution being hindered by the disappearance of the person in question

    i. allow a prompt and effective investigation of the offence or of the conduct of the person in question

The prompt and effective investigation condition may be satisfied if there are grounds to believe that the person:

- has made false statements or statements that cannot be easily verified
- may steal or destroy evidence
- may intimidate, threaten or make contact with witnesses or
- it is necessary to obtain evidence by interviewing

Where the suspected offence is *indictable*, this condition may justify arrest if there is a need to:

- enter and search premises occupied or controlled by the person
- search the person
- prevent contact with others or take fingerprints, footwear impressions, samples or photographs for comparison purposes

On 12 November 2012 a revision of PACE (Code G) was implemented demanding more detailed consideration of the necessity test by arresting officers than was previously required. Arresting officers must consider facts and information tending to indicate the person's innocence as well as their guilt (including whether any use of force was lawful and reasonable), and consider practical alternatives to arrest, such as street bail or conducting a voluntary interview with the suspect.

Each case must be decided on a case-by-case basis according to the circumstances existing at the time, using professional judgment and discretion concerning the necessity and proportionality of arrest. The importance of documenting decision making for future scrutiny cannot be underestimated.

## 9.3 **Voluntary Interviews**

Necessity to arrest and necessity to interview are two separate issues, therefore if arrest is not considered necessary a suspect could be interviewed voluntarily under caution.

Code G now clarifies the situation of what to do if a 'volunteer' leaves the interview before its conclusion, having been told (under Code C) they are not under arrest and are free to leave at any time. Leaving the interview could now justify arrest (under Code G) if there is a necessity to continue questioning, but this must be judged on the circumstances of the individual case existing at the time.

Necessity to arrest should be kept under continuous review during the interview. Circumstances could change making arrest necessary, eg threats made to others necessitating arrest to prevent physical harm, or denials requiring corroboration necessitating detention for a prompt and effective investigation (these are not exhaustive examples).

Voluntary interviews should be planned and conducted as thoroughly as for a person under arrest. Attendees should not be treated with any less consideration than an arrested person. It is the interviewer's responsibility to ensure any vulnerability is identified and appropriate safeguards are in place, including any requirement for an appropriate adult, interpreter etc. Voluntary attendees also have an absolute right to outside communication and legal advice.

### KEY POINTS

Special Warnings under sections 36 and 37 of the Criminal Justice and Public Order Act 1994 (CJPO) only apply to suspects under arrest; therefore they do not apply to voluntary interviews. Planning to deliver special warnings may therefore justify necessity to arrest.

Adverse inferences from silence may apply when a person is interviewed voluntarily as they can access legal advice if they wish.

## 9.4 **Planning and Conducting Arrests**

Arrest plans depend on the nature of the offence and what is known about the suspect. The primary objective is to gather as much evidence as possible from the arrest whilst minimising any identified risks.

Generic considerations include the timing and location of arrest, recording significant statements, searching suspects and premises, transporting suspects, preventing forensic cross-contamination, location of detention; briefing Custody Officers, checking personal property and seizing relevant items (eg mobile phones); physical and forensic medical examination and evidential samples, photographing injuries; considering urgent or emergency interviews; holding incommunicado, fitness to interview, appropriate adults, interpreters, interview strategies, fast track actions and forensic submissions etc.

The first stage of planning is researching the suspect and the likely place of arrest, including who or what may be present to inform the risk assessment. Although each case differs, some generic intelligence requirements includes the following.

### Checklist—Suspect intelligence profile
- Name, age, date of birth
- Other names used or known by
- Full physical description
- Known intelligence (including any medical conditions/vulnerabilities, habitual drug use etc)
- Recent photograph
- Current residence
- Details and layout of the location of arrest (eg owner, other occupants, risks and hazards such as children, pets, likely substance abuse, hiding places, outbuildings and gardens, access and exit points, previous

police visits and outcomes, local community/neighbourhood details etc)
- Vehicles owned, used or accessed
- Other premises and places frequented
- Known associates and their profiles including descriptions
- Criminal history including modus operandi and behaviour on arrest
- Current intelligence
- Warning markers, eg use of violence, weapons or access to firearms
- Previous responses in police interviews

## 9.4.1 Timing of arrests

The best time to arrest a suspect is ideally as soon as possible after the offence has been committed during the 'golden hour' period. This reduces the loss of material and is always in the public's best interest.

The timing of an arrest should meet the needs of the investigation whilst being balanced against the risk posed by the suspect to the victim, witnesses, the general public and the arresting officers. Additionally, any likelihood of further offences being committed or evidence being concealed, destroyed or falsified requires consideration. The circumstances must be kept under continuous review should circumstances change.

Reasons to delay arrest could include pursuing other lines of enquiry, using covert tactics, coordinating the simultaneous arrest of multiple suspects, gathering further evidence to conduct a more effective interview, and reducing the possibility of using pre-charge bail. A record should be maintained outlining the reasons with justification for the delay.

**KEY POINT**

Any decision to delay arresting an identified suspect must be fully justified. If they commit further preventable offences it may be difficult to defend the decision, so it is extremely important to make a record of the decision and its rationale (see also 'Problem solving in Chapter 3).

### 9.4.2 Location of arrest

The arrest location is influenced by its timing, eg whether the suspect is likely to be at home or at another location during a particular time of day. In some sensitive areas the impact of the arrest on the wider community needs consideration and consultation in advance with the Community Cohesion Officer or Neighbourhood Policing Team Inspector to manage the consequences.

Juveniles should generally not be arrested at their place of education unless it is unavoidable, in which case the Principal or their nominee must be informed (PACE Code C, 11E).

### 9.4.3 Powers of entry

Excluding entry under a search warrant, powers to enter and search premises to arrest for an indictable offence are available under section 17 PACE. Reasonable force may be used if necessary where there are reasonable grounds to believe the person sought is on the premises. Searches must only be to the extent reasonably required to locate the suspect.

Powers of entry are available for certain non-indictable offences, namely:

- prohibition of uniforms in connection with political objectives, section 1 Public Order Act 1936
- offences relating to entering and remaining on property, sections 6 to 8 or 10 Criminal Law Act 1967

- fear or provocation of violence, section 4 Public Order Act 1986
- driving under the influence of drink or drugs, section 4 Road Traffic Act 1988
- failure to stop when required by a constable in uniform, section 163 Road Traffic Act 1988
- offences involving transport system workers being over the prescribed alcohol limit, section 27 Transport and Works Act 1992
- failure to comply with an interim possession order, section 76 Criminal Justice and Public Order Act 1994
- certain offences relating to prevention of harm to animals, Animal Welfare Act 2006

Premises can also be entered and searched for a suspected person with the written permission of a person able to provide consent (PACE, Code B, 5.1 to 5.4), and to capture persons unlawfully at large, save life and limb or prevent serious damage to property (section 17 PACE).

### 9.4.4 Arresting officers

There are no rigid rules on the most appropriate person to conduct an arrest, eg an interviewing officer or someone not involved in the interview process, and there are advantages and disadvantages to each. Whoever is tasked must be fully briefed, ensuring they form their own opinion of the grounds and necessity; otherwise the arrest may be unlawful.

### 9.4.5 Significant statements/silence

Significant statements and unsolicited comments have been discussed in Chapter 4 and do not require further elaboration, except to say when planning arrests an officer should be nominated to record in writing all significant statements and unsolicited comments, and to maintain a contemporaneous record until the suspect has been booked into custody. They are of tremendous value to the subsequent interview, and even denials when arrested can form the basis of a challenge when presented later.

### 9.4.6 Urgent interviews

Arrested persons must not be interviewed except at a police station or other authorised place of detention, unless delay would be likely to lead to interference with, or harm to evidence connected with an offence, interference with or physical harm to other people, serious loss of or damage to property, alerting other suspects not yet arrested, or hindering the recovery of property obtained as a consequence of an offence.

If any of these criteria is satisfied, an 'urgent interview' can be conducted, eg questioning to locate and recover a firearm discarded by a suspect before anyone finding it is caused harm. Critically, questioning must cease once the relevant risk has been averted or the necessary questions have been put (PACE, Code C, 11.1). Urgent interviews should therefore not be used to ask evidential questions about other lines of enquiry.

When planning arrests involving urgent interviews, consideration must be given to practicalities, including the method of recording, such as contemporaneous notes or portable visual recording/audio equipment.

### 9.4.7 Interviews prior to requested legal advice at a police station

When a detainee requests legal advice at the police station, they cannot be interviewed until they have received it, unless the grounds above apply, and authorisation has been provided by a Superintendent or above (not necessarily independent of the investigation).

---

**KEY POINTS**

- Should the criteria apply, PACE allows urgent interviews to be conducted away from the police station, such as at the location of arrest. There is no reference in the Act to any authority being required in such circumstances.
- At the police station, after legal advice has been requested, urgent interviews need to be authorised by a Superintendent (or above) and use the caution '*You don't have to say anything but anything you do say may be given in evidence*'. This means adverse inferences cannot be drawn from the interview.
- Urgent interviews are infrequently used except in missing persons, kidnap, abduction and terrorism cases and are likely to be closely scrutinised by the courts.

---

## 9.4.8  Searches

Searching detainees and their premises and vehicles is a routine activity requiring little expansion here. Searches are an opportunity to gather evidence linking suspects to alleged offences and, although it seems obvious, when planning arrests, full details of items sought should be supplied to the search team. Specific tasks and responsibilities should be designated to individuals ensuring nothing is overlooked and opportunities missed through wrongful assumptions and misunderstandings (see also Chapter 12, section 12.6).

## 9.4.9  Location of detention

Suspect arrest planning includes considering the location of detention if multiple suspects are to be arrested simultaneously. Ideally, detention should be at different locations to prevent collusion and forensic cross-contamination. If this is impracticable and the same location is used, the Custody Officer should be briefed in advance to prevent the investigation being disadvantaged.

---

Particular facilities and resources may be required which is worth considering as part of the arrest strategy. Forensic kits and cells that are not regularly used may be ideal when it is necessary to maximise forensic examination opportunities. Access to interviewing facilities with downstream monitoring capability may also be a consideration.

## 9.4.10  Pre-briefing the Custody Officer

In pre-planned operations the Custody Officer and their staff should be briefed in advance, including the grounds for arrest, to prevent unnecessary information being asked for and revealed in the presence and hearing of the suspect.

A Custody Officer briefing is an opportunity to raise issues concerning the detention, such as managing multiple suspects, availability of cells including 'dry cells', forensic considerations, welfare and risk management.

## 9.4.11  Arrest team briefing

All personnel involved in the arrest operation, including any specialist resources such as Crime Scene Investigators (CSIs) and others if involved should be briefed by the officer responsible for the investigation or their nominee. An operational 'order' or briefing document is often prepared using a recognised structure such as IIMARCH or SAFCORM.

Effective briefings can have a positive or negative impact on success. Questions about roles and responsibilities should be encouraged and dealt with at the briefing. Documents and records are subject to disclosure rules, and care must be taken to ensure no briefing material is inadvertently left at the subject premises (which has embarrassingly happened in the past).

**Checklist—Arrest and search team briefing agenda**

- Introductions
- Operational objectives
- Details of the investigation
- Current situation
- Details of suspect(s) to be arrested, including recent photograph(s)
- Background details on persons expected to be at an address
- Powers of arrest and the grounds
- Powers of entry
- Precise wording for arresting officer(s)
- Search strategy and parameters (if applicable)
- Details of items sought and how they are to be dealt with
- Documentation including any warrants and search record numbers
- Roles and responsibilities
- Risks and control measures
- Communications including Airwave channels and contact telephone numbers
- Arrangements for collecting material under the Criminal Procedure and Investigations Act 1996 (CPIA)
- Debriefing location and time

The control room/command centre for the relevant area should be informed in advance should assistance be required. The local policing team manager should be informed and any local community issues considered.

## 9.4.12  Arrest and search team debriefing

A structured debriefing of staff involved in the arrest operation ensures all evidential opportunities have been maximised and relevant information disseminated:

**Checklist—Debriefing agenda**

- Any significant statements
- Other persons present
- Potential witnesses spoken to
- Search results
- Details and location of any items seized
- Fast track actions identified
- Other investigative material identified
- Potential special warning material identified
- Completing and collating evidential statements
- Completing the Premises Searched Record
- Intelligence gathered
- Other pertinent information (eg callers to the address and spoken to)
- Handover and collection of any relevant material under CPIA
- Welfare/health and safety issues
- Local community impact information

### KEY POINT

Arrests and searches provide opportunities to conduct other enquiries, including speaking to other people at the address who could be witnesses or potential intelligence sources. Neighbours and any visitors can be spoken to at the same time to see if they have any useful information about the detained person, such as movements, habits, associates, vehicles used etc. Conducting house-to-house (H-2-H) enquiries with neighbours can be useful for the same purpose.

## 9.5 Proactive Hunts for Suspects

Often swiftly locating and arresting a known suspect(s) is paramount due to the risk they present to the safety of the public. These cases can attract significant public and media attention and involve substantial resources, particularly if firearms are involved.

The offence under investigation could be a 'crime in action', meaning the offender is or may be continuing to commit the offence or further crimes whilst the investigation is in progress, eg an abduction where a victim's whereabouts are unknown, or there is reason to believe there may be further victims, or the same victim remains at risk of further harm.

The priority consideration is potentially increasing the risk to others by generating publicity and identifying the suspect. Additionally, there are consequences for the investigation, including the impact on any subsequent identification procedures and obtaining and coordinating the necessary resources.

Any high-impact 'person or manhunts' are potential critical incidents and are usually the responsibility of a Senior Investigating Officer (SIO) involving Crown Proscution Service (CPS) and Association of Chief Police Officers (ACPO) level consultation in a Gold Commander role.

## 9.6 **Detention Management**

### 9.6.1 **Briefing the Custody Officer**

Whilst recognising the Custody Officer's obligations when authorising detention, the content of the custody record (which is available for inspection by legal representatives) should be managed to prevent it having a negative impact on any subsequent pre-interview disclosure briefing. PACE Code G, Note 3 now specifically states:

An arrested person must be given sufficient information to enable them to understand they have been deprived of their liberty and the reason they have been arrested, as soon as practicable after their arrest, e.g. when a person is arrested on suspicion of committing an offence they must be informed of the nature of the suspected offence and when and where it was committed. The suspect must also be informed of the reason or reasons why arrest is considered necessary. Vague or technical language should be avoided. When explaining why one or more of the arrest criteria apply, it is not necessary to disclose any specific details that might undermine or otherwise adversely affect any investigative processes. An example might be the conduct of a formal interview when prior disclosure of such details might give the suspect an opportunity to fabricate an innocent explanation or to otherwise conceal lies from the interviewer.

When briefing the Custody Officer, any information which could impact on the investigation should not be supplied within hearing of the suspect. Additionally, other matters affecting the suspect's detention should be included in the briefing.

### Checklist—Custody Officer briefing

- Nature of offence
- When and where committed
- Significant statement(s) made by the suspect
- Welfare, vulnerability, risk assessment and any requirement for:
  - appropriate adult
  - interpreter
  - strip search
  - intimate search
  - delayed intimation
  - delayed access to legal advice
  - conducting an urgent interview
  - forensic considerations (eg intimate and non-intimate samples, medical examination, photographing injuries or identifying features etc)

It is helpful (as well as courteous) to provide a contact number for custody staff to make contact with the lead investigator if necessary.

## 9.6.2 Strip searches

A strip search is the removal of more than a person's outer clothing. It is authorised by the Custody Officer when considered necessary to remove an article which the detainee would not be allowed to keep because it may present a danger to themselves or others, might be used to assist escape, or be evidence relating to an offence. The conduct of strip searches is covered by PACE Code C, Annex A.

## 9.6.3 Intimate searches

Intimate searches are the physical examination of a person's body orifices (other than the mouth). They are authorised by an Inspector or above with reasonable grounds for believing the detained person may have concealed on them anything they could and might use to cause physical harm to themselves or another, or a Class A drug which they intended to supply to another or export.

There must be reasonable grounds for believing an intimate search is the only way of removing the item(s), and the detainee must be told before the search that it has been authorised, along with the grounds.

If the intimate search is for drugs, before being asked to consent, the detainee must be warned that refusal without good cause may harm their case if it comes to trial, and their consent must be provided in writing.

**KEY POINTS**

- Intimate searches seeking items the detainee might use to cause harm may only be conducted by a registered medical practitioner or registered nurse, unless an Inspector or above is satisfied *as a last resort* that the risks associated with allowing the item to remain with the detainee outweigh the risks associated with removing it, and it is not practicable for a doctor or nurse to conduct the search. In such cases an officer of the same sex as the detainee may carry out the search.
- A drugs search can only be conducted at a hospital, surgery or other medical premises by a healthcare professional.

## 9.6.4 Delaying intimation/incommunicado

Detainees may have one friend, relative or other person known to them or interested in their welfare informed of the location of their detention as soon as practicable. This can be delayed when the offence is *indictable* and an Inspector or above believes communicating the information is likely to lead to interference with or harm to evidence or other people, alerting others suspected of committing the offence but not yet arrested, or hindering the recovery of stolen property.

The officer may also authorise delay where they have reasonable grounds for believing the detained person has benefited from their criminal conduct, and the recovery of the value of the property constituting the benefit will be hindered by telling the named person of their arrest.

Intimations must not be delayed for more than 36 hours and cannot be delayed once the grounds have ceased.

**KEY POINT**

With arrested juveniles, the person responsible for their welfare must be informed of their detention.

## 9.6.5 Right to legal advice

Delaying legal advice is only permitted if the detainee is in police detention for an *indictable offence* and authorisation has been provided by a Superintendent or above. Reasonable grounds are required to believe delay might lead to interference with, or harm to, evidence connected with an indictable offence, interference with, or physical harm to other people, serious loss of, or damage to property, alerting other people suspected of having committed such an offence but not yet arrested for it, or hindering the recovery of property obtained in consequence of the commission of such an offence.

The officer may also authorise delay if they have reasonable grounds to believe the person detained for the indictable offence has benefited from their criminal conduct, and the recovery of the value of the property constituting the benefit will be hindered by allowing access to legal advice.

Once sufficient information to avert the risk has been obtained, questioning must cease until the detainee has received legal advice.

---

**KEY POINT**

Where legal advice has been requested but denied, adverse inferences from silence cannot be drawn. The interview must be conducted using the shortened caution, 'You do not have to say anything but anything you do say may be given in evidence'.

---

Where a solicitor nominated or selected by the detainee cannot be contacted, or has previously indicated they do not wish to be contacted or, having been contacted, has declined to attend, and the detainee has been advised of the duty solicitor scheme but has declined to ask for the duty solicitor, an Inspector or above may authorise the interview to proceed. Adverse inferences may be drawn in these circumstances because legal advice is not being denied.

---

Where a detainee who has requested legal advice changes their mind, the interview may be started or continued without delay provided they agree in writing or on the interview record, and an Inspector or above has enquired about the reasons and authorises the interview to proceed. Confirmation of the detainee's agreement, the reasons (if any) for changing their mind and the name of the authorising officer shall be recorded in the interview record. Adverse inferences may be drawn because legal advice is not being denied.

---

**KEY POINT**

If a solicitor arrives at the station to see a particular person, that person must be informed of their arrival and asked if they would like to see the solicitor, whether they are being interviewed or not (unless Annex B applies). This applies even if the detainee has declined legal advice, or if, having previously requested legal advice, they have agreed to be interviewed without it. The solicitor's attendance and the detainee's decision must be noted in the custody record.

---

## 9.7 **Forensic Strategy**

Depending on the requirements of the investigation, a forensic strategy to prove or disprove a suspect's involvement in the offence may be required. Any necessary authorities should be planned for in advance and the attendance and briefing of a forensic medical examiner and CSI coordinated. All requirements should be made clear to fully exploit any opportunities.[1]

---

[1] Recovering forensic evidence from people including suspects is described in Chapter 6.

## Checklist—Suspect forensic considerations

- Forensic material available eg clothing, jewellery, trace evidence through swabbing for blood or fibres
- Relevant authorities required
- Cross-contamination control plan
- Coordinate attendance and brief/de-brief FME and/or CSI (if required)
- Full body examination (body mapping) noting marks, scars or injuries
- Record descriptions of any tattoos or other identifying marks
- Describe any injuries using conventional medical terms and layman's language in brackets
- Measure and photograph all injuries with a scale
- General body photographs of detainee's front, back, hands, feet, legs, head, including full length images
- Medical staff to record the detainee's height, weight and build
- Sample of blood/urine for evidence of intoxication or misuse of substances relevant to the investigation
- Buccal swab
- Firearms discharge/explosive residue swabs
- Swabs from palms and backs of both hands
- Fingernail scrapings
- Fingernail cuttings
- Combed head hair
- Plucked head hair
- Cut head hair
- Swabs from body sites suspected of being connected to an assault
- Body impression
- Dental impression
- Continuity and storage of exhibits

## 9.8 **Managing Legal Advisers**

The solicitor's role in the police station is to protect and advance the legal rights of their client. On occasion this may require giving advice which has the effect of avoiding their client giving evidence which strengthens the prosecution case (PACE, Code C).

In fulfilling their obligations, solicitors probe the evidence and actively enquire into the investigation, including the police conduct towards their client. They assess their client's vulnerability (if any) and ability to communicate during interview, and identify the safest defence. This could be to answer questions, produce a prepared statement or remain silent.

Furthermore the solicitor will attempt to gain the most favourable disposal by influencing the police not to charge, or obtaining the most favourable alternative, eg caution. If their client is charged they will seek the most favourable position, such as granting bail.

### 9.8.1 **Pre-interview briefings**

Solicitors will seek as much information as possible about the case from all sources including custody staff, investigators and the suspect. Custody Officers should only provide information on the *grounds* for detention and matters relating to the custody record. Any requests for further information should be referred to the investigating officer for consideration of the pre-interview briefing (PIB).

A PIB is the meeting between an investigator and the legal representative before the interview. This is when the reason(s) for arrest and the purpose of the interview are outlined.

This briefing should be conducted in a suitable location like an office or interview room, where it can be held in private without interruption. Discussions at custody desks in full view and hearing of others with surrounding distractions are not good practice.

The content of the briefing should be contained in a typed or written document, a copy of which is provided to the legal representative and signed by all parties present. Best practice is to audio record the process so an accurate record is available for future scrutiny if necessary. This may be impractical for all cases due to resource restrictions (particularly in volume crime investigations), but as a minimum a written briefing should be provided.

A record of the PIB including any information provided or withheld with the reasons should be recorded on form MG6a and submitted with any prosecution file.

Although there is no legal obligation to provide any information about the *investigation* prior to interview, it may be beneficial to disclose certain material so the solicitor can provide realistic informed advice to the suspect.

The content of the briefing is therefore a matter of professional judgment, decided on a case-by-case basis considering:

- the material available or likely to become available to the investigation
- the impact on the interview of disclosing the information
- what the suspect already knows about the investigation, in which case there is probably limited value in withholding this information
- the material gathered by the investigation which the suspect is unaware of, in which case the decision is when and how to reveal this information
- if the suspect is vulnerable, this may influence the amount of information provided to prevent allegations of confusing them
- with multiple suspects a common pre-interview disclosure strategy may be initially required
- the content and timing of any media releases may impact on the content of the PIB and timing of the interview

- whether phased disclosure over a series of interviews is an appropriate tactic to use
- care must be taken not to mislead the solicitor or to over-state the importance of any evidence disclosed

### KEY POINTS

- A balance must be drawn between providing sufficient information for a solicitor to provide realistic advice, whilst preventing a suspect fabricating a defence based on the information disclosed.
- Solicitors are aware the police are not legally obliged to provide further information but often press for further disclosure and question the strength of the evidence. Such requests should be politely and professionally resisted.

### 9.8.2 Disclosure to unrepresented suspects

Providing a form of PIB to suspects who are not legally represented has generated some debate. The ACPO position is that providing disclosure to unrepresented suspects is not recommended. Legal advisers are experts in law and can therefore properly advise their clients on the strength and significance of any evidence revealed. Unrepresented suspects could misunderstand the content of a PIB and its significance for the interview; they may have questions on the information provided which in themselves risk becoming an interview.

### 9.8.3 Legal advice during interview

Solicitors may intervene during interview to seek clarification, challenge improper questions (or the manner in which they were put), advise their clients not to reply to particular questions or to provide further legal advice. Their role is clear and does not include questioning the interviewer on the conduct of the investigation or the content of the PIB.

### 9.8.4 Exclusion from interview

Solicitors can only be required to leave an interview if their approach or conduct prevents or unreasonably obstructs proper questions being put to the suspect, or their response being recorded. Examples of unacceptable conduct include answering questions on the suspect's behalf, or providing written replies to quote (this does not include introducing a prepared statement).

If this happens the interview should be stopped and a Superintendent or above consulted if readily available, or if not an officer not below Inspector and not connected with the investigation. After speaking with the solicitor, the officer consulted decides if the interview should continue with that solicitor present. If it is decided to exclude them, the suspect is allowed to consult another solicitor and have them present during interview.

Removing a solicitor from interview is a rare and serious step; a court may need to be satisfied that the decision was properly made. The officer making the decision may therefore need to witness the solicitor's conduct by listening to a recording of the interview.

## 9.9 **Interviewing Suspects**

Interviewing is a constantly evolving discipline and beyond the scope of this section to cover in more than cursory detail. As with victims and witnesses, the PEACE framework and principles of investigative interviewing described in Chapter 8 also apply to suspects.

### 9.9.1 Planning suspect interviews

All interviews must be properly planned with achievable topic-based objectives to meet the needs of the investigation. Planning should never be sacrificed or dismissed as too time consuming (which it is not).

The following checklist contains some generic planning considerations but is not exhaustive:

### Checklist—Interview Planning

- Review available material/facts already established
- Review the suspect's antecedents/background information to identify:
  - evidence of bad character
  - any vulnerability which may impact on the interview
  - age
  - gender
  - domestic circumstances
  - educational attainment/intellectual ability
  - physical and mental health
  - trauma
  - intelligence linking the suspect to other offences
  - previous contact with the police and responses when interviewed
- Examine the custody record
- Establish fitness to interview
- Review detainee's property for relevance to investigation
- Review detainee's physical description for relevance to investigation
- Identify any injuries/marks for potential special warning
- Review detainee's clothing for relevance to investigation
- Identify significant statements/silences
- Identify special warning material
- Visit the scene
- Identify all possible offences
- Determine points to prove

- Consider possible defences
- Identify interview objectives/facts to be determined:
  - significant statement/silence
  - suspect's account of the event
  - victim
  - scene
  - time parameters (movements/alibi)
  - introducing evidence suggesting involvement in the offence
  - introducing forensic evidence
  - introducing exhibits
  - other investigative areas
  - other information required from the suspect (eg mobile phone numbers, PIN codes and passwords, medical release permissions, authority to examine financial records, consent to identification procedures, handwriting samples etc)
- Consider innocent/reasonable explanation
- Identify exhibits required for the interview
- Consider the suspect's potential responses and how to respond:
  - admissions
  - denials
  - no comment
  - production of a prepared statement
  - reasonable/innocent explanation
- Prepare an interview plan
- Pre-interview briefing:
  - method of recording
  - information disclosed
  - information withheld
  - handling requests for further information
- Resources and practical arrangements:
  - interview room
  - recording equipment
  - timing of the interview

- o sequence of multiple suspect interviews
- o exhibits
- o photographs
- o notepaper
- o exhibit labels
- Coordinate others required:
  - o appropriate adult
  - o interpreter
  - o solicitor
- Roles and responsibilities:
  - o lead interviewer
  - o co-interviewer
  - o downstream monitor(s)

### 9.9.2 Juveniles/mentally disordered or otherwise mentally vulnerable people

Vulnerable suspects should be treated as being at some risk during the interview and given special consideration. Although often capable of providing reliable evidence, they may without knowing or wishing to do so also provide information that is unreliable, misleading or self-incriminating.

An appropriate adult must be involved where there is any doubt about a person's age, mental state or capacity. Their role is not passive; they are present to ensure the interview is conducted fairly and to facilitate communication.

If the appropriate adult is present at the police station during the reception process, the rights and entitlements must be completed in their presence. If they are not present, the process provisions must be completed again when they arrive.

Fitness to interview is the responsibility of the Custody Officer, in consultation with the officer in charge of the investigation and appropriate health care professionals as necessary. This includes identifying any safeguards required to allow the interview to take place.

### 9.9.3 Foreign languages

Unless authority to conduct an urgent interview has been granted, a person must not be interviewed without an interpreter if they have difficulty understanding English, the interviewer cannot speak the person's own language or the person wants an interpreter present.

---

**KEY POINT**

Where possible, interpreters should be obtained from the National Register of Public Service Interpreters (NRPSI) or the Council for the Advancement of Communication with Deaf People (CACDP), Directory of British Sign Language/English Interpreters.

---

### 9.9.4 Significant statements/silences

At the beginning of the interview after caution, any significant statement or silence which occurred in the presence and hearing of a police officer or other police staff, before the start of the interview should be put to the suspect (unless put in a previous interview). The suspect should be asked to confirm or deny the statement/silence and if they want to add or dispute anything. This may also be expanded on later in the interview.

### 9.9.5 Special warnings

Some evidence has more significance than other elements of the investigation when an explanation is requested during interview. These areas may be the subject of special warnings under the CJPO.

When a suspect who is interviewed *after arrest* fails or refuses to answer such questions, or fails to answer them satisfactorily after being given due warning, a court or jury may draw a proper inference.

Section 36 applies when a person is arrested by a constable and there is found:

1. on their person, in or on their clothing or footwear, or otherwise in their possession, or in the place where they were arrested, any objects marks or substances or marks on such objects,
2. which a constable investigating the case reasonably believes may be attributable to the person participating in an offence specified by the constable, and
3. the person fails or refuses to account for the objects, marks or substances found when requested to do so by a constable who informs them of their belief.

Section 37 applies when an arrested person was found by a constable:

1. at a place at or about the time the offence for which he was arrested is alleged to have been committed, and
2. a constable investigating the offence reasonably believes their presence at that place at that time may be attributable to their participation in the offence, and
3. the constable informs the person of their belief and the person fails or refuses to account for their presence at that place when requested to do so.

For an inference to be drawn, the suspect must be informed by the interviewing officer using ordinary, clear non-technical language:

- the OFFENCE under investigation
- what FACT the suspect is being asked to account for
- the belief this FACT may be due to the suspect taking part in the commission of the offence
- a court may draw a proper INFERENCE if the suspect fails or refuses to account for that fact
- the interview is being RECORDED and may be given in evidence if the case goes to trial

**KEY POINTS**

- The arresting officer and person giving the special warning do not have to be the same person.
- Special warnings do not apply to suspects who are not under arrest so cannot be used in voluntary interviews.
- Under the Police Reform Act 2002, designated non-warranted investigators can administer special warnings.
- Situations where a suspect's DNA is found on the victim's clothing was clarified in the case of *R v Abbas* (CLR 2010) where the court of appeal directed this did not fall within the definition of section 36 and therefore a special warning should not be given in these circumstances.
- The delivery of any special warnings and any suspect response should be highlighted in the record of interview and brought to the attention of the CPS on the form MG6.

## 9.9.6  Bad character evidence

Bad character is defined by section 98 Criminal Justice Act 2003 as 'evidence of, or a disposition towards misconduct'; this is not restricted to previous convictions and includes other reprehensible conduct. Supporting evidence is available from many sources, such as employment/disciplinary records, previous arrests which did not result in charges, previous charges and acquittals, and other information which demonstrates a propensity to be untruthful.

There are seven gateways through which a defendant's bad character may be introduced into evidence depending on the matter in issue:

a) All parties agree to it being admissible.
b) It is adduced from the defendant himself, or is given in answer to a question asked by him in cross-examination and intended to elicit it.
c) It is important explanatory evidence without which the fact finders could not reasonably be expected to understand the background to the case.

d) It is relevant to an important matter in issue between the defendant and the prosecution.

e) It has substantial probative value in relation to an important matter in issue between the defendant and another co defendant.

f) It is evidence to correct a false impression given by the defendant.

g) The defendant has made an attack on another person's character.

---

### KEY POINTS

- Raising bad character is generally best left to the end of the interview to assist editing if the court does not admit it into evidence.
- When framing questions, the relevance of the bad character material when compared with the subject of the interview should be pointed out and comment invited. There is little value in merely reading out lists of previous convictions which generally attract a 'no comment' response.
- Bad character information is recorded and supplied to the CPS on form MG16.

---

### 9.9.7 Prepared statements

If a prepared statement is tendered and read out by the suspect or solicitor at the start of the interview (although they may be introduced at any stage) it should be dealt with as follows:

- Accept the prepared statement, or copy (although solicitors cannot be forced to supply it)
- Confirm the statement was made by the suspect
- If not already signed, ask the suspect to sign it (although they cannot be forced to do so)
- The statement should be exhibited by the interviewer
- Conclude the interview informing the solicitor that the statement and the need for further interview will be considered

- Analyse the statement, identifying any missing information, gaps and anomalies and revise the interview plan
- Conduct a further interview based on the revised interview plan

---

**KEY POINT**

Prepared statements are rarely sufficiently detailed to answer all relevant questions. The interview should continue despite any indication that no further comment will be made. The threshold for ceasing questioning is when it is reasonably believed there is sufficient evidence for a realistic prospect of conviction. This is wider than the previous threshold of sufficient evidence to charge.

---

## 9.9.8  Refusal to be interviewed

A suspect may choose not to answer questions but the police do not require their consent or agreement to be interviewed (PACE, Code C, 12.5).

If a suspect attempts to prevent questioning by leaving the interview room or refusing to leave their cell, they should be advised that their consent or agreement is not required. They should be cautioned and informed that if they fail or refuse to cooperate, the interview may take place in the cell and their failure or refusal to cooperate may be given in evidence. If they continue to be uncooperative, they should be interviewed in the cell using portable recording equipment. If this is not an option, a contemporaneous record of questions and answers should be recorded on form MG15.

---

**KEY POINT**

If a suspect refuses to be interviewed, it is still necessary to put relevant questions to them and provide an opportunity to answer for adverse inference applications to be made at court.

---

## 9.10 **Detention Times**

Generally a detainee's relevant time is calculated from their time of arrival at the police station (section 41 PACE). Exceptions are when a person wanted in one police force area is arrested and detained in another; their relevant time would start from the time of their arrival at the first police station in the area where they are wanted, or 24 hours after their arrest, whichever is earlier.

A different situation arises when a person is arrested for an offence in one police force area and found to be wanted for a different offence in another force area. In these circumstances, provided they are not interviewed about the second offence whilst in the first police area (or in transit), a fresh detention clock commences and their relevant time starts when they arrive at the first police station in the second force area, or 24 hours after they leave the station in the first police force area, whichever is the sooner.

---

### KEY POINT—'RELEVANT TIME'

'Relevant time' should not be confused with 'authorised time' which is the time the Custody Officer authorises the detention of an arrested person and is the point from which periodic review times are calculated.

---

### 9.10.1 **Detention reviews**

Periodic reviews of detention must be conducted:

- no later than six hours after detention was first authorised (the first review), then
- no later than nine hours after the first review (the second review), and
- subsequently at intervals of not more than nine hours.

Where the detainee has not been charged, the review officer is an Inspector or above not directly involved in the investigation; but after charge, reviews are the Custody Officer's responsibility. The state of investigations should be communicated regularly to review officers to allow them to effectively discharge their responsibilities.

## 9.10.2  Extensions of detention

Some investigations may require detention without charge beyond 24 hours for enquiries and interviews to be progressed.

Any time after the second review has been conducted (so no later than 15 hours) a Superintendent or above with responsibility for the police station holding the detainee may authorise extended detention without charge for up to a further 12 hours, where they have reasonable grounds for believing:

a) an offence for which the detainee has been arrested is an indictable offence; and
b) further detention without charge is necessary to secure and preserve evidence or to obtain evidence by questioning; and
c) the investigation is being conducted diligently and expeditiously.

Detaining a juvenile or mentally vulnerable person longer than 24 hours depends on the circumstances of the case and additional consideration of the person's vulnerability, any representations made on their behalf (including the views of the appropriate adult) and any alternatives to police custody.

Review officers must conduct extensions of detention in person, including considering any representations, and should be briefed in a timely manner on the progress and conduct of the investigation. This includes what further enquiries and interviews are considered necessary whilst the suspect is in custody and the timescales involved. This briefing may include providing information with a request that it is not revealed to the detainee or their legal representative.

---

**KEY POINTS**

The maximum extension that can be granted is 12 hours (total detention time 36 hours), but shorter periods may be authorised depending on the circumstances of the case.

Reviewing officers need sufficient time to consider requests and attend the custody office in person, which needs advance planning. Police forces have their own arrangements, particularly outside office hours when a Superintendent or above could provide PACE cover for the entire force area and have conflicting demands to manage.

An extension of detention cannot be authorised beyond 24 hours purely to obtain a charging decision.

---

### 9.10.3 Warrants of further detention

A person can only be detained without charge beyond 36 hours for an indictable offence, under the authority of a Warrant of Further Detention (WOFD) issued by a Magistrates Court (sections 43 and 44 PACE), who must be satisfied there are reasonable grounds for believing further detention is justified because all three of the following criteria are met:

1. An offence for which the person is under arrest is indictable.
2. Detention without charge is necessary to secure or preserve evidence relating to an offence for which the person is under arrest, or to obtain such evidence by questioning them.
3. The investigation is being conducted diligently and expeditiously.

A WOFD can be issued for such a period as the court thinks fit (not automatically 36 hours) and should relate to what the police intend to do to progress the investigation.

If there are sufficient grounds, further applications can be made up to an overall maximum detention period of 96 hours from the relevant time.

### 9.10.3.1 Court procedure

- Applications are made by a constable (or other rank) on oath and supported by information.
- A court cannot hear an application unless the detained person has been supplied with a copy of the information and has been brought before the hearing.
- The detained person is entitled to legal representation at the hearing.
- An application may be made:
  - (a) at any time before the expiry of 36 hours from the relevant time; or
  - (b) where:
    - i. it is not practicable for the court hearing the application to sit at the expiry of 36 hours after the relevant time; but
    - ii. the court will sit during the 6 hours following the end of that 36-hour period; the application may be made before the 6 hours have expired.
    - iii. if an application is made after the 36 hours have expired (but within the additional 6 hours) and it appears to the court that it would have been reasonable for the police to have made the application within 36 hours from the relevant time, the court shall dismiss the application.
- Applications should be made between 1000 hours and 2100 hours and if possible during normal court hours.
- If it appears a special sitting is required outside normal court hours but between 1000 hours and 2100 hours, the justice's clerk should be notified of this possibility, while the court is sitting if possible.
- It will not usually be practicable to arrange a special court sitting outside 1000 hours and 2100 hours.

### 9.10.3.2 Information supplied

The information supplied to the court and the detainee includes:

a) the nature of the offence;
b) the general nature of the evidence on which the person was arrested;
c) enquiries relating to the offence that have been made and what further enquiries are proposed; and
d) the reasons why continued detention is believed necessary to conduct further enquiries.

A general summary outlining what the investigation has achieved so far and what needs to be completed within the timeframe of the proposed extension is necessary to support the application. This includes any time scales for results such as forensic tests or hi-tech examinations that will be available for further interviews. The information supplied to the court needs careful consideration as it may impact on future pre-interview disclosure.

The term 'diligently and expeditiously' may have to be justified under cross-examination and means enquiries are being conducted as quickly as possible in an industrious manner. This could involve explaining how several areas of investigative activity are being conducted simultaneously and investigators are working extended tours of duty to facilitate this.

The checklist below provides some suggestions but is not exhaustive:

### Checklist—WOFD supporting information

- Whether the investigation was pre-planned or a spontaneous incident
- The number of investigators and other resources engaged on the enquiry
- Extensive forensic examinations and testing is being conducted
- CSIs are dedicated to the incident
- Forensic scientists have been deployed to the scene(s)
- A post mortem examination is to be/has been conducted

- Witness testimony from significant/key witnesses has been/is being recorded in accordance with ABE
- H-2-H enquiries have/are being conducted with extensive parameters
- CCTV identification, recovery and analysis is in progress
- Checking of fingerprints
- Checking detainee's replies against other material
- Correlating information obtained from other detainees in the same case
- Checking alibis
- Communicating with other police forces (in the UK or abroad)
- Obtaining interpreters to conduct interviews with witnesses and suspects
- Translating documents

**KEY POINTS—'WOFD'**

- The application is made at the time an officer is sworn in to give evidence. This is important when managing applications involving multiple suspects who are appearing separately, to ensure their detention time does not expire before their application commences.
- If granted, the time of the WOFD commences when it is signed by the magistrate.
- Planning a WOFD should consider the logistics and timeframes involved; it is often prudent to make early applications, taking account of the court's availability.
- Police forces will have their own documentation to supply the required information for an application which has to be authorised by a Superintendent or above.
- As a contingency it is advisable to conduct a 'wash up' interview with the suspect(s) before the application to ensure all critical questions have been put in case further detention is not authorised.

## 9.11 **Intelligence Interviews**

An 'intelligence interview' with a person in police detention is voluntary. The objective is to obtain information about criminal activity other than the offence(s) for which they have been arrested, therefore they do not fall within the PACE definition of an interview and are not conducted under caution or recorded.

Police forces have individual policies balancing the integrity of the investigation in progress whilst exploiting the opportunity to obtain potentially actionable information from an intelligence interview. Considerations include not conducting the interview until after the investigation phase has concluded, using officers not connected to the investigation (usually Intelligence Bureaux or Dedicated Source Unit staff) and managing the content of the custody record so the safety of a detainee who agrees to an intelligence interview is not compromised.

---

### KEY POINT—INTERVIEW ADVISERS

Interview advisers (PIP 2, Specialists) can provide assistance with all aspects of interview strategies and should be consulted as early as possible in complex investigations.

---

# Chapter 10
# Types of Crime Investigation

## 10.1 Introduction

The basic principles of investigation such as decision making and the 'five building blocks' discussed in Chapter 4 are the foundation of all enquiries. However, crime is diverse and some enquiries involve processes and policies which do not apply to others. This chapter outlines some specific considerations for certain types of crime investigation that should prove useful to investigators.

## 10.2 Volume Crime

Volume crime is 'any crime which through its sheer volume has a significant impact on the community and the ability of the local police to tackle it'. These offences are managed through the Volume Crime Management Model (VCMM) and include acquisitive crime, such as burglary, theft and street robbery, and other 'volume' offences, like criminal damage and assault.

The VCMM links to the National Intelligence Model (NIM) where a Tasking and Coordination Group (TCG) identifies local volume crime priorities and allocates resources to tackle them. It is designed to improve performance by ensuring everyone involved in the process knows what is expected of them, including minimum standards of investigation and supervision.

An investigator's role in the VCMM depends on where in the process they are deployed, eg primary and/or secondary investigation, processing suspects or a combination of these.

Reported crimes are assessed against a range of 'solvability factors' which inform decisions on allocation and further investigation. These factors include whether any of the following are immediately available to link a suspect to the offence:

- forensic material
- identifiable property stolen or recovered
- material left at the scene by the offender(s) which could lead to their identification
- a witness who may identify the offender(s) by viewing photographs or describes them in sufficient detail to compile an E-Fit
- the suspect is known or their identity is likely to become apparent, or a suspect's vehicle is located, described or identified
- a linked series of offences is identified, including repeat victims
- CCTV or other passive data sources to identify suspects are available

Crime reports with limited solvability factors not requiring resources to attend may be allocated for 'primary investigation', including telephone investigation to identify potential lines of enquiry, repeat victims and other possible linked offences. An investigation plan is then recorded before allocation for secondary investigation with suggested disposal options and, where a suspect is known, evidence collated and an arrest package prepared.

Individual force policy may allocate certain crimes for secondary investigation where there are no solvability factors, such as those which impact on public confidence and satisfaction like dwelling burglary, hate crime and repeat victimisation.

Crime reports allocated for secondary investigation should contain an investigation plan documented in a simple format describing what further enquiries should be conducted before finalisation and be flexible to develop as the enquiry progresses.

Typical plans for acquisitive crime are likely to contain actions concerning the scene and stolen property such as the following:

- Preserve and assess the point of entry for forensic and physical evidence and Crime Scene Investigator (CSI) examination.
- Establish with the victim anything the offender has touched, moved or brought to the scene and preserve any forensic opportunities.
- Identify the approach/egress routes and search for foot-wear marks, blood, tools brought to the scene and articles removed or discarded by the offender.
- Search possible locations where stolen property could be concealed for later collection eg wheelie bins.
- House-to-house (H-2-H) enquiries in the immediate area and route taken by the offender.
- If available, obtain a detailed description of any suspect(s) from witnesses.
- Obtain comprehensive details of stolen property including serial numbers and unique identifying marks (including photographs if available).

Following initial attendance:

- With the complainant, review and update the crime reports stolen property list (where applicable) with details of further missing property, items located that were previously believed stolen and any additional descriptions not previously available.
- Circulate property details ensuring a Police National Computer (PNC) record is created for any stolen plant (agricultural and construction), engines, trailers, firearms, marine craft (including jet skis and rigid inflatables) and animals (which are registered with a marking company).

- Attempt to locate stolen property by enquiring at outlets such as second-hand dealers, pawnbrokers, Cash Converters and similar outlets, antique dealers, car boot sales, classified advertisements, EBay/other internet sites, trade journals, trade auctions, jewellers, markets, auction rooms, scrap metal dealers and convicted/suspected handlers.
- Preserve any recovered stolen property for CSI examination.
- Circulate details of distinctive stolen property in the local media.
- Check property registers, including the systems of neighbouring Basic Command Units (BCU) or forces where appropriate.
- Update crime reports concerning any recovered property and amend the investigation plan as a result of new solvability factors and lines of enquiry identified.
- If stolen property is recovered, obtain an identification statement from the owner specifically containing how they can identify the item (serial numbers, identifying marks).

## 10.3 **Offences against the Person**

Violent crime may form part of a control strategy within the VCMM and, regardless of the severity of injury, is broadly divided into three types:

1. Stranger attacks where the alleged offender and victim do not know each other.
2. Acquaintance assaults where the alleged offender is known to the victim, but is not a relative or intimate partner.
3. Domestic violence (DV).

Identifying these broad circumstances helps prioritise lines of enquiry for each case, for example identifying the suspect in a stranger attack compared to dealing with a reluctant victim of domestic violence where the suspect has been immediately arrested.

The core investigative and forensic strategies should always be considered, ensuring the following are completed wherever possible:

- Treat the victim as a crime scene, including collecting any available forensic evidence (eg clothing)
- Obtain early injury photographs
- Obtain evidence of a victim's injury from a CSI or attending police officer
- Obtain a statement of complaint from the victim as soon as possible after the incident
- Obtain an initial account if the victim is unable to provide a statement at the time
- Obtain statements from any witnesses to the incident
- Obtain evidence from a health care professional describing the victim's injuries, any treatment provided and their prognosis
- Submit all intelligence, including locations of violence to identify 'hot spots', for the tasking and coordination process, and assist in developing multi-agency solutions for violent crime reduction

## 10.4 **Domestic Violence**

The definition of domestic violence (DV) by the Association of Chief Police Officers (ACPO) is:

> Any incident of threatening behaviour, violence or abuse (psychological, physical, sexual, financial or emotional) between adults, aged 18 years and over, who are or have been intimate partners or family members, regardless of gender and sexuality.

Family members include a mother, father, son, daughter, brother, sister and grandparents, whether they are directly related, in-laws or stepfamily.

The priority of the police when responding to DV is to protect the lives of both adults and children at risk, investigate all reports, facilitate effective action to hold offenders to account and to adopt a proactive multi-agency approach to prevention and reduction.

As well as identifying and mitigating risks faced by the victim and any children in the family, challenges may include overcoming the victim's reluctance to prosecute, which is particularly relevant as initial responding officers have an obligation to take positive action in all DV cases and exercise a power of arrest where one exists.

Sufficient evidence to prosecute may have to be obtained from other sources to support a 'victimless prosecution', but forensic material may have limited value if the suspect and victim are living together.

## Checklist—DV sources of evidence

- Attending officers (including head/body-worn cameras)
- Photograph/video of disturbance at the scene
- Recordings of 999/101 calls
- Injury photographs including further photographs when injuries are more apparent
- Recovery of torn/damaged/bloodstained clothing
- Analysis of blood pattern distribution to corroborate a physical assault
- Recovery of potential weapons (which may be ordinary domestic items) and forensically linking to the suspect
- Linking suspected weapons to victim injuries through the National Injuries Database
- Evidence of previous violent incidents, such as records of previous calls to the police, including those with prior partners
- Police intelligence systems
- Incidents of sexual violence not previously disclosed

- Incidents witnessed by children
- Incidents witnessed by other family members, friends or colleagues
- H-2-H enquiries
- Incidents outside the home or occurring in public
- CCTV/passive data recordings
- Child contact agreements or disputes
- Civil injunctions
- Medical information that may constitute evidence
- Evidence of social isolation, eg lack of contact between the victim and their family, friends, neighbours or schools, medical appointments that have not been made, or made but not kept, or where the suspect accompanied the victim (to maintain control and prevent them disclosing information)
- Evidence held by other agencies
- Evidence of previous victims held on any data source

Conflicting accounts and counter-allegations where each party claims to be the victim may be presented. Dual arrests should be avoided without conducting a full investigation, which should include a separate evaluation of the claims to establish if justifiable force was used in self-defence and an attempt to identify the primary aggressor, including recording:

- severity of any injuries inflicted by either party
- whether either party has made threats to another party, child or other family/household member
- whether either party has a prior history of violence
- whether either party has made previous counter-allegations
- whether either party acted defensively to protect themselves or a third person from injury

**KEY POINTS**

- Specialist Domestic Violence Officers and/or Police Domestic Violence Coordinators can provide DV investigation advice, including identifying, categorising and monitoring risk and safety measures, engaging in the tasking and coordination process to address high-risk and persistent offenders and appropriately sharing information with partner agencies/organisations.
- All DV cases fall within the pre-charge Crown Prosecution Service (CPS) advice scheme even when a guilty plea is likely. CPS will also decide whether there is sufficient evidence to proceed without the support of the victim so all available material should be collected.
- DV is frequently repeated, making homicide potentially preventable. Any precursor incidents including police action and decisions will be closely scrutinised by a Domestic Homicide Review now obligatory under section 9 Domestic Violence, Crime and Victims Act 2004.

## 10.5 Protection from Harassment Act 1997

The Protection from Harassment Act 1997 (PHA) can be used to address harassment or fear of violence caused to a victim on at least two occasions. Harassment is not defined, but causing alarm or distress are elements; therefore if a suspect's behaviour does not involve specific threats but causes the victim harassment the offence is committed, eg silent telephone phone calls or following the victim around.

**KEY POINT**

Where a person's actions amount to an offence under the Offences Against the Person Act 1861, the Public Order Act 1984 or the Criminal Damage Act 1971, proceedings should not be instigated under the PHA.

## 10.6  **Hate Crime**

A hate crime or incident is defined as:

> One which is perceived by the victim or any other person to be motivated by prejudice or hate, e.g. racism, homophobia, religion or faith, sexual orientation, a disability or some other intolerance that manifests itself in hatred towards others.

An allegation from any party (not just a victim) is sufficient for a hate *incident* to be recorded; however, an incident must only be recorded as a *crime* where there is evidence that an offence has been committed or attempted etc.

Hate incidents/crimes are potential critical incidents, particularly where repeat victimisation is involved, and whilst making enquiries to identify the offender the investigation should also:

- identify repeat victimisation and/or linked incidents ensuring all necessary steps are taken to prevent a reoccurrence
- identify any risks to the victim, their family or community as a whole
- allay the fears of the victim and mitigate any identified risks with protective measures where appropriate, eg covert monitoring measures, personal attack alarms and overt tactics such as high visibility patrols
- where appropriate visually record the victim's interview
- not question victims of homophobia about their sexuality and not disclose this information to their family/ friends without permission in case they are unaware of the victim's sexual orientation
- identify and report any concern about community tension
- update the victim on an ongoing basis
- submit any information into the intelligence system using the 5 x 5 x 5 grading system
- refer any crime which involves an element of hate to the CPS for the charging decision

## 10.7 **Honour-based Violence and Forced Marriage**

The terms 'honour crime', 'honour-based violence' (HBV) or 'izzat' (Arabic for honour) are generic terms for crimes, where the victim is punished by their family or community for bringing shame or dishonour on them by transgressing perceived correct codes of behaviour. Such offences are prosecuted under the relevant law, eg assault, false imprisonment, kidnap, murder etc.

> **KEY POINT**
>
> HBV has recently become a very topical subject; a high profile example is the case of 17-year-old Shafilea Ahmed, who went missing in Warrington, Cheshire in 2003. Six months later Shafilia's body was found in a Cumbrian river and in 2012 her parents were found guilty of her murder for 'dishonouring the family in the community'.

A forced marriage is when one or both spouses do not consent and duress is involved to force the victim into the marriage; this may involve physical, psychological, sexual and emotional abuse which continues after the marriage.

Forced marriage can occur within the UK or by taking the victim abroad, often not knowing in advance that they are to be married. Once outside the UK they may find it impossible to return and be unable to communicate with others.

All agencies encountering victims of forced marriage and HBV must follow the 'one chance' rule, meaning they may only have one chance to speak to the victim and thus only have one opportunity to save their life.

Reports of forced marriage should only be handled by officers qualified to deal with such cases through experience and specialist training. Police forces have their own protocols including multi-agency working, but any investigator could find themselves in a situation where they receive an initial report of forced marriage/HBV.

In these circumstances it is essential to remember the 'one chance' rule and take immediate action, including gathering the information in the checklist suggested in this section, and contacting a supervisor according to local force protocols for specialist resources and senior investigative oversight.

The safety and welfare of the person under threat takes priority and confidentiality must be maintained with only necessary personnel informed. The family of the person under threat, or a person acting on their behalf (possibly innocently) may attempt to locate them, including reporting the victim as a missing person or the perpetrator of a crime. No information should be supplied and any incident logs should have restricted access.

Protective measures include removing the victim to a place of safety, or, in the case of a child, taking them into police protection. High-risk cases may be managed by a Multi-Agency Risk Assessment Conference (MARAC) or by Multi-Agency Public Protection Arrangements (MAPPA) with only essential personnel involved. The Forced Marriage Unit at the Foreign and Commonwealth Office is an important source of advice and should be contacted.

### Checklist—HBV information to be gathered

- Details of the person making the report and their relationship with the individual under threat
- Details of the person under threat including:
  - date of report
  - name
  - nationality (including any dual nationality which has implications for consular assistance abroad)
  - age
  - date and place of birth
  - passport information, including ascertaining if they have two passports and which one they will be travelling on

- ○ school
- ○ employment
- ○ full details of the allegation
- ○ name and address of parents or those with parental responsibility
- ○ National Insurance number
- ○ driving licence number
- ○ distinguishing features
- ○ recent photograph and any other identifying documents
- A list of trusted friends and family and their contact details
- A code word to authenticate future contacts
- A way of establishing discreet future contact that will not put the person at risk of harm
- Background information, including any involvement with adult or children's social care, doctors or other health services
- Addresses of the extended family in the UK and any known phone numbers
- Details of any threats, abuse or other hostile action against the person, whether reported by the victim or a third party
- The nature of the risk level (eg pregnancy, if they have a secret boyfriend/girlfriend or if they are already married)
- Any other family members that are at risk of forced marriage, or if there is a history of forced marriage and abuse
- Visually recorded interview (vulnerable/intimidated witnesses)
- Voluntary DNA sample and fingerprints

If the individual is going abroad imminently and this cannot be avoided, obtain where known:

- a photocopy of their passport and encourage them to keep details of the number and place and date of issue

- any address they may be staying overseas
- potential spouse's name
- name of potential spouse's father
- date of proposed wedding
- addresses of the extended family overseas and any known phone numbers
- information that only the victim would be aware of (to corroborate their identity if later interviewed at the British Embassy/High Commission and prevent a similar person being produced pretending to be them)
- details of any travel plans and people likely to accompany them
- name and address of close relatives remaining in the UK
- a safe means of contact, eg a mobile phone that will function overseas and be kept hidden
- advise them to take emergency cash, in local currency and also hard currency (pounds, dollars, euros) for use in the country of destination if problems arise
- if reported by a third party, their details in case the person contacts them from overseas, or on their return
- details from the person under threat of a trusted friend/advocate in the UK who they can maintain contact with and who can be approached if they do not return
- estimated return date with request they make contact without fail on their return
- written statement from the person explaining they want the police, adult/children's social care, a teacher or third party to act on their behalf if they do not return by a certain date
- provide contact details of the department and person handling the case (with advice to avoid discovery of the information)

- supply the address and contact number for the nearest British Embassy/High Commission
- encourage them to memorise at least one telephone number and email address, preferably the British Embassy/High Commission if they are a British national
- explain the implications of dual nationality which limits consular assistance
- if they are not a British national, encourage contact with the Forced Marriage Unit
- contact any identified friend/advocate and obtain a statement of their support before the person departs
- take contact details with them of a person they can trust in the country of destination
- provide a copy of the Forced Marriage Unit's leaflet 'Forced Marriage Abroad' and advise them to contact the Forced Marriage Unit

**KEY POINTS**

- There is a difference between forced marriage and arranged marriage, as the latter implies there is consent of both parties and involves choice.
- There is no specific criminal offence of forced marriage, although at the time of writing this is under government consideration.

## 10.8  Rape and Serious Sexual Offences

Generally serious sexual offences fall into one of six types which impact on the investigation strategy when prioritising lines of enquiry:

1. Stranger—where the victim has no previous knowledge of the suspect, has not met them before the offence, and is unable to name them or provide information about their identity or whereabouts.

2. Acquaintance—where the victim is able to identify the suspect as a person known to them.

3. Domestic—committed by people who are, or who have been intimate partners or family members of the victim.

4. Drug-assisted—where alcohol and/or drugs are intentionally administered to the victim before committing the offence, including offending against an incapacitated victim who does not have the capacity to consent.

5. Child victim under 18 years old.

6. Multiple offenders—involving more than one offender, either in the actual offence or the commissioning of the offence.

These categories have no separate legal status but are useful to consider when prioritising enquiries, eg the priority in stranger offences is to identify the suspect, so forensic recovery from the victim and fast track analysis is a high priority. With acquaintance offences, the identity of the offender is probably known so although forensic recovery from the victim would be completed, fast track submission may not be as productive as other lines of enquiry, such as obtaining evidence of early complaint.

The investigation plan should include whichever of the core investigative strategies are appropriate. However, depending on the individual case, the following checklists may provide further considerations.[1]

---

**Checklists—Serious sexual offences investigation**

**Checklist 1—Stranger (unconnected and unknown) offender**

- Obtain and attempt to cross-match DNA samples from the scene and victim with the National DNA Database (NDNAD)

---

[1] While these have been separated into groups for ease of reference, there may be overlaps.

---

- Check for any fingerprints, finger marks and other physical trace evidence at crime location and on victim
- Conduct a 'Query Using Enhanced Search Techniques' (QUEST) or postcode search on the Police National Computer (PNC) for offenders within a given area
- Trace any reported sexual health problems with sexual health clinics if the suspect has transferred (or contracted) a sexually transmitted disease to or from the victim
- Assess any suspect connections to and targeting of the crime scene(s) or victim, ie as per the 'problem analysis triangle' (see Chapter 3)
- Research any links, eg targeting by victim type, location and time of offence, prowlers, indecent exposures, suspicious activities etc
- Establish if time and date of the offence is significant or coincides with something else (eg local pubs/nightclub activities, special events)
- Check if there are any sex workers operating nearby who may have knowledge of suspect
- Consider mode of transport of offender, eg vehicles, taxis and public transport. Check nearby car parks and stolen/abandoned vehicles around relevant times
- Liaise with Public Protection Teams to identify possible suspects or associates of a suspect, paying particular attention to similar modus operandi
- Consider E-Fits of offender, forensic drawings of items or photographs of matching items regarding vehicles, clothing, unusual marks, peculiarities, hairstyles or tattoos
- Search intelligence databases (particularly the Police National Database (PND))
- Map the scene, routes in and out used by the victim and suspect, identify possible search zones, scene features and nearby premises

- Produce sequence of events charts and timelines (including chronology of the suspect, victim/witness and parallel or sequential significant events)
- Conduct stop checks, covert surveillance or reconstructions on relevant times, dates and anniversaries relating to the original offence, to identify witnesses routinely in the area, or as a method of checking for future offences, revisits or further offending
- Search for any objects reported missing by the victim
- Circulate details of any missing items in force bulletins and particularly to specialist burglary investigators
- Develop a suspect priority matrix and TIE (trace, interview, eliminate) strategy based on known information
- Consider intelligence-led DNA screening (if no match on NDNAD)
- Consider familial DNA (fDNA) analysis (if no match on NDNAD)
- Assess the possibility of the suspect being employed locally (maybe temporarily contracted to work in the area) and subsequently re-locating and changing employment due to police investigation
- Conduct case comparison (including comparable case analysis, analysis of series, identification of common denominators, search databases of offences for similar modus operandi
- Consult outside experts and specialist resources—National Crime Agency (NCA) Crime Operations Support Team, Serious Crime Analysis Section (SCAS), Child Exploitation and Online Protection Centre (CEOP), Behavioural Investigative Adviser (BIA), forensic clinical psychologist or geographic profiler

### Checklist 2—Acquaintance offender

- Investigate the circumstances of how victim met the offender

- Check for evidence of targeting of the victim by the offender
- Examine the offender's method of contacting the victim, eg internet dating agencies, singles clubs, evening classes etc
- Consider attempts to contact the victim post-offence (possibly justifying or minimising their actions)
- Seek behavioural information from the suspect's current or previous partners
- Gather information about the suspect's routines, employment, hobbies, financial transactions, telephone records, internet access, social media usage, social habits and fetishes
- Check other force areas where the offender may have come to notice for similar offences or behaviour via the PND

## Checklist 3—Domestic-related

- Identify any witnesses, including children, relatives, friends and neighbours
- Link the history of any reported domestic violence
- Investigate any history of violence not reported to the police which could be corroborated by records from other agencies, eg medical information held by GPs
- Trace witnesses to any previous offences
- Identify other family members (including children) who the suspect has had close access to, both currently and in the past
- Obtain information from previous partners about their relationship and specifically sexual behaviour, including changes in sexual behaviour
- Research any previous allegations against the suspect which have been withdrawn or discontinued

- Seek assistance from any other useful partner agencies that might be involved in connected areas of DV, family, relationship problems, health or education

### Checklist 4—Drug-assisted

- Use early evidence kits to secure samples at the earliest opportunity
- Use a forensic physician to examine the victim at a Sexual Assault Referral Centre (SARC) and identify any symptoms of drug ingestion and obtain toxicology samples
- Examine victim's and suspect's (if identified) clothing for traces of drugs used for intoxication (blood and hair samples also)
- Seek evidence of the offence(s) being photographed or recorded by the suspect using video, digital camera or mobile phone etc
- Develop sequence of events to account for lost time (eg CCTV and mobile phone records and note that drugs tend to take 15 to 20 minutes to take effect)
- Identify any associated offence(s) such as abduction, kidnap or sexual exploitation
- Profile persons known to have drug connections
- Investigate possible serial offending by checking records for any similar offences or attempts
- Look for possible links to other serious sexual assaults (seek SCAS assistance)
- Identify any theft of non-valuable items from the victim and check property records
- Check for the use of internet sites supplying drugs and advice about their use and effectiveness
- Request information from the suspect's (if identified) current or previous partners
- Examine the suspect's connections to internet pornography
- Check internet and credit card purchases

**Checklist 5—Multiple offender serious sexual offences**

- Obtain and attempt to cross-match DNA samples from the victim's forensic medical examination with the NDNAD
- Cross-match any unidentified fingerprints, finger marks and other physical trace evidence
- Examine the possibility of the offence being drug-assisted
- Consider the possibility of several scenes
- Examine any possible links between TIEs or suspects
- Identify any similar modus operandi (not necessarily multiple offender based)
- Seek intelligence about any sexual exploitation group which might be linked
- Identify any vehicles or premises used
- Identify the primary or dominant suspect (usually the first to commit a serious sexual offence on the victim)
- Investigate the possibility that the dominant suspect has a previous conviction for a sexual offence against an individual victim
- Identify any suspect who appears to have been coerced into committing the offence and interview them first, where possible

## 10.9  Missing Person Enquiries

The ACPO definition of a missing person is:

> Anyone whose whereabouts is unknown whatever the circumstances of the disappearance. They will be considered missing until located and their well being or otherwise established.

The majority of missing persons are quickly located or return unharmed of their own accord. Some cases do not require any police action, eg relatives losing contact where referral to other support agencies is the most appropriate action. Other missing people are never located and in a small number of cases are the victims of serious crime, including murder.

It cannot be overemphasised that some missing person reports can and do escalate into major investigations and critical incidents. In a number of high-profile cases the initial response to a missing person report has led to criticism of the police handling of the case, particularly around early searches and the gathering of intelligence and evidence (eg 12-year-old Tia Sharpe enquiry, South East London in August 2012, where her body was found in the loft of a house that had already been searched by the police).

---

**KEY POINT**

If in any doubt, the worst possible scenario must be considered to ensure investigative opportunities are fully exploited and nothing is missed during the early stages of a missing person enquiry. Time is critical, statistics show most murders occur quite soon after a person goes missing, particularly children and young persons.[2]

---

A missing person investigation begins on first notification to the police. Accurate information must be obtained about the circumstances, including any known reasons for the disappearance, which determines the scale and immediacy of the response.

Reports are graded as high, medium or low based on risk factors including:

- information that the person is likely to self-harm or attempt suicide
- whether the person is suspected to be the victim of a crime in progress, eg abduction

---

[2] CATCHEM database. CATCHEM stands for 'Centralised Analytical Team Collating Homicide Expertise and Management', a dataset maintained by the National Crime Agency (NCA).

- vulnerability due to age, infirmity or any other factor
- any inclement weather which would seriously increase the risk to health, particularly concerning children or elderly people
- whether the missing person needs essential medication or treatment not readily available to them
- presence of any physical illness, disability or mental health problems
- person's ability or inability to interact safely with others, or in an unknown environment
- involvement in a criminal, violent, homophobic and/or racist incident or confrontation immediately prior to disappearance
- subject to ongoing bullying or harassment
- where the person has disappeared AND suffered or was exposed to harm
- any behaviour that is out of character or departure from normal patterns (often a strong indicator of risk)
- lack of any legitimate reason to go missing
- indications that preparations for absence have been made
- known intentions of the missing person when last seen and failing to complete them, eg going to the shops
- any family and/or relationship problems or recent history of family conflict including abuse
- victim or perpetrator of domestic violence
- on a child protection register
- drugs or alcohol dependency
- work, school, college, university or relationship problems
- employment, financial or other depression problems
- any local concerns or community issues
- links to serious criminality or OCG activity
- any other factor(s) which would influence the risk assessment

The risk levels as described in the ACPO Manual of Guidance for the Management of Missing Persons are:

1. **Low**—no apparent threat of danger to either the subject or the public. For disappearances assessed as low risk, in addition to recording information on the PNC, the person reporting should be advised that, following basic enquiries, unless circumstances change, further active enquiries will not be conducted.

2. **Medium**—risk posed is likely to place the subject in danger or they are a threat to themselves or others. These cases require an active and measured response by the police and other agencies to trace the subject and support the person reporting, including the missing person's family.

3. **High**—risk posed is immediate and there are *substantial* grounds for believing the subject is in danger through their own vulnerability, or the risk posed is *immediate* and there are *substantial* grounds for believing that the public are in danger. High-risk cases require the immediate deployment of significant resources and may include the appointment of a Senior Investigating Officer (SIO).

---

**KEY POINT**

All missing person reports should be continually reviewed as risk can increase or decrease with the passage of time. High-risk cases must be quickly identified and brought to the attention of supervisors and senior investigators (if believed suspicious) as soon as practicable.

---

To formulate an appropriate response, it is important to establish why the missing person is not where they are expected to be. Generally people are missing for one of four reasons:

1. They are lost and temporarily disorientated, eg they do not know where they are but want to be found.

2. They have control over their decisions and are voluntarily missing, having decided on a course of action, eg they wish to leave home or commit suicide.

3. They are missing due to accident, injury or illness, eg someone who has wandered off due to a medical condition such as dementia.
4. They are missing against their will or may be under the influence of a third party, eg an abduction or murder victim.

A key line of enquiry is establishing the circumstances of the last sighting, including the demeanour and intentions of the missing person at that time. This is most likely to form the basis of further investigation with appropriate resourcing. The '5WH' questions need asking, such as: Were they intending to catch a train or a bus? Were they accompanied by anyone else? Were they behaving out of character? What was their direction of travel? Were they in an unfamiliar area? Why could they have gone missing? What have they got with them? etc.

It is important to consider whether the person reporting the person missing has a motive for providing false or misleading information. Experience has shown missing person reports may be made to cover up a crime.

### 10.9.1 Missing person searches

Thorough and systematic searching is a vitally important element of missing person investigation, including ensuring a comprehensive search is made of the person's home, the immediate area and any other relevant locations such as the place they were last seen. The objective of this search is to locate the missing person (ensuring they have not returned home) or any material which might assist the enquiry eg a suicide note or letter.

---

**Checklist—Searches**

**Phase 1**—Routine search of the missing person's home and immediate area.

---

**Phase 2**—Hasty but thorough search based on the most likely circumstances of the disappearance, responding to early information gathering and likely to include the LAST KNOWN POSITION (LKP) of the missing person.

**Phase 3**—Scenario-based fully managed intelligence-led Police Search Advisor (PoLSA)-searches of likely locations by trained search teams and (any other assets considered necessary) to a high level of assurance that the missing person is not present.

---

**KEY POINTS**

- Search levels increase according to identified vulnerability and concern (ie high-risk missing persons). Advice should be sought at the earliest opportunity from in-force PoLSA plus the NCA National Search Adviser who can provide free help and advice if required, including use of technical and specialist search assets.
- The LKP should always be searched and areas can be widened to include locations where previously found.

---

## 10.9.2  Lines of enquiry

Depending on the circumstances of the disappearance, some suggested lines of enquiry, in no order of priority, include the following:

- Review initial report and actions already taken.
- Identify and prioritise relevant lines of enquiry:
  - search, including places of concealment
  - H-2-H
  - trace/interview (T/I) last person to see the person alive (always to be treated with caution and scepticism)
  - T/I witnesses to movements
  - timeline their recent movements
  - T/I friends/associates
  - places habitually frequented
  - education establishment
  - place of employment/education/social clubs

  ○ other places of interest to the missing person
  ○ passive and communications data (eg social media sites) opportunities.
- Investigate and confirm the circumstances of the last sighting, including time, location and direction of travel.
- Validate any reported sightings to avoid following false trails and have a 'sightings policy' stating how such reports are to be dealt with and managed (eg accurate descriptions, noting if the person reporting knows the missing person, anything noticed or said etc).
- Record written statements (take statement) where appropriate.
- Obtain full description (check accuracy before any media release) including DNA, fingerprint and dental records.
- Establish if there is a reason to go missing (eg threatened suicide, financial or domestic problems, school or cyber bullying etc).[3]
- Establish if the disappearance is out of character.
- Establish if preparations for absence from home have been made by taking clothing (description), holdall/carrier (description), money/bank cards, cheque books, mobile phone/charger (obtain number and supplier), medication, personal possessions, passport, laptop/tablet.
- Victimology information—identifying friends, associates, places frequented, habits/routines, access to transport, relationships, places habitually used for hobbies/interests, drinking, eating, sleeping, shopping (including using loyalty cards), banking/finances, social media usage, medical conditions and medication used.
- If previously reported missing, enquiries at locations previously found.

---

[3] Note: the use of hypotheses can be considered as to possible reasons and explanations; see also Chapter 3, section 3.5.

- Locations with a previous or emotional attachment, eg cemeteries where loved ones are interned, holiday locations and other familiar areas.
- Significant events/anniversaries possibly linked to the date of disappearance.
- Any useful information in diaries, computers, data storage devices, phones, receipts, letters, travel documents.
- Checks with establishments such as hospitals, doctors, welfare agencies, hotels/guest houses, transport companies, financial institutions.[4]
- Communications data enquiries including last calls made to/from the missing person's home address and specialist location services (access will be influenced by the high, medium or low (HML) grading), telephone billing and subscriber information for the missing person and associates.
- Text or record a message on the missing person's phone to make contact if they are safe and well.
- Circulations:
  - PNC
  - PNC marker on vehicles owned or used by the missing person
  - PNC audits for checks by others on the missing person
  - Special Circulation Bulletin within force and to other forces
  - Police Gazette
  - Interpol/Europol
  - media appeals (local/regional/national including social media sites).
- Notifications:
  - UK Missing Persons Bureau (**IMPORTANT and MANDATORY**)
  - Missing People Charity (formerly NMPH).

---

[4] The NCA Crime Operations Support team has a matrix to use as an aide-memoire for conducting these types of enquiry, aka 'proof of life' template.

---

When located, missing persons should always be interviewed to establish whether they have been a victim or committed crime before or whilst missing, where and by whom they have been harboured and any information which may lead to their early discovery should they disappear again. Intelligence records including COMPACT and the National Missing Persons Bureau should be updated and relevant support put in place to avoid a reoccurrence.

---

**KEY POINTS**

- When an adult missing person is located, their whereabouts must not be disclosed to others against their wishes. Some people are reported missing to the police so they can be located for reasons that are not in their interest, eg a person fleeing honour-based violence. If consent is not provided, the person reporting should be informed that the subject has been located and reassured concerning their wellbeing.
- Be mindful of child sexual exploitation (CSE) involving young vulnerable missing persons, especially those who frequently go missing from care placements and who may be the target of sexual predators and systematic or organised abuse.
- The **UK Missing Persons Bureau** (MPB) is a vital resource and must be contacted and notified. They provide a range of services including coordinating enquiries and cross-matching with other unidentified persons. They act as the centre for the exchange of information between forces and organisations, including provision of general advice, guidance and support (<www.missingpersons.police.uk>).

---

### 10.9.3 Other agencies

Young people in care and other people such as the elderly, people with mental health problems or learning difficulties are likely to be vulnerable when missing from their residential settings. Police forces have local protocols concerning multi-agency responsibilities, including adopting a problem-solving approach in these circumstances which should be researched.

---

**KEY POINT—RISK ASSESSMENT**

Any risk assessment must be kept under dynamic review to cater for any changes in circumstances during the course of the investigation. Any emerging or developing information should be brought to the attention of a supervisor as soon as possible, and immediately if the risk is deemed to be high.

---

## 10.10 **Criminal Use of Firearms**

Many incidents involving firearms, such as domestic murder and armed robbery can be properly investigated using standard major investigation principles. However, additional issues need consideration for other types of 'gun crime', including so-called 'bad on bad' shootings linked to territorial disputes and drugs, often involving power, status and respect in a gang culture. In extreme cases the investigation may involve the meticulously planned and executed contract killing of a selected target.

All reports of firearms usage must be fully investigated. Difficulties encountered often include offences not being reported; late or third party reporting when forensic material has already been disposed of by the offender(s); victims and witnesses refusing to cooperate through fear of repercussions; criminals' knowledge of conventional police investigation techniques enabling them to take forensic countermeasures; the increased use of technology to organise shootings; and the mobility of criminals who may travel to other parts of the country to carry out attacks.

Covert policing techniques can be considered as part of the reactive investigation strategy. However, to protect their sensitivity and future effectiveness, these tactics are not revealed in this handbook and this section only provides general overt suggestions.

Often, in advance of shootings, warning signals are available, including heightened tension in communities from new drug dealers, the prison release of notorious gang members or an overt act of disrespect. If these signals are identified and properly assessed using the National Intelligence Model (NIM), firearms incidents can be prevented, possibly by issuing a threat to life (aka TTL or Osman) warning.

---

### KEY POINTS

- The link between the criminal use of firearms and the supply of drugs is often evident, and an effective strategy to tackle 'gun crime' may depend on an effective police response to drug dealing and territorial control.
- Some larger forces (eg GMP—Operation Xcalibur, MPS—Operation Trident) have specialist units investigating gun and gang crime. It is strongly recommended that advice is obtained from them on best practice.
- In firearm discharges, stray bullets can and do travel much further than a target or victim location. Proposed search areas for bullet heads may need to be significantly extended—a fact worth considering when setting cordon parameters.

---

Different scenarios likely to be encountered with the criminal use of firearms include:

- gunshots heard but no evidence to substantiate a firearms discharge
- gunshots fired with evidence of a firearms discharge (no bullets or cartridge casings)
- gunshots fired but no victim or offender (cartridges, bullets or casings recovered)
- gunshots fired with an identified victim but no offender
- gunshots fired with a victim and suspect (no weapon)
- persons reported with injuries that are gunshot wounds (eg by doctors and medics) including ones that are accidentally self-inflicted (eg when firearms are activated when concealed in clothing or when being demonstrated or tested)

- a suspect with a weapon (with or without a victim)
- recovery of weapons or ammunition
- weapons trafficking

---

**Checklist—Firearms incidents**

- Gather as much information as possible from the source of the report
- Resources deployed are based on initial risk assessment with preservation of life a priority (see Chapter 4)
- Obtain advice from a firearms tactical adviser
- If the offence is in progress, instigate procedures for authorities, firearms silver command and control, risk assessment and intelligence capabilities
- Scene risk assessment to be conducted by attending officers
- Identify, secure and protect scene(s):
  - victim
  - suspect
  - weapon and ammunition (considering safety and security)
  - location
  - hospital (victim may be in hospital and still under threat from suspects/gangs)
- Forensic recovery of evidence including weapon and ammunition:
  - any firearm or suspected firearm must be recovered by a trained officer to certify it has been made safe; weapons must be secured whilst maintaining their evidential integrity; details of the precise procedures followed should be recorded
  - identify and evidence whether the firearm was loaded or unloaded, and what position the barrel (if revolver) was in
  - exhibit each weapon, component part and item of ammunition, stating where they were found

---

- o photograph firearms and component parts along-side a scale to indicate dimensions and include cop-ies of photographs with the case file
- Forensic opportunities to be fully exploited (finger-prints/DNA/ firearms discharge residue (FDR)):
  - o fingerprint examination
  - o DNA recovery
  - o Quasar testing
  - o medical examination of suspects for gunshot inju-ries and marks around the hands for weapon recoil marks and bruises
  - o examination of suspects' external skin and recovery of clothing for FDR (eg pockets and waistbands)
  - o establishing compatibility of the firearm with any ammunition recovered
- Weapon identification
- Submit samples for forensic examination by a Foren-sic Service Provider (FSP) and the National Ballistics Intelligence Service (NABIS), considering fast track submission in urgent cases for comparison analysis
- Identify witnesses at an early stage and arrange for their care and safety
- Interview witnesses (consider video recording). Wit-nesses to specified gun and knife offences are auto-matically categorised as intimidated under section 17(5) of the Youth Justice and Criminal Evidence Act 1999 (YJCEA) (as inserted by the Coroners and Justice Act 2009) unless they want to opt out (see Chapter 8, section 8.7)
- Fast track identification of the victim and provisions made for their safety (further attempts on their life)
- Develop a full intelligence package/profile on the victim
- Interview the victim including a hostile/reluctant vic-tim/witness strategy (consider video recording)
- Fast track identification of suspects

- Prepare suspect profile
- Suspect management strategy (sterility and avoidance of cross-contamination is vitally important, especially when swabbing for FDR on external bodily surfaces and seizing clothing)
- Set intelligence requirements including passive data/ social network opportunities
- Community Impact Assessment
- Media management strategy
- Hot debrief of all officers involved
- Adopt a positive prosecution strategy; consider prosecution without the cooperation of hostile victims or witnesses
- Incident finalisation code (firearms) to be completed on incident logging systems
- Arrange intelligence support to the investigation and management of incoming information including a single point of contact (SPoC) for firearms intelligence
- Analyse the potential significance of the report, unless it is proved to be false or malicious, including future risk analysis and predictive intelligence capability (repercussions/reprisals)
- Identify if the incident is part of a series and linked to others via NABIS—establish weapon/ammunition profile (forensic history/ballistics comparison) including mandatory national data sharing

## 10.11  **Terrorism and Extremism**

Terrorism is the use or threat of action (including outside the UK) where:

(a) it involves serious violence against a person, serious damage to property, endangers a person's life (other than the person committing the action), creates serious risk to the health and safety of the public or a section of the public, or is designed to seriously interfere with or seriously disrupt an electronic system;

(b) it is designed to influence the government or an international governmental organisation, or to intimidate the public or a section of the public; and

(c) it is made for the purpose of advancing a political, religious or ideological cause.[5]

The diverse nature of terrorism includes individuals and groups affiliated to, or inspired by international terrorist organisations such Al-Qaeda (AQ), Dissident Irish Republicans (DIR) in Northern Ireland to extreme right wing (XRW) activity in the UK.

Terrorists can operate in organised cells receiving instructions from others in a hierarchy; they could be individuals or a group inspired by an ideology but not directed by a core leadership, or operate individually as 'lone wolves'.

The challenge of investigating terrorism is different to other types of crime; due to its global reach the investigation could have international dimensions and multiple centres of simultaneous activity at locations throughout the UK spanning several police force areas.

Investigations are generally a fusion of covert and overt activity with clearly defined command and coordination structures operated on a strictly 'need to know' basis to prevent compromise. Terrorism powers including arrest, detention and search are different to powers under the Police and Criminal Evidence Act 1984 (PACE) and are not generally familiar to police personnel outside of the counter-terrorism (CT) investigation structure.

Countering terrorism and extremism is not the sole responsibility of investigators working in the Counter Terrorism Command (CTC) of the Metropolitan Police and the regional Counter-Terrorism Units (CTUs); it is a team effort. All police staff have a role to play through develop-

---

[5] Terrorism Act 2000, s 1.

ing community intelligence and remaining vigilant whilst conducting their day-to-day activities and reporting suspicious activity.

Planned terrorism investigations are conducted by specialist officers, but any investigator could identify intelligence or become involved in the initial stages of an unplanned spontaneous incident, eg through discovery whilst conducting other enquiries, such as searching premises, vehicles or people.

All investigators should be aware of suspicious activity which could transpire to be terrorist reconnaissance and attack planning of potential targets, fundraising, acquiring storage facilities, or purchasing vehicles, chemicals and components to construct an improvised explosive device (IED).

This section is only intended to raise awareness amongst all investigators that terrorists do reside in our communities and operate throughout the UK. History has proved that intelligence opportunities are available and investigators in whatever capacity should always remain vigilant.

---

**KEY POINT**

Any officer suspecting terrorist activity should immediately contact their Force Special Branch/CTU no matter how insignificant they feel the information is. It could be an important link that prevents an attack.

---

## 10.12 **European and International Enquiries**

Increased freedom of movement throughout the European Union, together with illegal entry and asylum seekers, means it is no longer unusual to conduct enquiries with some kind of international dimension.

Force Intelligence Bureaux have International Liaison Officers who should be consulted for advice and guidance, including access to restricted intelligence opportunities that are not for publication.

Regularly encountered situations are summarised in this section to provide basic guidance and awareness.

### 10.12.1 European Arrest Warrants and extradition

All police forces now have the responsibility for dealing with European Arrest Warrants (EAWs) when intelligence suggests a wanted person is within their force area.

The Extradition Act 2003 places countries into two categories:

1. Within the European Union and Gibraltar.
2. Those outside the EU.

EAWs are issued for two types of person:

1. Those who have been sentenced to imprisonment and are circulated, either because they have escaped or have been sentenced (possibly in their absence) and are to be returned to serve their sentence.
2. Those who are accused of criminal offences and are to be returned to the issuing state to stand trial or to be interviewed.

People circulated as wanted under an EAW are increasingly likely to be encountered. The Serious Organised Crime Agency (SOCA—soon to be merged with NCA) receives EAWs from other countries; after ensuring the warrant is legal and can be executed anywhere in England and Wales, they circulate the suspect as wanted on PNC and conduct intelligence checks to identify where they are residing.

If intelligence suggests a suspect is residing in a particular area, the EAW is sent to that force's extradition single point of contact to action enquiries and the arrest. It is important to know which type of warrant has been issued, as this determines if any premises are to be searched, the extent of any search and items that can be recovered.

A PNC marker indicating 'Subject to Sirene Circulation', means the originating European country has insufficient information to progress their enquiry, or SOCA are in the process of certifying the EAW prior to circulating for arrest on PNC. The person must not be arrested in these circumstances, but detailed information obtained, including their description, marks and distinguishing features, residence, travel plans and any persons accompanying them.

When persons are arrested or circulated as wanted for an offence in the UK and an EAW also exists, caution should be exercised. The EAW takes precedence over any UK offences for which the subject has been arrested and results in them being taken to London for extradition procedures as soon as practicable. Generally the UK offence should be arrested for first and arrest under the EAW made later after consultation.

All persons arrested under an EAW should be cautioned using the words:

> You are under arrest under the Extradition Act 2003. You do not have to say anything. Anything you do say may be given in evidence.

The subject should then be asked:

1. 'What is your name?'
2. 'What is your date of birth?'

These questions and answers must be recorded in the arresting officer's statement for the court. If there is any doubt that the arrested person is not the person sought by the requesting country they will be released by the Extradition Magistrate in London. Confirmation of the person's identity is therefore crucial, so any supporting documents, including their passport or identity card, should be seized and referred to in the arresting officer's statement.

An arrest for extradition is not a PACE arrest, but the detainee should be taken to a designated custody suite, and a new custody record opened and the Extradition Act Codes of Practice adhered to.

A full copy of the EAW (English version together with one in the language of the issuing country) and a copy of the accompanying SOCA certificate must be served on the suspect as soon as possible by physically handing it to them. Contact must be made with SOCA (24/7) and the force SPoC for extradition according to local policy.

Fingerprints, DNA and photographs must be taken by a police officer (not a Detention Officer) to assist with confirming identity. The Custody Officer should ensure arrangements are made for transport to the City of Westminster Magistrates' Court.

A court file consisting of an MG1, MG5, MG7 and MG11 is required, including how identification has been established, whether a passport/ID card has been seized (exhibit relevant documents and include a copy of the passport with the case papers) and if the suspect requires a solicitor and/ or interpreter.

An EAW will not be issued in the UK for the arrest of a foreign national in a member state for an offence committed in the UK unless a domestic warrant (Warrant of First Instance) has been obtained first; this applies even though powers of arrest for the offence in the UK do not require a warrant.

The offence must be an offence for which extradition may be sought under the Extradition Act 2003, be of sufficient seriousness for the relevant police force to undertake collection of the suspect, be 'trial ready' and the Prosecuting Authority (including the CPS) must have indicated they are willing to pursue the case once the suspect has been returned and it satisfies the tests contained in the Code for Prosecutors.

It is a responsibility of the CPS to obtain the EAW and it is a matter of law that an extradited person can only be dealt with after their return to the UK for offences detailed in the

EAW; all offences under investigation or suspected should therefore be listed.

If the location of the fugitive is known, the EAW requires translation into the relevant language and circulation through SOCA.

---

**KEY POINT**

Although EAWs may be issued for minor offences, they should still be dealt with as a priority to avoid high-level criticism from the requesting country. This is currently being reconsidered by the UK government.

---

Requests for extradition from Category 2 countries must be submitted through the Home Office Judicial Cooperation Unit, provided:

- there is sufficient existing evidence for a realistic prospect of conviction
- it is in the public interest to prosecute and a domestic warrant has been issued
- reference has to be made to the treaty or convention under which the request is made, to determine whether the offence is one for which the person can be extradited
- the requesting force is responsible for preparing the case in conjunction with the CPS, who will advise on the charges for which extradition is sought

The requesting force is responsible for collecting the person and/or any seized items from the arresting authority, plus all associated costs. Advice should be sought from the Metropolitan Police Service (MPS) Extradition and International Assistance Unit concerning risk factors to consider and manage which may not be immediately apparent.

## 10.12.2 International letters of request

The UK is a signatory to a number of international treaties and conventions which provide the legal framework for mutual legal assistance overseas, and govern the exchange of evidence between the UK and other countries both inside and outside the EU. Police forces cannot initiate enquires in an overseas jurisdiction without the necessary permissions.

An International Letter of Request (ILOR) is a written request from one judicial authority to another requesting enquiries to obtain evidential material from jurisdictions outside the UK which cannot be completed on a police-to-police basis.

If it appears that an offence has been committed or there are reasonable grounds for so believing, and proceedings/investigation have been instigated, any judge or justice of the peace in England or Wales may issue an ILOR on the application of a prosecuting authority (or, where proceedings have been instituted, a person charged in those proceedings).

A designated prosecuting authority itself (including CPS) may issue an ILOR if it appears that an offence has been committed, or there are reasonable grounds for so believing and proceedings/investigation have begun.

The CPS will advise on mutual legal assistance, including which states will accept an ILOR, the procedure for making requests, plus any grounds for refusing assistance and restrictions on the use to which the assistance may be put.

An ILOR contains an outline of the case, the evidence requested and any legislation that needs to be adhered to, ensuring it is admissible in the requesting state's proceedings. It must contain specific information on the assistance required.

Although there are no hard and fast rules on when or when not to use an ILOR, they are generally used to obtain evidence or data which is not in the public domain, or to conduct enquiries which require coercive powers. Examples include taking statements, seizing evidence, searching premises, surveillance and covert operations, obtaining information from closed databases, banking information, company records, ISP and email content, and transfer of consenting persons in custody to give evidence in criminal proceedings. Requests for intelligence gathering as opposed to evidence should not be made in an ILOR.

The police draft the ILOR for scrutiny and finalisation by the CPS who, in making the request for assistance, are exercising a statutory power and stating the evidence requested is required for use in the proceedings or investigation. This is not a 'rubber stamping' exercise as it is the prosecutor's request, not the police.

---

**KEY POINTS**

- The CPS should be approached as soon as it is known evidential enquiries will be required abroad. ILORs require considerable care to draft. Although there are measures in place to transmit them abroad in cases of urgency, they can take some time to execute. An ILOR is a legal document and failure to comply with its requirements could lead to legal challenge, including the admissibility of any evidence obtained.
- If it is necessary for UK police officers to travel abroad on enquiries, they do so at the invitation and with prior permission from the relevant state. They do not have any more power than a citizen of the country they are visiting, and in the majority of cases will be assisting and cannot initiate action themselves in the foreign jurisdiction.
- Investigators may also be required to gather evidence in the UK on behalf of a requesting nation via an ILOR.

---

## 10.12.3 Circulation notices

International circulations must be submitted through the force International Liaison Officer whose advice should be sought regarding the relevant notice, summarised below:

---

**Checklist**

**Red Notice**—Seeks the arrest or provisional arrest of wanted persons with a view to extradition, these allow the warrant to be circulated worldwide.

**Green Notice**—Provides details of criminals who are not currently wanted, but are of international significance and may be of interest to law enforcement agencies in member countries, or are likely to commit offences affecting several countries.

**Blue Notice**—To collect additional information about a person's identity or activities in relation to crime, eg unidentified offenders.

**Yellow Notice**—Issued to locate adult missing persons, missing minors or to help identify persons who are unable to identify themselves.

**Black Notice**—Provides details of unidentified bodies or deceased persons who may have used a false identity.

## 10.12.4 Convictions

It is the officer in the case's responsibility to obtain previous convictions of EU nationals who are defendants, suspects, victims or witnesses and attach them to the case file. These are obtained via the ACPO Criminal Records Office International Conviction Exchange and should be requested at the earliest opportunity in accordance with local force protocols.

Non-EU convictions from countries having a criminal register for criminal proceedings and other purposes should also be requested at the earliest opportunity in accordance with local force protocols.

# Chapter 11

# Investigating Sudden and Unexplained Deaths

## 11.1 Introduction

Deaths that occur outside medical settings and unexpectedly are often referred to as 'sudden and unexplained deaths'. They all require some form of investigation even though the death may not be suspicious or associated with criminality. The majority of deaths actually occur from natural causes, and the role of the investigator is to confirm that no criminal offences have been committed, particularly homicide.

Where there is potential third party involvement, eg due to the nature and type of visible injuries and/or information available, the incident must be treated as suspicious. Most forces have specialist units (some working under collaborative agreements with neighbouring forces) to deal with these types of enquiries and the investigation is handed over to a senior detective (ie Senior Investigating Officer (SIO)) usually of Superintendent or Chief/Inspector rank.

However, not all homicides are easily identifiable; people who are deceased aren't able to offer any information, so caution and scepticism are required. Mistakes in the initial investigation of murder always prove costly and affect chances of success, which rely heavily upon accurate assessments and methodical processes. Crime investigators must therefore acquire a good level of understanding, professional knowledge and expertise for when they are called upon to deal with a sudden and unexplained death.

It would be extremely difficult to condense all the necessary information and guidance into one chapter, so the aim is to at least cover the basic knowledge and skills required. Sections on suicides and child deaths have also been included, which can prove complex and challenging to deal with. Should further information be required on any of the topics covered, there are dedicated manuals and practical guides that contain more detailed content, such as T Cook and A Tattersall, *Blackstone's Senior Investigating Officers' Handbook* (2nd edn, Oxford University Press, 2010) and the *Murder Investigation Manual* (ACPO/Centrex, 2006).

## 11.2 Types of Death Investigation

Figure 11.1 gives an outline of the various routes a death investigation can take, accepting they may switch from one to another if the circumstances change. For example, during a coroner's investigation, if it transpires during post mortem that a homicide has occurred, then the coroner's investigation will cease and a murder enquiry will commence.

### 11.2.1 Special Procedure Investigations

Category 2 in Figure 11.1 shows what are sometimes termed 'special procedure investigations'. Some forces deem certain types of unexpected deaths to merit a higher level of response and investigation (see column 2). This may include early notification and involvement of a more senior detective (eg of Detective Inspector rank) who is expected to assume early responsibility for supervising and conducting the investigation. These types of deaths require a higher level of investigation and may include:

- deaths of any person under 18 years of age
- deaths in healthcare settings
- deaths in police custody or prisons

- illicit drug-related deaths
- accidental deaths (other than road collisions)
- deaths that occur out-of-doors
- suspected suicides
- deaths of vulnerable persons
- deaths of prominent or famous people
- deaths in Ministry of Defence establishments
- deaths that become critical incidents

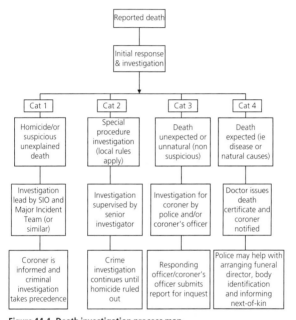

**Figure 11.1  Death investigation process map**

The aim is to ensure a more thorough investigation is conducted to eliminate mistakes and any possibility of criminal involvement. This is because these types of deaths are often more difficult to judge and prone to more suspicion because of the circumstances in which they occur, the types of individuals involved and higher degree of risk. Such cases carry a more substantial level of accountability and are likely to attract public and media interest.

---

**KEY POINT**

If an investigator considers that an enquiry into a sudden death they are dealing with would benefit from the input and advice of a more senior detective, either in person or via a communications link, then they shouldn't hesitate to contact one.

---

## 11.3 Post Mortems

The post mortem process is what in most cases will help determine the cause of death and confirm the type of investigation. Post mortem means 'after death' and is the examination of a body to determine what caused death.

There are two types of post mortems: those done on behalf of the coroner in hospital-based mortuaries by a general pathologist; and those done on behalf of the police. It is usually for the coroner to decide the type of post mortem and whether one is necessary. If, for example, a patient dies of a disease that has been treated by a medical practitioner prior to death, then the doctor who was treating them can certify the cause of death for the requirements of a coroner. If, however, a medically qualified person is not able to certify the cause of death, then a general post mortem must be conducted.

The police can make a request to the coroner for the benefit of their investigation that a forensic post mortem by a Forensic Pathologist is required. Procedures are similar, except they are far more rigorous with an emphasis on the collection of evidence as well as determining cause of death.

Forensic post mortems are generally sanctioned via consultation and agreement between a senior detective (eg on-call SIO) and the coroner. This is because they tend to be more medically intrusive, costly and time consuming. If the death is classified as a category 1 (ie homicide or suspicious) there is nearly always a forensic post mortem; categories 2 and 3 are discretionary (ie could be forensic or general); and for category 4 a post mortem may not be necessary at all.

### 11.3.1  Role of Forensic Pathologist

Forensic Pathologists used to be known as 'Home Office pathologists' because they were registered with the Home Office. This term has since been replaced by consultant Home Office Registered Forensic Pathologist. However, many judges, juries and lay people probably still know and understand the previous terminology.

A Forensic Pathologist is a medically qualified doctor who is an expert in identifying the patterns of natural disease and unnatural trauma in the human body and uses their skills and knowledge to assist investigations and the legal process. The Forensic Pathologist is essentially a medical adviser and potential expert witness. The police and pathologist work as a close team, while maintaining the professional integrity and impartiality of the Forensic Pathology role.

The investigation into a suspicious death has two separate components. The role of the coroner is to identify the deceased and establish a cause of death, whereas the role of the police is to investigate and establish if a criminal offence has occurred. The Forensic Pathologist is involved in both and is acting under the authority of, and on behalf of, the coroner, but provides evidence and guidance to the police to assist with their criminal investigation.

---

**KEY POINTS**

- Forensic Pathologists can usually only be authorised and requested by senior detectives (eg SIOs) in consultation with coroners
- Pathologists prefer to visit the scene and view the body and surroundings in context

---

> • If unsure about a cause of death (ie whether suspicious) a safe
>   option is to forensically remove the body for forensic post mor-
>   tem while keeping the scene protected and sterile—then if the
>   death is found to be a homicide, the scene is still intact

## 11.4 Cause and Manner of Death

Two terms that need to be understood so they are not confused are 'cause of death' (COD) and 'manner of death'
(MOD). A medical COD is the pathological condition which
causes the death; whereas the MOD is the instrument, physical agent or other means used. It is important to distinguish
between the two. The medical cause of death could be, for
example, a head injury, and the manner of death repeated
punching, strike by metal bar, fall from tall building etc.

The manner of death is generally divided into five
categories:

1. Natural death (ie natural process or disease)
2. Accidental death (unintentional or inadvertent actions)
3. Suicide
4. Homicide
5. Unascertained or unknown (cannot be determined with
   reasonable certainty)

Medical cause of death and evidential interpretation as to
manner of death play a crucial role in coroners' verdicts and
criminal proceedings. If, for example, a person falls down a
flight of stairs, the cause of death may be determined at post
mortem as severe head injury, whereas the determination
as to manner of death would have to be aided by the police
investigation. The result could point to either an accidental
fall or them having been deliberately pushed by a third
party. To establish the manner of death, a combination of
police investigation and pathological findings is required
to complete the evidential picture.

# 11.5 **Sudden Deaths—Initial Actions**

Those who receive notification of a death must ensure comprehensive information is obtained and relevant questions are asked (ie '5WH'—see Chapter 3). Any potential for obtaining valuable information and securing evidence should be quickly recognised and all factual details accurately recorded.

Response officers who attend have to first check whether there is the slightest indication of signs of life, in which case first aid should be attempted and medical assistance summoned. People can and do appear dead when their life signs are barely visible, for example in hypothermia cases. The police are not medical experts and must always refer to those who are. Sometimes death may have already been certified or is obvious due to heavy decomposition, skeletisation, vital body parts missing or when submerged in water, in which case the task of conducting an investigation into who they are and how their death occurred can quickly begin.

---

**KEY POINTS**

- First task is always to confirm death and check whether any necessary medical assistance has been given. Preservation of life is an overriding priority
- Clear instructions need to be provided to those who report finding a deceased person so that potential evidence is preserved pending arrival of initial response officers
- It must be remembered that in a large number of cases the person reporting the death has been the person who was responsible for causing it

---

## 11.5.1 **Pronouncing life extinct**

Only qualified medical experts can formally declare and certify a person clinically dead. Medical doctors, pathologists or qualified paramedics officially declare, pronounce and legally certify that 'life is extinct'. The precise time and date and by whom death is certified becomes a very important piece of information and one that is used as a starting point for setting the 'relevant time' (ie significant period during which death might have occurred).

In order to administer first aid, to check for signs of life and to certify death, some movement of or interference with a deceased may be necessary. This may involve attaching monitoring devices, medical equipment or physically moving a body. These processes may interfere with or contaminate forensic evidence collection and leave extra marks and traces that need to be accounted for. Defibrillators, for example, leave heavy bruising on the chest area.

Therefore it is important to debrief medical practitioners who have been involved in the initial response. An account should be obtained of:

- who the person(s) were who administered medical treatment
- what their initial assessments and findings were
- what treatments, equipment, dressings or drugs were used and why
- what equipment, packaging or dressings they left at the scene
- what actions they took and what if anything was found, noticed, moved or removed on or from the body or surroundings in which it was found
- who pronounced life extinct
- what precise time death was certified as
- what notes, details, sketches or photographs were made/taken
- who they saw or spoke to or what they were told
- what is known about the deceased's medical history and doctor's details
- what else was seen or heard that might be of use to the investigation

---

**KEY POINT**

Medical professionals may be asked for their opinion as to what may have caused a death based on their knowledge, experience and assessment. They may have noticed something that gave them cause for concern. Though never conclusive, their opinion can help provide an early indication as to what may have been the COD. They should not be encouraged, however, to begin examining the body after death is certified as this may interfere with forensic examination processes required later.

---

## 11.5.2 Initial investigation

Implementing correct procedures by methodically preserving a potential crime scene and body is always the safest option. The following golden rule applies ...

> **If in doubt ... think murder!**

With anything other than a category 4 death (death natural and expected due to disease or old age) where there is sufficient doubt or insufficient information, this rule MUST APPLY until such time cause and manner of death are established. Once a decision has been made to treat a death as suspicious then the scene(s) should be identified, secured and protected (ISP principle), leaving the body undisturbed. A senior supervisory detective should be summoned to assume control of the investigation. The responsibility for continuing the investigation then transfers to that person. Relevant specialists and experts, such as a Forensic Pathologist and Crime Scene Investigators/Managers (CSIs), forensic specialists and photographers can also be summoned. The investigation status and resources required will be escalated until such time criminal involvement can be ruled out.

---

### 11.5.3 Scene and body assessment

If a cause of death is uncertain, depending on local policy, an option is to make a careful assessment of the scene where the death has occurred. Wherever possible, this should only be conducted under the supervision of a competent CSI.

This assessment may include a brief examination of the body to check for obvious wounds, injuries or signs of recent trauma. This should be limited to a visual inspection of exposed areas of the body such as head, face, neck and forearms, provided it appears safe to do so and suitable protective clothing (ie gloves as a minimum) are worn. Any touching, moving or disturbance of a body should be kept to an absolute minimum and a body SHOULD NEVER BE TURNED OVER or subjected to any other movement that might allow body fluids to be released (eg out of the nose or mouth) and cause contamination.

Visual inspections are never totally conclusive, but it is useful to look for tell-tale signs. This will not implicate or eliminate the possibility of homicide, as only a Forensic Pathologist at a post mortem (after death) can do that. Some causes of death, for example strangulation, poisoning, lethal drugs injection or internal bruising and bleeding caused by blows from a fist or blunt instrument, are difficult to detect externally, even on an examination table.

### 11.5.4 Scene management

As much information from the scene(s) and surroundings must be gleaned as possible, remembering what a 'scene' might include (see Chapter 5). Many of the actions required are common to the procedures followed at any crime scene and it is the crime investigator's role to ensure those procedures are applied.

Once a death is deemed suspicious, certain prescribed procedures apply with the scene(s) being secured so there is no risk of interference. Indoor scenes are easier to identify, secure and protect (ISP), whereas outdoor scenes tend to be more difficult. CSIs will help in advising on protecting scenes, taking visual recordings and still photography before anything is moved or touched, helping secure a common approach path (CAP) and using stepping plates to secure a route around the body and preserving evidence.

Rough sketches can be made to note the position of a body relative to its surroundings and other objects and furniture in context, such as weapons, damaged items, footwear marks and blood markings etc. This assists in answering the 'where' and 'how' questions (5WH matrix). Positioning of the body in context helps in determining whether it has been moved before (ante) or after (post) death (mortem). For example, information may be gained from the distribution of blood in relation to the position of the body, which may indicate blows and the use of a weapon.

Bodies at hospitals (eg in accident and emergency units) pose different considerations when preserving evidence; both for the body and anything that may come from it, eg clothing or possessions. It is advisable to track down the whereabouts (in the hospital) of the body and possessions quickly. Even in a hospital or medical clinic, a body must be treated as a crime scene. Once medical treatment has finished and death certified, hospital staff become less involved with a deceased's body so arrangements need to be made in conjunction with a CSI to secure and protect it (in a body bag) ready for transportation to a mortuary. Grieving relatives and friends may add further complications, depending on the circumstances of the death and religious or cultural considerations.

> **KEY POINT**
>
> A deceased's body is a crime scene and usually the most valuable piece of potential evidence in any death investigation.

## 11.5.5 Gathering and analysing information

The investigator's role is to conduct a trawl for information to help determine how and why a person died. Making good use of the interrogative pronouns 5WH provides a structured approach to seeking, analysing and recording information. A list of possible questions can be raised relatively quickly and information gaps identified.

### Checklist—5WH questions

- Who certified death, at what time, where and when?
- What medical treatment has been given, why and who by?
- Where is the body now and who is with it?
- What arrangements are in place for preserving and securing the scene(s)?
- What appears to have happened? (*What are the likely hypotheses as to cause and manner of death? How and why did death occur?*)
- What clues and information are available?
- Who is the deceased? (*Where do they live? What is their social and medical history?*)
- Who are their next of kin? (*When were they told and how? What were they told and who by? Where are they now? What support have they been given?*)
- Who does the deceased live with? (*Where are they now? What do they say about the death? What background information can they provide?*)
- Who is/are the deceased's partner, close friends or associates?
- Who found the body? (*What is their relationship to the deceased? What is their background and character? How, why and when did they make the find? What have they said in their initial account?*)
- When was the deceased last seen alive, who by, where and under what circumstances?
- Where has death taken place? (*What signs are there of the deceased having been or died elsewhere, eg mud on their clothing, drag or scuff marks, blood trails etc?*)

- When did the death taken place? (*What dated articles are lying around eg mail and newspapers in the house or behind the front door?*)
- How long has the person been dead for?
- Why was the body not found sooner?
- What is noticeable at the scene? (*eg theft, disturbance traces, forced entry or insecurity, missing items, clean up, blood distribution corresponding to the position of the body?*)
- What significant items of property are present or missing? (*eg personal items, wallet, purse, mobile phone, cash, medical items/aids etc?*)
- What was the deceased doing before they died?
- What is known about their last movements, moods, problems and behaviour?
- What could be a motive for them having been attacked or murdered?
- What evidence suggests anything other than a natural or accidental death occurred?
- What recent activities or events might be linked to their death?
- What other information is available?
- Who has informed the coroner and what have they been told?
- Who else has been informed or requested?
- What enquiries have been conducted?

## 11.5.6 Identification of the body

A quick and accurate identification of a body is necessary, not only to help the investigation, but for the next of kin to be informed as quickly as possible. Checking for personal possessions (eg mobile phones) and seeking information from those who might know them can help make an early identification. This is important, as failure to do so could cause unnecessary distress to the deceased's close family

and relatives and unsettle their relationship and cooperation with the police investigation.

Continuity of a body, if being transferred to a mortuary,
is necessary and upon arrival it needs to be 'identified' to
the mortuary staff and/or pathologist. This duty is performed before formal identification, viewing or post mortem takes place. This is usually done by an officer travelling
with the body to the mortuary in order to provide continuity in handover to the care of the mortuary staff. Some
forces have arrangements agreed by the coroner for attaching identity bracelets. Funeral directors are usually involved
in this process as they are used to transport bodies to and
from mortuaries, which is normal procedure as they have
the appropriate experience and most suitable vehicles and
equipment for the purpose (and it is more dignified).

Police identification is made by a person who observes the
body at the scene, whereas personal identification is performed
by a relative or person who knew the deceased. In practice, the
latter is conducted at a mortuary in a suitable viewing room
once the external examination of the victim has been completed and all necessary external swabs and samples have been
obtained (ie if a forensic post mortem is required).

The formal identification process is a statutory responsibility for coroners. Visual identification may not always be
possible because of injuries sustained or decomposition.
Coroners decide on acceptable processes to establish or
confirm the identity of a deceased and there are a number
of alternative methods.

### Checklist—Methods of body identification

- Facial reconstruction, facial image analysis, artist's
  impression
- Personal effects (clothing, jewellery, spectacles, wal-
  lets, watches, phones, keys)
- External physical characteristics
- Internal organs and soft tissue (eg surgical operations
  and body art or modification)

- Odontology (teeth, gums, contents of oral cavity)
- Osteology (study of the human skeleton—sub-discipline of anthropology)
- Biological samples (blood, biochemistry, toxicology, or DNA)
- Prints (ie finger and palm prints)
- Radiological imaging (for use in osteology, odontology, and facial reconstruction)
- Computed tomography (ie CT scans for two- and three-dimensional imaging)
- Podiatry (using foot analysis for diseases, walking gait, abnormalities etc)
- Environmental information (specialist examinations to identify likely environment within which a person lived, eg stable isotope fingerprinting to identify geographic region, or pollen, soil, and botanical samples to do the same)
- Missing Persons Bureau assistance
- Media appeals

## 11.6 **Families and Relatives**

Establishing and managing effective family liaison is important throughout an investigation into a death, particularly in homicide or suspicious cases. The police have a clear duty to communicate effectively and inclusively with a bereaved family. One of the most significant relationships the police have to develop is the one with families, relatives and close friends of a deceased person during what is a very distressing and upsetting time and one they never forget.

High standards of service delivery are expected when dealing with families and relatives, so police roles and responsibilities must be conducted professionally and relationships managed effectively. If things go wrong with the police/family relationship it will take a long time to recover.

A priority is to identify the deceased and notify their next of kin and relatives promptly to establish an early trusting relationship with them. There are many methods and sources of communication, eg via social media sites, for them to find out for themselves, so investigators must try to stay one step ahead of digital communication forums that may relay information about a person's death.

When a deceased's identity is known or suspected, an option is for the next of kin to be informed that a body of a person *matching the description* of their relative or spouse etc has been found. This is what happens in some missing person cases. It is a preferable choice to not telling the family anything and them finding out via a non-police source (eg the media). Caveats can be given to tactfully manage their expectations.

Families and relatives need information which must be given to them provided doing so does not undermine or interfere with the investigation. Families themselves are also an important *source* of information, eg about the deceased's background and lifestyle for what is often termed 'victimology' enquiries.

---

### KEY POINTS

1. Providing inaccurate information is to be avoided. It is much better to explain why details cannot be provided rather than having to make corrections later. Explaining why it is necessary to withhold information is preferable to giving no/mis-information that leads to a loss of trust and confidence.
2. **Never delay** in informing the next of kin and family if there is a strong indication of who the deceased is. Often this can be quickly established by carefully checking personal possessions (eg wallet, purse, phone or information received).

---

## 11.6.1 Identification of the family

A deceased's family has to be considered in the broadest sense and generally includes partners, parents, guardians, children, siblings, members of the extended family, and any others who may have had a direct and close relationship. This can, however, become complicated, with split marriages, ex-partners and children dispersed across geographic locations, or possible association with cultural or lifestyle diversity, eg gay, lesbian, bisexual or transgender community, or faith group.

Some families are complex in their make-up and relationship, eg when parents are separated or divorced. Communication and contact need to be managed tactfully so as not to cause friction or animosity by showing favour to one or the other.

## 11.6.2  Role of a Family Liaison Officer

In homicide and suspicious death cases, Family Liaison Officers (FLOs) are usually deployed. It is useful to know what this role entails, as some of the same working principles can be adopted in other types of death investigations, eg when managing the initial stages of an unexplained or sudden death that has yet to be designated suspicious, or merits a 'special procedure' investigation.

FLOs are specifically trained to deal with the day-to-day management of the interaction between investigators and families to ensure they are treated appropriately, professionally and the police are respectful of their needs. The primary role of a FLO is that of an *investigator* to help an enquiry team meet it's aims and objectives (see also *Family Liaison Officer Guidance Manual* (ACPO/NPIA, 2008)).

### Checklist—Role of a FLO

- Provide families with full details and updates on the investigation
- Provide reassurance the investigation is being conducted diligently and expeditiously
- Give or facilitate practical support

- Consider any threats or concerns for their safety and welfare
- Assist in arranging and escorting the family for identification of the body
- Deal with requests for organ donations
- Gather antecedent information and evidence of identification
- Gather 'victimology' type information
- Offer information and advice re supporting agencies
- Monitor relationship between family/police investigation
- Deal with requests or complaints (from the family)
- Establish liaison with the coroner and make arrangements for release of the body or body parts seized under the Human Tissue Act 2004 (HTA)
- Consider funeral arrangements and police attendance/involvement (eg flowers and messages)
- Liaise with family re media issues and shield from unwarranted media intrusion
- Manage exit strategy (eg case officer to continue liaison)

## 11.7 **Faith, Culture and Diversity**

A deceased, their family and friends may be part of any number of nationalities, cultural groups or faiths, or have no faith at all. Assumptions or biases should not be made or applied around any beliefs or lifestyle choices. It is advisable to find out about associated beliefs, cultures and any matters relating to diversity which might need managing sensitively and tactfully when dealing with deaths.

People's differences, beliefs and individual requirements must be considered, although the nature of some types of deaths may mean it is not always feasible for any wishes to be met in the early stages of an investigation. As progress is made, however, it may become more likely that these requirements can be taken into account.

A range of local resources and advisers are usually available to give advice and offer support to ensure the most appropriate course of action is taken. Local race and diversity units, for example, may be consulted and they can make use of contacts and networks of key representatives and advisers. There may be local force policy that provides specific guidance and details of procedures.

## 11.8 'Victimology' Enquiries

The phrase '*Find out how a victim lived…and you'll find out how they died*' refers to those important clues that are available when delving into the background of a deceased person. An objective is to seek as much detail about a deceased as possible, a process which is often referred to as 'victimology'. This involves seeking personal and intrusive information, a process that often requires careful and tactful management. It can entail a thorough search of the victim's belongings and/or room, house, etc to look for any information that helps the investigation. Reasons for doing this must be carefully explained to a deceased's family and relatives, informing them how it can provide valuable leads and lines of enquiry.

Researching a deceased's background and lifestyle is a strategy that features in the list of main lines of enquiry (MLOE). Obtaining these details, if unknown, must be a 'fast track' (or high priority (HP)) action. It is an unfortunate by-product as a murder victim that investigators have to delve through someone's personal life to seek clues. However, these enquiries often generate productive leads by piecing together final movements, associates, lifestyle, habits, family tree etc.

### Checklist—'Victimology' information

- Full name(s), address(es), description (and recent videos or photographs), social background, education, qualifications, specialist skills, character and personality, premises or businesses linked to, places frequented

- Lifestyle, previous convictions, criminality, previous incidents of note, employment, habits, social activities, hobbies and interests, vehicle details, means of transport, likes and dislikes, drug abuse or other vices, habits, secrets, sexual orientation and preferences, risk-taking, financial information, investments, premises and businesses
- Close associates and relationships, current, intended and previous romantic or sexual relationships and partners, dating agencies
- Routines, daily activities, places visited, who they came into contact with and when, last known movements, when last seen and what they said and their mood
- Involvement in precursor events, incidents or activities
- Personal possessions, phones, diaries, secure storage places, laptops, tablets, computers, where money and expensive items are kept, who had access to their belongings, any missing items
- Medical details and history, details of doctor (GP), any illnesses, level of fitness, physical and mental health, surgery and operations, prescribed medicines, deformities, allergies, unusual marks or scars, tattoos, piercings, dental history and details of dentist
- Vulnerabilities or disabilities
- Any specific information, such as, if female, had they been pregnant or had a termination
- Digital and communications data profiling information from social media usage, itemised phone billing, computer usage (eg gaming) websites visited or access to any other passive data digital recording devices, Facebook contacts etc

## 11.9 **Official Categories of Murder**

The ACPO official categories of murder are useful to know. These tend to relate more to command and control and resourcing than decision making, but nonetheless have been widely adopted and are regularly used in police major crime terminology.

| | |
|---|---|
| Category A+ | A homicide or other major investigation where public concern and the associated response to media intervention are such that 'normal' staffing levels are not adequate to keep pace with the investigation. |
| Category A | A homicide or other major investigation which is of grave concern or where vulnerable members of the public are at risk; where the identity of the offender/s is/are not apparent, or the investigation and the securing of evidence requires significant resource allocation. |
| Category B | A homicide or other major investigation where the identity of the offender(s) is not apparent, the continued risk to the public is low, and the investigation or securing of evidence can be achieved within normal resourcing arrangements. |
| Category C | A homicide or other major investigation where the identity of the offender(s) is apparent from the outset and the investigation and/or securing of evidence can easily be achieved.<br>*Murder Investigation Manual* (ACPO/Centrex, 2006) |

## 11.10 **Suicide Deaths**

Committing suicide is not a crime per se, provided the motives are genuine, whereas assisting suicide is. Some homicides are disguised and staged to appear as suicide, or the suicide is attributable to some form of assistance, threats, bullying or harassment. There have been many cases where murders have been committed and made to look like suicide, which is why these types of deaths need a cautious approach. Facts presented must not be taken at face value (ie applying the **ABC** rule).

As in all death investigations, and suicides are no different: **if in doubt think murder!** In any case, a final determination of suicide can only be made by a coroner aided by pathology and police investigation reports. Evidence will come from the death scene and in the circumstances leading up to the death, plus the pathological examination of the body (eg checks for defensive marks on hands and arms).

In some suicides the cause and manner of death (COD/MOD) are not always straightforward and conclusive (unlike simple asphyxiation through hanging or massive brain damage via a *single* gunshot wound to the head). Investigators need to be on the look out for other possible explanations, such as where victims have been pushed not fallen down some stairs; or who have been thrown off a balcony and not slipped or committed suicide; or who have been strangled by a ligature and then hoisted up to look like a suicidal hanging (in which case there will be two rope lines around the neck, and the offender, possibly the person reporting, may have rope marks/abrasions/cuts around their hands).

Any determination of suicide must be based upon a linked series of factors that eliminate homicide, accident, third party involvement or natural causes. To assist, investigators can apply three basic considerations that help establish the manner of death in suicide cases:

## Checklist—Three suicide considerations

1. Close proximity to the body of the weapon or means of causing death.
2. Injuries or death wounds that appear self-inflicted AND could have feasibly and practically been inflicted by the deceased.
3. Existence of a motive or intent on the part of the deceased to take their own life.

Motive and intent can be established by examining movements, activities and behaviour of a deceased leading up to their death. For example, sourcing a ligature (eg rope) and fixings to hang themselves, purchasing flammable materials to set themselves on fire, visiting buildings or bridges from which to jump to their deaths, telling others of their intent, writing notes, researching suicide websites, history of previous failed attempts, significant changes in behaviour, excessive use of drink or drugs, severe depression and mood swings etc.

There are a number of possible motives in suicide cases:

| | |
|---|---|
| • Depression | • Severe emotional crisis |
| • Drug abuse | • Psychological problems |
| • Alcohol problems | • Physical deterioration |
| • Relationship/domestic problems | • Loss of a loved one |
| • Frustration | • Death of a child |
| • Fear/anger/resentment | • Financial problems |
| • Hostility | • Teenage/adolescence problems |
| • Guilt (eg of a crime) | • Loss of employment |
| • Terminal illness | • Despair and general inability to cope |
| • Illness in the family | |

## 11.10.1 Suicide notes

Suicide notes are indications of suicide provided they are genuine. That they were actually written by the deceased and voluntarily **needs to be confirmed**. Any note should be recovered in a manner to preserve forensic evidence, including DNA and fingerprints. Past writings of the deceased should be collected for comparison purposes and there are specialists who can compare not just handwriting but comparative writing style and grammar.

There is sometimes the possibility that suicide notes (and the means of committing the suicide) may be removed or destroyed prior to police attendance. Investigators should be mindful of family members who can, in some circumstances, experience difficulty in accepting their relative or loved one has committed suicide and remove or destroy evidence. It has also been known for relatives of suicide victims to accuse the police of a cover-up, or poor investigation and request a formal review, with the hope they can change a coroner's verdict.

Diaries, letters, text messages, communications and social media data and similar material can be examined for information that may corroborate details in a suicide note. Any stated or inferred intention of a person to take their own life and sudden and strange precursor activities are important investigative information.

Recovered articles and material can help contribute to compiling a 'psychological autopsy' of the deceased. This is a collaborative procedure involving law enforcement and mental health experts who attempt to determine the state of mind of a person prior to their fatal act.

## 11.10.2 **False reports of suicide**

Some people commit a murder and try and stage it to appear as a genuine suicide, then feel duty bound and compelled to report the death due to their alleged finding of the body and/or relationship to the victim (eg spouse/lover/relative/close friend etc). What they say and do can be very useful evidential information for (dis)proving their honesty and truthfulness. This emphasises the importance of obtaining the full contents of any report or emergency call to the emergency services (police, ambulance), which must be carefully scrutinised for precise wording and detail via a transcript/recording (if available) of the exact words used. Studies have shown that mistakes are often made by offenders in how they report these deaths and how they behave, as indications of guilt can come from their words, language, tonality and general behaviour that can be recognised.[1]

---

[1] Further details and advice can be obtained from the SOCA/NCA COS team.

## 11.11 **Child Deaths**

A sudden and unexpected death of an infant (SUDI) or child (SUDC) is defined as:

The unexpected death of an infant (under one year) or child (less than 18 years old) which:

- Was not anticipated as a significant possibility, eg 24 hours before the death, or
- Where there was a similarly unexpected collapse or incident leading to or precipitating the events which led to the death.[2]

The majority of child deaths are not suspicious and sadly many result from accidents, natural causes and medical conditions, including 'cot death' which is defined as:

The sudden and unexpected death of a baby for no obvious reason. The post mortem examination may explain some deaths. Those that remain unexplained after post mortem examination may be registered as sudden infant death syndrome (SIDS), sudden infant death, sudden unexpected death in infancy (SUDI), unascertained or cot death.[3]

Child deaths broadly fall into three investigative groups:

- Natural non-suspicious, including sudden infant death syndrome, natural or medical causes where there are no concerning factors
- Suspicious child deaths that may feature criminal offences, other than the four homicide offences below
- Homicide—criminal offences of murder, manslaughter, infanticide and familial homicide

---

[2] HM Government, *Working Together to Safeguard Children. A guide to inter-agency working to safeguard and promote the welfare of children* (DCSF Publications, 2010).

[3] Foundation for the Study of Infant Death (FSID), fact sheet available at <www.fsid.org.uk>.

SUDI/SUDC investigations should never be considered straightforward. It is essential to keep an open mind and search for the truth, which may not be readily apparent. Investigators are in the sensitive position of providing care and support to families and persons connected with the child, whilst simultaneously preserving and obtaining evidence as to the cause of the death, which in extreme cases could identify the parents as suspects.

---

**KEY POINT**

Five common principles pertinent to child deaths, especially when having contact with family members are:

1. Being caring and sensitive particularly to those who are grieving.
2. An inter-agency response—working together and sharing information.
3. Keeping an open mind and adopting a balanced approach.
4. Ensuring a proportionate response to the circumstances.
5. Preservation of all potential evidence.

---

*Working Together to Safeguard Children*,[4] often referred to as 'Working Together', is a guide to inter-agency working to safeguard and promote the welfare of children in accordance with the Children Acts of 1989 and 2004. Chapter 7 relating to the child death review processes and Chapter 8 regarding serious case reviews of certain child deaths are designated as statutory guidance, which is underpinned by section 16 of the Children Act 2004.

Investigations into childhood death involve professionals from different agencies with distinct roles to perform, working together to share information and professional knowledge to establish how and why a child died, including the four key questions:

---

[4] HM Government, *Working Together to Safeguard Children. A guide to inter-agency working to safeguard and promote the welfare of children* (DCSF Publications, 2010).

1. Why did the child die?
2. What was the cause of the death and the circumstances?
3. Are there any criminal offences disclosed?
4. If so, who was/were responsible for committing those offences?

The linked processes of child death review have been compulsory since 1 April 2008 and operate across England but are coordinated on a local geographical basis, within the Local Safeguarding Children Board (LSCB) and Child Death Overview Panel (CDOP). There are similar processes in Wales, Scotland and Northern Ireland.

The term 'child' encompasses children and young people up to the age of 18 years, but excludes 'babies who are still born and planned terminations of pregnancy carried out within the law'.

'Working Together' states that an appropriate balance should be drawn between the forensic and medical requirements and the families' need for support. Families should be treated with sensitivity, discretion and respect at all times and professionals should approach their enquiries with an open mind, but in all cases enquiries should:

- seek to understand the reasons for the child's death
- address the possible needs of other children in the household
- consider the needs of all family members and
- identify any lessons learnt about how best to safeguard and promote children's welfare in the future

## 11.12 **Rapid Response and Child Death Overview Panel**

There are two categories of rapid response and CDOP processes.

### 11.12.1 Rapid response

This is a multi-agency response intended to take place as soon as possible after the unexpected death of a child or young person and aimed at establishing the cause of death, safeguarding other siblings, coordinating support for families and gathering information for the CDOP.

A rapid response meeting involves a multi-agency collaboration of professionals with attendees determined on a case-by-case basis chaired by a designated paediatrician. Many of these professionals will have contributed to the actual rapid response itself, more often than not at the hospital. Consideration is given to a joint home or location of death visit by the police and paediatrician or other healthcare professional within 24 hours.

### 11.12.2 Child Death Overview Panel

This is a sub committee of the LSCB whose function is to review all child deaths in their area against national criteria to inform local strategic planning on how best to safeguard and promote the welfare of children. The process is a paper-based review, parents do not attend the CDOP meeting and all cases are anonymised prior to discussion. The CDOP reviews all child deaths, but the rapid response process only relates to sudden and unexpected deaths.

---

**KEY POINT**

The police are statutory partners with the LSCB and have a duty to safeguard children so must take 'Working Together to Safeguard Children' into account and only depart from it if they have clear reasons.

---

Investigations into child deaths where factors arouse suspicion are police led and require detailed investigation into the circumstances. Such enquiries are particularly challenging where there is no direct evidence or grounds to suspect a specific criminal act, but there are factors that raise the possibility that a criminal act may have contributed to the death, and thereby merit more detailed investigation of the circumstances.

Investigations into SUDI/SUDC will usually be undertaken by investigators in family protection/child abuse units supervised by a Detective Inspector. Investigations involving suspicious child death or homicide, including causing or allowing the death of a child or vulnerable adult under section 5 of the Domestic Violence, Crime and Victims Act 2004 (child under 16) should be led by an SIO (PIP Level 3).

The presence of the following factors *may* raise levels of concern regarding whether or not a death is 'suspicious'. Their presence is not conclusive proof of a criminal act, but may justify a more detailed investigation when seen in the context of a particular set of circumstances.

### Checklist—Factors that may increase suspicion

- History of domestic abuse, including violence towards children
- Accounts and behaviour from those caring for the dead child that are inconsistent with the physical findings, and may vary on questioning
- Mental health issues within the family or parent/carers
- History of hospital or GP visits when symptoms ascribed to the child cannot be verified by independent observation or investigation. Numerous visits to different hospitals/medical practices may occur
- History of alcohol/drug abuse or a criminal record for the parent/carer
- Deaths of children over the age of one year (commonly more suspicious than those less than a year old)
- The child or the family are known to Social Services and children in the family may be on a child protection plan, at risk, or recent events or intelligence suggest this should be the case

- Child comes from a family in which a previous child has died unexpectedly
- Inappropriate delay in seeking medical help

Suspicious physical findings include:

- Bruising in a baby too young to be independently mobile, multiple bruises, bruises in unusual sites, eg behind the ears or on the trunk/abdomen, or bruises of obviously different ages without a clear plausible explanation of how they occurred
- Petechiae or retinal haemorrhaging, eg in the eyeballs
- Blood on the face (pink frothy blood is often found in non-suspicious deaths but thicker blood warrants further investigation)
- The child has been dead longer than stated
- Fractures identified from a radiological skeletal survey prior to post mortem
- Evidence of bleeding over the surface of the brain, between two of the membranes that surround the brain (subdural haemorrhage), bleeding into the inside surface of the back of the eye (retinal haemorrhage) and brain swelling identified by diagnostic imaging before autopsy
- Identification of prescription or recreational drugs (other than those used in attempted resuscitation) in samples taken for toxicological analysis

Also to be considered if relevant:

- Home environment/conditions
- Stressors, eg financial debt
- Mode of death, position of child, its surroundings and general condition
- Family dynamics
- Strange interaction between the parents/their demeanour or behaviour
- Foreign body in upper airway
- Suicide attempt

- Comments made (verbal/text/written)
- Prior unusual or unexplained illnesses
- Apparent life-threatening event (ALTE)
- Signs of neglect, eg growth, hygiene, lack of food
- Previous physical abuse
- Previous neglect

Whilst the 'five building block principles' (see Chapter 4) continue to underpin the investigation process, a child homicide contains considerations that are different to that of an adult homicide and may impact on the investigation:

- The initial circumstances may show no obvious cause of death or be immediately apparent, even after the post mortem. It may take some time to establish if death is through a crime or natural causes
- The vulnerability and small size of very young children makes it possible to obscure the cause of death and the circumstances
- Sensitive management is required due to the highly emotional nature of child death and uncertainty in establishing the cause of death and circumstances
- Investigators require specialist knowledge
- Specialist post mortem procedures, including a paediatric pathologist, are required
- Issues concerning parents handling the deceased child and access to the body that would not arise in adult cases
- Forensic opportunities that are of limited value when a family member is responsible for the death
- Risk to other siblings if the child is unlawfully killed by a parent or carer
- Multi-agency response with possible issues concerning conflicting priorities, information sharing and communication
- Suspects within the family which present issues for family liaison

- Reliance on experts, particularly medical experts, where there are limited witnesses to the circumstances surrounding the death
- Criminal offences relating solely to children
- Faith and child-rearing practices
- Parallel proceedings in the Criminal and Family Courts which may create issues in relation to disclosure and access to siblings who may be witnesses
- Media reporting

### Final Checklist—Sudden death investigations

- Consider any dangers and risks before approaching the body or location (eg, fires, dangerous environments, premises or terrain, diseases, body fluids, insects, needles, electric or gas appliances, water, animals etc)
- Check for signs of life and give consideration to administering first aid/medical assistance (unless death is so obvious, eg decomposed, skeletal remains or vital organs/body parts missing)
- Prevent unnecessary contamination of the scene
- Confirm death certified, time recorded and by whom
- Make a visual inspection of exposed parts and avoid touching anything unless absolutely necessary (record what has/has not been touched)—always use protective gloves
- Make a careful note of any obvious and visible marks or injuries
- Make a careful note of the position of the body, state of clothing or undress and anything else that might be relevant (eg visible bloodstaining, broken or missing furniture or items, room temperature, lighting on or off, curtains closed or open, medication lying around, drugs paraphernalia)
- Note and preserve (where necessary) any physical evidence in the area (eg a mobile phone, suicide note, weapon)

- Establish if anyone witnessed the death
- Determine if there are any other potential crime scenes and take appropriate action
- Establish if anyone has touched or moved the body or any items prior to arrival (eg first responders, paramedics, medical examiners, family and friends, witnesses etc)
- Establish details of person finding the body and last person to see the deceased alive
- Make enquiries to establish the identity of the deceased and next of kin details
- Establish what enquiries have been made to contact the next of kin (if there is some degree of certainty as to who the deceased is, the next of kin can be tactfully informed *who it might be*—until formally identified—*without delay*)
- Make enquiries into background and last known movements of deceased, including medical history and GP details
- Identify or confirm what type of death investigation process is required
- Consider what additional resources are required
- Ensure the coroner has been informed of the death and liaised with
- Keep any bereaved parties informed of progress of the investigation
- Accurately record all relevant detail and information available
- Suicides can be staged to cover up murders
- Child deaths require a different approach, more sensitive handling and a multi-agency approach to the investigation
- In all sudden death investigations keep an open mind—**if in doubt think murder!**

## References

T Cook and A Tattersall, *Blackstone's Senior Investigating Officers' Handbook* (2nd edn, Oxford University Press, 2010)

*Family Liaison Officer Guidance Manual* (ACPO/NPIA, 2008)

Foundation for the Study of Infant Death (FSID), fact sheet available at <http://www.fsid.org.uk>

HM Government, *Working Together to Safeguard Children. A guide to inter-agency working to safeguard and promote the welfare of children* (DCSF Publications, 2010)

*Murder Investigation Manual* (ACPO/Centrex, 2006)

# Chapter 12
# Proactive Investigation

## 12.1 Introduction

In reactive investigations the police respond to reports of crimes that have already been committed, initial reports are taken and responded to, then further investigations are conducted.

In proactive investigations the police initiate action against some kind of continuing criminal activity; this could be targeting suspected offenders or targeting a particular type of crime where the offenders are unidentified.

Proactive investigation is not confined to covert operations, such as surveillance. A range of overt proactive options to prevent, detect and disrupt crime are available, including activities like executing search warrants, high visibility patrols, road checks and exercising stop and search powers.

Other proactive options include consulting and working with specialists in covert operations, confiscation of criminal property, dealing with threats to life (TTL) and managing dangerous offenders through Multi-Agency Public Protection Arrangements (MAPPA).

Complex investigations may require an integrated approach and use every available technique at some stage.

The National Intelligence Model (NIM) recognises three levels of criminality:

- Level 1—local crime issues that can be managed within a Basic Command Unit (BCU)
- Level 2—cross-border issues where organised criminality affects more than one BCU and potentially crosses boundaries into neighbouring forces

- Level 3—serious and organised crime operating on a national or international level

These NIM levels influence the tasking and coordination process, including the deployment of local, regional and national specialist assets in targeted operations. This does not mean proactive techniques are the sole preserve of specialists, but it does mean investigators will face competing demands for resources when submitting applications at whatever NIM level.

Investigating crime is not a 'one size fits all' or 'tick box' activity; creative problem solving (see also Chapter 3) is to be encouraged, including the properly managed use of proactive techniques.

This chapter aims to provide mainstream investigators with an overview of considerations but is not exhaustive.

## 12.2 **Covert Investigation**

Covert operations can be used as a stand-alone tactic or to complement conventional lines of enquiry depending on the needs of the investigation, eg developing intelligence to potentially convert into evidence where overt techniques cannot or are unlikely to achieve the required objective. In simple terms, overt investigation gathers evidence that implicates suspects and covert investigation obtains evidence of suspects implicating themselves.

Some covert tactics such as the use of mobile and foot surveillance, static observation points and covert human intelligence sources (CHIS) are generally known, and some even more sensitive techniques have been revealed in television documentaries.

Preservation of tactics is essential to ensure their future effectiveness and minimise the risk of compromise and possible harm to those involved. Knowledge of certain methods is restricted even within police circles and it is inappropriate to mention these in this handbook. Investigators encountering or involved in covert operations at whatever level must strictly adhere to the 'need to know' (as opposed to 'nice to know') principle, including amongst their colleagues.

Due to the intrusion on Article 8 of the European Convention on Human Rights (ECHR), right to respect for private and family life, covert investigation at whatever NIM level has to be authorised and will be closely scrutinised. The evidence obtained is often compelling, so defence tactics at trial may seek its exclusion by questioning the integrity of the process and challenging police adherence to the procedures involved. This includes not just authorisation and the actions of operatives but the disclosure obligations under the Criminal Procedure and Investigations Act 1996 (CPIA).

Balancing a defendant's right to a fair trial alongside the management of sensitive material is challenging and may necessitate a Public Interest Immunity (PII) hearing to prevent certain information being disclosed to the defence. Early consultation with the Crown Prosecution Service (CPS) is essential.

The principle legislation governing covert investigation can be summarised in two parts:

- Police Act 1997, Part III, which empowers authorities to interfere with private property in circumstances which would otherwise be trespassing (this may be necessary to facilitate actions under the Regulation of Investigatory Powers Act 2000 (RIPA 2000)); and
- RIPA 2000, which empowers investigators to use specific methods to acquire evidence without the subject of the investigation being aware.

The basic covert methods of investigation under RIPA are:

- interception of communications (not discussed in this chapter)
- directed surveillance

- intrusive surveillance
- covert human intelligence sources (CHIS)

## 12.2.1 Authorisation

All covert investigation methods must be authorised before their use. Generally the higher the level of intrusion sought, the higher the level of authority is required, which is balanced with the increased seriousness of the crime.

Police forces have individual authorisation protocols involving either a central designated on-call Authorising Officer (AO) or local arrangements. Investigators should familiarise themselves with these.

The authority levels are broadly summarised in the table that follows: contingencies in cases of urgency are strictly controlled to avoid abuse of the system and applicants and AOs must be members of the same organisation, eg the same police force.

**Summary of authority levels**

| Method | Authority level |
|---|---|
| Interception of communication | • Home Secretary |
| Intrusive surveillance | • Chief Officer of Police subject to prior approval of the Chief Surveillance Commissioner—authorisation period three months unless renewed. |
| | • Designated deputies (Deputy Chief Constable/Assistant Chief Constable (DCC/ACC)) if urgent provisions apply—authorisation period 72 hours. |
| Directed surveillance | • Superintendent—authorisation period three months unless renewed (72 hours if authorised orally unless renewed). |
| | • Inspector if urgency provisions apply—authorisation period 72 hours unless renewed by Superintendent. |

| Method | Authority level |
|--------|-----------------|
| CHIS | • ACC—for juvenile CHIS—authorisation period one month (CHIS under 16 years of age are prevented from providing information on an adult with parental responsibility for them). |
| | • Superintendent—for adult CHIS—authorisation period 12 months (72 hours if authorised orally unless renewed). |
| | • Inspector—for adult CHIS if urgent provisions apply—authorisation period 72 hours unless renewed by Superintendent. |

## 12.2.2 Surveillance

Surveillance is only covert when it is conducted in a manner calculated to ensure the subject is unaware it is taking place and is defined by RIPA 2000, section 48(2) as including:

- monitoring, observing or listening to persons, their movements, their conversations or other activities or communications;
- recording anything monitored, observed or listened to in the course of surveillance; and
- surveillance by or with the assistance of a surveillance device.

### KEY POINTS—NOT CONSTRUED AS SURVEILLANCE

- Any conduct of CHIS for obtaining or recording any information which is disclosed in their presence, whether a surveillance device is used or not.
- The use of CHIS for obtaining or recording information.
- Entry onto or interference with property or with wireless telegraphy which would be unlawful unless it was authorised property interference under Part III of the Police Act 1997 (as amended by RIPA 2000).

### 12.2.3 Directed surveillance

Directed surveillance is the lowest level of intrusion within the framework of covert methods and can be authorised for the purpose of preventing or detecting crime, preventing disorder or to apprehend the suspected offender, RIPA 2000, sections 28(3), 81(2) and 81(5).

Directed surveillance is also permitted:

- in the interests of national security
- in the interests of the economic well-being of the UK
- in the interests of public safety
- for the purpose of protecting public health
- for the purpose of assessing or collecting certain fiscal levies

Outside the police service these additional statutory reasons are restricted to specific agencies and are not generally available, which may need taking into consideration if planning joint operations, for example with Trading Standards, but does not require further elaboration here.

Directed surveillance is:

- covert but not intrusive
- undertaken for the purpose of a specific operation or investigation
- will or is likely to obtain private information about any person, not just the subject of the operation
- does not include observations conducted in immediate response to spontaneous events

For example, if an officer on routine duties witnesses an offence and whilst in pursuit of the suspect conceals themselves to watch where they go, this would not be directed surveillance, as the officer's actions are in immediate response to a spontaneous event and not pre-planned.

Private information is defined by RIPA 2000, section 26(10) as *any information relating to a person's private or family life or personal relationships with others.*

Directed surveillance can be conducted anywhere except:

- inside any premises at the time being used as a residence, no matter how temporary, including hotel accommodation, tents, caravans, a prison cell or even railway arches;
- in any vehicle which is primarily used as a private vehicle, either by the owner or a person having the right to use it (this does not include taxis);
- outside such premises or vehicles if conducted by remote technical means (eg a long-range microphone) which enables events and conversations inside the residential premises and/or private vehicle(s) to be monitored from outside, and the product is of the same quality as would be obtained by devices or persons inside the premises or vehicle(s).

The fact that an individual is in a public location (eg a car park) does not diminish their right to an expectation of privacy, and surveillance should only be conducted if authorised. This should be considered when using local authority CCTV cameras; although their presence to the public is known, a directed surveillance authority is required if they are used in a pre-planned operation.

Applicants and AOs must acknowledge potential collateral intrusion into the privacy of third parties who may be present in the surveillance arena but not subjects of the operation. It must be demonstrated that actions taken are proportionate and a necessary breach of the right to privacy, with measures used to minimise any collateral intrusion and its consequences.

### 12.2.4 Observation posts (*R v Johnson*)

An Observation Post (OP) is a position from which to observe, record and report activity at a given location or area; it must be staffed by a minimum of two specially trained operatives with the relevant RIPA 2000 authorisation, and arrangements to record, preserve and produce any evidence obtained including the use of surveillance logs.

To safeguard against the location of the OP being disclosed and exposed in court, which could put any occupants or persons connected to the premises at risk, certain requirements derived from the 1988 case of *R v Johnson*[1] must be followed:

- The police officer in charge of the observations should be a sergeant or above, responsible for issuing logs and equipment in accordance with the surveillance authority, and briefing and debriefing the officers conducting the surveillance.
- This officer must be able to testify that prior to the observations commencing they visited all observation posts and ascertained from the occupier(s) of the premises their attitude towards the use being made of the premises, and the possibility that subsequent disclosure may lead to the identification of the premises and occupant(s).
- The officer in charge may inform the court of any difficulties encountered in a particular locality and of any problems obtaining assistance from the public.
- Immediately before any trial a Chief Inspector or above must visit the places used for observations and be able to testify that they ascertained:
  - whether the occupant(s) was the same as when the observations took place;
  - their attitude to possible disclosure of the use made of the premises and any facts which could lead to the identification of the premises and occupants.
- A statement of evidence will be submitted to the CPS outlining these points and the officer may be required to present this evidence if an application to exclude the evidence is made.

## 12.2.5 Intrusive surveillance

Intrusive surveillance is by definition more intrusive than directed surveillance, and as such can only be used

---

[1] [1989] All ER 121.

for the investigation of serious crime with a higher level of authority.

Serious crime is defined by RIPA 2000, section 81(3) as:

- offences for which a person aged 21 years or over with no previous convictions, could reasonably expect to be sentenced to three years imprisonment or more; or
- involves the use of violence; or
- results in substantial financial gain; or
- is engaged by a large number of people pursuing a common purpose.

Intrusive surveillance is activity that intrudes on a person's private life, and is:

- covert
- carried out in relation to anything taking place within a *residential* premises or in any *private* vehicle
- involves the presence of an individual or any surveillance device on any *residential* premises or in any *private* vehicle or
- is carried out in relation to anything taking place on *residential* premises or in a *private* vehicle by means of any surveillance device that is not present on the premises or in the vehicle

## 12.3  Covert Human Intelligence Sources

The term CHIS covers undercover officers, test purchase officers and individuals formerly known as 'informers'. Nationally accredited training exists for undercover and test purchase officers, and ACPO guidance recommends that 'informers' are only handled and managed by trained staff assigned in Dedicated Source Units (DSU). This is due to the high risk of retribution if the CHIS is compromised, the tradecraft required and operational security surrounding the dissemination and storage of sensitive material.

Section 26(8) of RIPA 2000 sets out the full definition of CHIS, which in essence is:

- a person who establishes or maintains a personal or other relationship with another person for the covert purpose of facilitating anything that:
  - covertly uses such a relationship to obtain information, or
  - to provide access to any information or to another person, or
  - covertly discloses information obtained by the use of such a relationship or as a consequence of the existence of such a relationship.

Before authorising CHIS activity, AOs must believe it is necessary:

- in the interests of national security
- for preventing or detecting crime or preventing disorder
- in the interests of the economic well-being of the UK
- in the interests of public safety
- for the purpose of protecting public health
- for assessing or collecting any tax, duty, levy or other imposition, contribution or charge payable to a government department or
- for other purposes which may be specified by order of the Secretary of State

As with surveillance, most of the organisations empowered to deploy CHIS are limited to the statutory purposes of the prevention and detection of crime, and/or disorder.

Authorisation for the use and conduct of CHIS must be proportionate to what it is trying to achieve and if a particular conduct is not recorded on the authority it will not be authorised.

Potential dangers of using CHIS include possibly exposing and compromising a police operation by tasking them (double agent), the CHIS deliberately supplying misinformation, or receiving more information from the police than they supply, plus the instigation of crimes that would not otherwise be committed (agent provocateur).

Mainstream investigators should be alert to potential subjects for recruitment and referral to their DSU, but on no account should they handle CHIS themselves which would be outside RIPA 2000 and therefore unlawful.

The issue of 'status drift 'often arises where, as part of their normal duties, investigators speak with someone who provides information about local criminals. This is community information and does not require a RIPA authority, but if the investigator then asks the person to find out more information this could be deemed as tasking and require authority.

The pertinent question to consider is whether the person has established or is maintaining a covert relationship to obtain and pass on the information; if there is any doubt at all, advice should be sought from the DSU or AO.

**KEY POINTS**

- CHIS authorisation is necessary in all circumstances where the CHIS uses or exploits a personal relationship to acquire information from another person which that person would regard as private.
- All individuals fitting the RIPA definition must be managed as CHIS. The Office of the Surveillance Commissioners (OSC) have expressed dissatisfaction over terms such as 'confidential source', 'confidential contact' and 'tasked witness', which seem to indicate an attempt to manage individuals outside of the regulated provisions.

## 12.4 Developing a Covert Strategy

The first stage in developing a covert/proactive strategy is to establish clear objectives about what is trying to be achieved. Only then can appropriate tactics be considered to fill the intelligence or evidence gaps.

The general principles of deploying covert techniques are that they must be lawful, appropriate, necessary, proportionate and auditable. The process can be time consuming, involving tasking and coordination, pre-application feasibility studies, detailed risk assessment, planning for contingencies (including compromise and its consequences) and preparing and submitting applications.

Covert operations can be expensive both in monetary value and time; there will inevitably be other competing demands for resources and there should be a formal tasking through the NIM. Wherever possible, investigators should anticipate the need for covert activity early and identify relevant issues by asking themselves the following questions:

- What are the objectives to be achieved and how this is relevant to the investigation? eg:
  - identify suspects
  - identify subjects of interest
  - locate a subject or item or place of interest
  - obtain information about a subject
  - collect evidence
  - gather intelligence
  - develop/update existing intelligence
  - obtain evidence to support a conspiracy
  - identify evidence of planning
  - identify post-offence intelligence
  - recover evidence
  - recover weapon(s)
  - identify a stronghold
  - locate property
  - prevent commission of further offences, or arrest
  - control measure to minimise risk to the public
  - identify associates
  - obtain evidence of association
  - identify addresses
  - identify vehicles used
  - identify locations of interest

- attribute mobile phone use
- attribute ATM use
- identify further/new lines of enquiry
- covertly obtain biometric (ie DNA) material
- obtain lifestyle information
- Is the application based on reliable information/intelligence?
- Is the proposed action necessary and justified or can the material be obtained by other non-intrusive means?
- What is the least intrusive method of securing such evidence or information?
- What are the legal constraints?
  - RIPA 2000
  - Police Act 1997
  - Human Rights Act 1998
  - ECHR—Articles 2, 6 and 8
  - CPIA 1996
- What is the timeframe for the operation or is a unique window of opportunity available?
- Are sufficient trained and accredited staff available to properly conduct the operation?
- Is sufficient equipment and funding available?
- What are the risks to the organisation of deploying the tactics?
- What are the risks to the organisation's staff of deploying the tactics?
- What are the risks to the public or specified third parties of deploying the tactics?
- What are the risks to the subject of the investigation?
- Will the methods breach ECHR Article 8(1)?
- Is there justification for doing so provided by ECHR Article 8(2)?
- What is the risk of collateral intrusion and how will this be managed?
- How will the covert methods be protected at trial?
- What advice should be sought?

It is only by asking and answering these questions that an authorisation can proceed and a tactical plan be developed and implemented.

---

**KEY POINT**

Investigators considering covert tactics should seek advice from force surveillance specialists, Force Intelligence Bureaux, Covert Authorities Bureaux, and Technical Support Units or externally from the NCA Covert Advice Team.

---

## 12.5 Asset Recovery

Financial investigation is not only a line of investigation to complement mainstream enquiries; it can also be used proactively to deter and disrupt all levels of criminality by using powers under the Proceeds of Crime Act 2002 (POCA).

Generally POCA powers are under used due to a misconception that they only apply to high-level organised offending but this is not the case; opportunities are available to target all levels of offending, including NIM level 1 locally based individuals.

POCA provides a framework to conduct financial investigations, restrain and confiscate assets, seize cash in excess of £1,000, seek its forfeiture and tackle money laundering. This prevents the funding of further criminal activity, ensures crime does not pay and removes negative role models from communities.

Confiscation is not restricted to drug dealers, so in addition to the primary objective of detecting and prosecuting the offence another objective should be set to conduct a 'criminal lifestyle' investigation to identify and trace offenders' criminal assets, particularly when dealing with acquisitive crime.

The 'criminal lifestyle' investigation questions a person's ability to account for their assets, in simple terms to establish if expenditure exceeds identified legitimate income and can it be accounted for (apart from benefiting from crime). Any assets that cannot legitimately be accounted for may be seized as proceeds of crime.

Confiscation powers may be triggered where the suspect has been:

1. convicted of drug trafficking, money laundering, directing terrorism, people trafficking, arms trafficking, counterfeiting, intellectual property offences (copyright/patent/trademarks), pimping, brothel keeping, blackmail, theft, fraud offences or aiding, abetting, attempting, conspiring or inciting any of these; or

2. charged with an offence or a series of offences committed over a period of at least six months where they have obtained £5,000 from that offence or others taken into consideration at the same time; or

3. convicted of a combination of offences amounting to 'a course of criminal activity'. The suspect satisfies this final test if they have:
   (a) been convicted in the current proceedings of four or more offences of any description from which they have benefited, or
   (b) been convicted in the current proceedings of any one such offence and has other convictions for any such offences on at least two separate occasions in the past six years. In addition the total benefits from the offences and/or any others taken into consideration by the court on the same occasion (or occasions) must not be less than £5,000.

The form MG17 is used to refer potential asset recovery cases to specialist financial investigators who should always be consulted along with the CPS to select charges enabling a court to find that the defendant had a 'criminal lifestyle' within section 75 of POCA 2002 and apply confiscation.

Lines of enquiry to consider may include searching premises to acquire evidence of conspicuous wealth to show 'living beyond their means', eg receipts, banking details, luxury goods, high value motor vehicles etc.

The court may issue a confiscation order following the conviction of an offender who has benefited from criminal conduct. The court decides the value of the confiscation order based on the offences for which the defendant has been convicted and any others taken into consideration.

If the court determines a defendant has a 'criminal life-style' they assess their benefit from 'general criminal conduct'. This includes the specific conduct for which they have been convicted, but also their other criminal conduct at any time, all of which can be proved on the balance of probabilities.

The benefit can be calculated over a period of up to six years and can therefore be considerably more than the offence with which they are charged.

## 12.5.1 Money laundering

Money laundering is where the proceeds of crime are converted into assets which appear to have a legitimate origin. Criminal property is property (not just money) that has been gained as a result of or in connection with criminal conduct (in other words the proceeds of crime), and the offender knows or suspects the property constitutes or represents this benefit. This includes cash but can also include other property, eg a car, house or an interest in land.

The three common money laundering offences are:

Section 327 of POCA—Concealing Criminal Property etc is an offence committed when there are reasonable grounds to suspect any person is involved in concealing, disguising, converting, transferring criminal property or if they remove criminal property from the UK.

Disguising criminal property includes concealing or disguising its nature, source, location, disposition, movement, ownership or any rights connected with it. This means that a person who hides stolen goods (concealing) or puts false number plates on a stolen car (disguising) may be guilty of money laundering.

Property is obtained by a person if they obtain an interest in it, the prosecution need to prove the persons knowledge from the circumstances in which they came into possession of the property, but it is not necessary to prove the identity of the person who committed the crime that gave rise to the creation of the criminal property.

Possession means having physical custody of the criminal property, but a defence is available if the person acquired, used or had possession of it for 'adequate consideration'. There is no distinction between the proceeds of a person's own crimes and crimes committed by others, but the alleged offender must know or suspect the property represents such benefit.

Section 328 of POCA—Arrangements—a person commits an offence if they enter into or become concerned in an arrangement which they know or suspect will facilitate (by whatever means) the acquisition, retention, use or control of criminal property by or on behalf of another person.

This could cover a suspect allowing a third party to use their bank account for the transfer of cash.

Section 329 of POCA—Acquisition, use and possession—a person commits an offence if with the necessary knowledge or suspicion they acquire, use or possess criminal property.

---

### KEY POINTS

- The relationship between money laundering offences and handling stolen goods often raises issues that require careful consideration by the police, CPS and the courts in those cases where the charge could be money laundering based on possession under section 329 of POCA or an offence of handling stolen goods.
- The Code for Crown Prosecutors and CPS Legal Guidance advises that a money laundering charge may be appropriate

---

> when either a defendant has possessed criminal proceeds in large amounts or in lesser amounts but repeatedly, and where assets are laundered for profit.
> - In straightforward cases where 'A' has passed stolen goods to 'B', the appropriate charge will generally be handling stolen goods. Where there are aggravating factors such as a significant attempt to transfer or conceal ill-gotten gains, money laundering could be considered as an additional charge.

Under Parts 2 and 8 of POCA, Accredited Financial Investigators (AFI) may obtain production orders, search and seizure warrants, account monitoring orders, customer information orders and restraint orders which are only available to support a confiscation or money laundering investigation. They can only be applied for by an AFI and require the signed authority of a Crown Court Judge.

### 12.5.1.1 Production orders

A production order requires the specified person appearing to be in possession or control of it to produce confidential material such as bank accounts to an appropriate officer.

### 12.5.1.2 Search and seizure warrants

Search and seizure warrants authorise an appropriate person to enter and search specified premises, and to seize any material found, which is likely to be of substantial value (whether or not by itself) to the investigation.

Search and seizure warrants may be obtained if a production order is not complied with, or it would not be appropriate to obtain a production order as it is not practicable to communicate with any person against whom the production order may be made.

### 12.5.1.3 Account monitoring orders

Account monitoring orders require a financial institution to provide account information on a specified account, for a specified period not exceeding 90 days. The information is provided in a manner and at a time or times stated in the order.

### 12.5.1.4  Customer information orders

There is no single database in the UK that is guaranteed to provide a comprehensive list of all financial accounts an individual may hold. Customer information orders are used when there are reasonable grounds for suspecting that an individual is using financial accounts for criminal purposes (eg money laundering) at various banks in a particular area and in different names.

An order allows a notice to be sent to those banks in the area to ascertain if that individual holds an account(s) under any of the names provided. If identified the financial institution must provide sufficient account information for the investigator to obtain a production order.

### 12.5.1.5  Restraint orders

A restraint order prohibits a specified person dissipating any realisable assets held before they can be subject of a confiscation order.

A restraint order should be anticipated and considered at an early stage of the criminal investigation, they will not be needed in all cases and there must be a real risk that without the restraint order, assets may be dissipated.

Only accredited financial investigators are able to apply for a restraint order, the decision to obtain one is taken in conjunction with the CPS and authorised by a Superintendent, they are applied for by the prosecutor before a conviction is obtained.

---

**KEY POINT**

- Investigators should seek early advice and guidance from their Financial Investigation or Economic Crime Unit in accordance with local force policy on how this legislation can be exploited in support of an investigation.

---

## 12.5.2 Cash seizure

Investigators can seize cash for its evidential value under the Police and Criminal Evidence Act 1984 (PACE) where the following conditions apply:

- they are lawfully searching a person or premises and find the cash
- under the authority of a warrant to search for cash as evidence of a particular crime
- a specific search for cash under a magistrate's authority issued under sections 289 and 290 of POCA

A further power exists to seize and detain cash with a view to forfeiture under sections 294 to 298 of POCA where a constable or customs officer finds £1,000 or more in any kind of currency, cheques, postal orders, bankers drafts or bonds and suspects that it has come from or is intended to be used to commit crime.

Prior written authority to search should be obtained from a magistrate; if this is impractical approval can be given by an Inspector prior to the search, eg if the search is not pre-planned; if this is also impractical a search can be completed without authority and an Inspector informed afterwards, eg if there is a random find.

This is a civil procedure and does not require the suspect to be charged or convicted of a crime, and it can run in parallel with a criminal investigation.

In the majority of cases, cash seizure, detention and forfeiture will be dealt with by an accredited Financial Investigator. However, there is always a possibility that mainstream investigators may start the process, eg when there is an unplanned discovery of large amounts of cash (remember this is not just money) when searching persons, vehicles or premises.

An officer may seize cash under the following conditions:

- their presence is lawful (there is no power of entry under POCA)

- there are reasonable grounds to suspect the cash is recoverable property (obtained by unlawful conduct), or is intended for use by any person in unlawful conduct
- there appears to be £1,000 or more

Depending on the surrounding circumstances of the cash find, a person's possession of £1,000 or more may or may not be suspicious, depending on any explanation given. Cash seizure powers require some objective grounds and discretion may be required depending on the individual circumstances, particularly when considering the seizure of smaller amounts.

If the situation is encountered where several persons are together and each has an amount of cash, these amounts can be added together and if the total amounts to £1,000 or more the POCA provisions apply, eg four persons in a vehicle each with £500 in their possession.

Investigators should note:

- time the cash was first seen
- where it was found or concealed
- description of the cash

To establish ownership of the cash and whether it is 'recoverable property', the person found in possession of it should be asked to provide an explanation of its origins when deciding if there is reasonable cause to believe it is from crime or is to be used in crime. Relevant questions may include:

- How much cash is there?
- What types of notes or cheques are there?
- Who does it belong to?
- From what activities did the cash derive?
- How did it get there?
- Has the person touched or handled it?

When seizing cash it is advisable that:

- it is not counted (to prevent contaminating future drugs or other forensic examination) and the amount is estimated
- gloves are worn

- photographs are taken
- cash is double-bagged and sealed using clean tamper evident bags in the presence of the subject and if possible an entry signed in the officer's official note book
- cash should not be removed from any wrapping, bag or container, but if this is absolutely necessary the receptacle should be seized in the same manner
- two officers are present throughout the procedure and both sign the exhibit labels
- cash is lodged in a safe, a receipt is provided to the person as soon as possible and the search record completed

It is advisable to avoid:

- placing property on floors or other contaminated surfaces
- letting the person found in possession of the cash touch it
- handling the cash any more than is necessary
- using officers who have recently been in contact with drugs, explosives, firearms or other substances
- taking the cash into the custody suite to prevent contamination with drugs and other substances

### 12.5.2.1 Cash seizure forms

There are four forms investigators must consider:

1. Form A—First/Further Detention of Seized Cash—this is a legal document and a copy must be served on each individual from whom the cash has been seized *prior to them being released from custody*.
2. POCA Receipt for Cash—consists of two pages both to be signed by each individual and the officer serving. The top copy is forwarded to the Financial Investigator/cash seizure officer in accordance with local practice and the bottom copy is retained by the individual.
3. Court Notification—provides details of the hearing for continued detention at the magistrates' court, including the date and time.
4. Disclaimer—if any individual disclaims any right to the seized cash they should be asked to sign a disclaimer

form to be supplied to the Economic Crime Unit/cash seizure officer.

The first three forms are mandatory, but the disclaimer is optional depending of the circumstances.

### 12.5.2.2 Financial interviews

If appropriate, financial questions should be incorporated into the main PACE interview, such as where the person has been arrested for money laundering.

Where the cash seizure does not form part of a criminal investigation, although there is no power of detention for the purpose of questioning, a separate voluntary financial interview not conducted under PACE is undertaken.

Financial interviews are not conducted under caution but are tape recorded; as cash seizure and forfeiture is a civil process, investigators should not direct questions towards the person's possible criminality.

As the cash is believed to be derived from crime, the interviewer is entitled to ask questions about its origins. The person found in possession may be legally represented (but there is no guarantee they will receive legal aid) and is not obliged to answer the questions, but a court may draw inferences from a 'no comment' reply.

During the 'financial interview', in addition to questions concerning the origins of the cash, investigators should explore the person's legitimate income and financial situation, including their income, expenditure and assets. These questions are to establish if the person has more assets and expenditure than can be supported by any legitimate income. Investigators should consult their own force policy and procedures regarding 'financial interviews', which could be conducted using pro forma questionnaires, and, during office hours, by financial investigators.

A constable or customs officer must apply to a magistrates' court for a cash detention hearing which must be concluded within 48 hours of the officer first seizing the cash (not including Saturdays, Sundays, Christmas Day, Good Friday and Bank Holidays).

As this is a civil procedure, the CPS is not involved and the application can be contested by other parties. If the hearing is not completed within the 48 hours the cash must be returned, unless it is also being detained as evidence under section 19 or 22 of PACE.

Legally, any *police officer* can complete the paperwork and attend the magistrates' court for the cash detention hearing, but usual practice is for specialist officers to deal with this process. In most forces the Financial Investigation Unit provide this support, but in some areas appointed cash seizure officers are embedded within BCUs.

Investigators should contact the Financial Investigation Unit without delay following seizure to instigate the cash detention hearing. Contact outside office hours is usually by email or fax subject to local procedure.

It is a legal requirement that Form A (First Application for Continued Detention of Seized Cash) is served on the person found in possession of the cash and any other identified interested party. A copy must also be supplied to the court.

Form A informs the person that an application for further detention of the cash is to be made and where and when the hearing will take place.

Mainstream investigators may have to complete this initial process, particularly outside office hours when financial investigators may be unavailable. Investigators should ensure they have proof of service (a witness statement or receipt).

A right of appeal against the detention of the cash is available and a notice is also served informing the person how they can reclaim the seized cash. The use and format of this form varies from force to force.

Normally specialist financial investigators arrange and progress the application, including completion and submission of the required documentation. For information purposes the process is briefly summarised as follows:

- Information in support of application for further detention is prepared including:
  - grounds for the application
  - detailed description of the circumstances
  - enquiries already conducted (including information from any interviews)
  - enquiries to be completed
- The cash should be deposited in a bank account at the earliest opportunity (complying with individual force policy) unless it is required in its original state as evidence in the case, or it is to be submitted for drug testing or other forensic analysis.
- Cash detention hearing within 48 hours of the cash first being seen.
- If the magistrate grants an order for continued detention a Form B is issued with a Notice to Affected Persons for the Order of Continued Detention (Form C).
- If the magistrate decides the cash is not to be forfeited, they may direct it be returned to any person.
- Investigate the origins of the cash within the three-month period.
- A further detention hearing must be held within three months and further applications may be made in three-monthly increments up to a total of two years.
- The magistrate may order the forfeiture of the cash or any part of it if satisfied that it is recoverable property or is intended for use in unlawful conduct based on the civil standard of proof.
- Once an application for forfeiture is made, cash cannot be released under any circumstance until the forfeiture proceedings are concluded.

---

**KEY POINTS**

- The powers under POCA complement the powers normally used under PACE for evidential purposes, eg section 19 for the seizure of items in evidence, and section 22 for the retention of items for use in evidence.

---

> • Advice should be sought from the financial investigation/economic crime unit when considering obtaining POCA search warrants. This is a specialist area where prior authority may be required; a prior authority does not include the power to enter premises.

## 12.6 **Proactive Searches**

Searching premises is a routine activity for warranted and non-warranted investigators. This section provides general practical guidance on the application process, planning and executing search warrants.

Section 18 and 32 PACE searches are routinely conducted after arrests for indictable offences, but intelligence may also identify premises where criminal activity is suspected prior to the arrest phase.

Search warrants are applied for under various Acts of Parliament, but there are three general types, allowing some flexibility when planning a search:

1. A 'specific premises warrant'—a warrant to enter one premises on one occasion.
2. An 'all premises warrant'—a warrant to enter more than one premises, eg where it is suspected there is evidence of an offence, or a wanted person at more than one location.
3. A 'multiple entry warrant'—a warrant allowing entry to premises (or more than one premises) on more than one occasion, eg where it is suspected a significant amount of material may be found which will take multiple visits to recover.

### 12.6.1 **Application process**

The grounds to apply for search warrants often rely on information provided by third parties (including CHIS). Reasonable steps must be taken to check this information is accurate; an application may not be made on the basis of anonymous information unless corroboration has been sought from elsewhere.

An Inspector or above must provide written authority before an application to the magistrates' court is made. In urgent cases where they are not readily available the senior officer on duty may authorise the application.

Different provisions apply to applications under the Terrorism Act 2000, which are made to a judge and require the authority of a Superintendent or above.

When making an application there is no requirement to disclose the identity of any CHIS, but care should be taken when drafting the documentation to ensure a covert source is not compromised. Occupiers of premises are entitled to a copy of the warrant and supporting documentation is subject to disclosure rules under CPIA.

Applications are made in person to the magistrate's court, but in urgent cases out-of-hours applications to a magistrate (often at their home address) may be made. Whatever the circumstances, the constable must be in possession of the written authority for the application.

Applicants will be required to state on oath and can be questioned on:

- grounds for the application
- enactment under which the warrant would be issued
- if the application is for a 'multiple entry warrant', the reason why this is necessary and whether an unlimited number of entries are required or whether a maximum number is desired
- identity of the premises, including the grounds for making an 'all premises' application if this is relevant
- in so far as is practical, the articles or persons sought
- identity of the person occupying or in control of the premises; reasonable enquiries must be made to establish if anything is known about them
- nature of the premises, including whether they have been searched previously, and if so how recently

A search warrant is valid for three months, but if refused no further application can be made unless additional grounds are found.

A warrant to enter and search may be executed by any constable, but non-warranted investigators (with powers under Part 4 of the Police Reform Act 2002) must be in the company of, and under the supervision of a constable. An Inspector or above may direct a designated Investigating Officer not to wear a uniform for a specific operation.

### 12.6.2 Planning the search

Many searches are straightforward but others require detailed planning and risk assessment, particularly if dealing with a specialist method of entry to mitigate violent (possibly armed) occupants, dangerous animals, or if the search has community impact issues necessitating management of the consequences.

### 12.6.3 Before the search

- PACE requires an officer to be designated as being in charge of the search (OIC); they may be a supervisor or the most senior officer present, but can be delegated to a lower rank more conversant if this is more appropriate
- The OIC should consult the local police/Community Liaison Officer if there is reason to believe the search may have an adverse impact on the community (in urgent cases consultation can be as soon as practicable after the search)
- Based on the evidential/intelligence requirements of the investigation the specific objectives of the search, including items sought, should be identified
- Conduct intelligence checks on the occupier, premises, location of the search and any associated persons to identify any risk factors and possible links to other

offences, including any outstanding stolen property/
other evidence
- Identify measures to mitigate any risks
- Brief others involved in the search, including:
  - powers to be exercised
  - items being searched for (with descriptions); consider
    also POCA and possible other linked offences where
    property may be seized if lawfully on premises
  - individual responsibilities of the search team
  - Details of Exhibits Officer (EO)
  - extent and limits of the search
  - specialist resources (eg use of a Police Search Advisor
    (PolSA) and (Police Search Team) PST, drugs/firearms
    dogs etc)
  - identified warnings/risks and mitigation measures
  - it is good practice to sequentially number any briefing
    documents and ensure they are returned after the
    briefing, as there have been occasions when briefing
    materials have been left at the subject premises
- Obtain any necessary equipment (this is not an exhaustive
  list):
  - keys from a detainee's property to gain entry
  - method of entry tools
  - exhibit bags and packaging of assorted sizes
  - exhibit labels
  - ladders/steps
  - torch/lighting/search equipment
  - exhibits register
- Inform the control room/communications centre of the
  location and timing of the search in case urgent assistance is required
- Consider CSI/SOCO attending to photograph items in
  position, assist with any forensic recovery and visually
  record the conduct of the search, including any damage
  caused (or not caused)
- Obtain the next consecutive number from the premises
  searched register

### 12.6.4 Conducting the search

- Searches should be made at a reasonable hour unless this would frustrate the purpose of the search; departure from this rarely causes difficulty with justification but should be documented
- The number of officers involved in the search should be determined by what is reasonable and necessary in the circumstances
- The extent of the search is dictated by the offence under investigation and what is sought
- If the extent or complexity of the search indicates it is likely to take some time, including the volume of material to be examined, the OIC may consider using seize and sift powers (see section 12.7)
- Anything may be seized where there are reasonable grounds for believing it is evidence or has been obtained by or through the commission of an offence (if it is necessary to prevent the items being concealed, lost, disposed of, altered, damaged, destroyed or tampered with)
- No item can be seized if it is believed to be subject of legal privilege
- The OIC should first try to communicate with the occupier or person entitled to grant entry, unless they are not present, the premises are unoccupied or alerting them would frustrate the objects of the search or endanger others (including the search team)
- Reasonable and proportionate force may be used if necessary to gain entry where entry is refused, it is impossible to communicate with a person entitled to grant access or alerting them would frustrate the object of the search or endanger others
- The OIC should identify themselves and accompanying officers (producing identification if not in uniform) and state the purpose and grounds of the search
- Premises may be searched only to the extent necessary to achieve the purpose having regard to the size and nature of things sought

- A search may not continue once the objective of the search has been achieved
- A search may not continue once the OIC is satisfied that whatever is sought is not on the premises
- A friend, neighbour or other person must be allowed to witness the search if the occupier wishes, unless the OIC reasonably believes their presence would seriously hinder the investigation or endanger other people (a search need not be unreasonably delayed for this purpose)
- Searches provide opportunities to speak with any persons on the premises, visitors and neighbours to gain information that might be of use to the enquiry

## 12.6.5  After the search

- The occupier shall be supplied with a copy of the search warrant and Notice of Powers and Rights (unless impractical)—if they are not present the documents should be endorsed and left in a prominent place
- If the premises have been entered by force, the OIC must ensure they are secured by arranging for the occupier or their agent to be present or any other appropriate means (but do not enter into discussions regarding compensation for damage)
- On arrival at the police station the officer in charge of the search shall make or have a record made of the search in the search register maintained at each subdivision or equivalent; including:
  - address searched
  - date, time and duration of the search
  - authority used for the search
  - name of the officer in charge of the search
  - names of all other officers involved in the search
  - names of any people on the premises
  - grounds for refusing an occupier's request to have someone present during the search

- ○ list of articles seized or the location of a list, eg a property or exhibits register
  - ○ grounds for seizure
  - ○ whether force was used and the reason
  - ○ details of any damage caused and the circumstances
  - ○ location of the Notice of Powers and Rights, including who it was given to
- Debrief the search, including:
  - ○ the result of the search and items seized (if any) and who by
  - ○ location of seized items
  - ○ identifying material to develop for further lines of enquiry
  - ○ identifying stolen property for identification
  - ○ identifying items for forensic examination and development
  - ○ identifying material required for interviews with suspects highlighting any special warning material
- Check continuity of all items is maintained, including completion and signing of exhibit labels
- Securely store material recovered in accordance with local procedures

### KEY POINT

Some evidential items may need attributing to individuals in order to avoid defences of lack of connection, knowledge or contact. It is important to evidentially link suspects not only to the premises but also to the items and the places they were found, eg by evidencing other personal items or belongings located nearby.

## 12.7 **Seize and Sift**

Sections 50 and 51 of the Criminal Justice and Police Act 2001 allow for the seizure and removal of property found on premises or on a person where it is not reasonably practicable to complete a process of examination, searching or separation at the scene.

Section 52 includes a legal obligation to provide a written notice to the person from whom the property was seized; this includes a description of what has been taken and an application for any person with an interest in the property to attend the examination. All reasonable steps must be attempted to accommodate them subject to the need to prevent harm to, interference with or unreasonable delay to the investigation.

Although not specifically written into the Act when it was drafted, what is often overlooked is that seize and sift also applies to computer, tablet and wi-fi equipment examination and latterly to mobile phones, which in many cases now are basically small mobile computers. In all probability, they will contain material not connected with the offence under investigation so serving a section 52 notice on the person from whom it was seized should be considered.

---

**KEY POINTS**

- An example of seize and sift might be where a large number of documents are recovered and it is impractical to examine them at the location of the search, or where a computer is seized for subsequent examination by the High Tech Crime Unit.
- Officers must be careful only to exercise seize and sift powers if it is essential and not to remove any more material than is necessary. Removal of large amounts of material (particularly if not relevant) may have serious implications for the owners, particularly if it concerns their business activity.

---

## 12.8 **Prolific and Priority Offenders**

In 2002 the 'Narrowing the Justice Gap' programme first established the definition of a persistent offender as a person aged 18 years or older, who has been convicted of six or more recordable offences in the previous 12 months. This definition has developed both nationally and locally, but continues to be based on the premise that, however defined, a large proportion of crime is committed by relatively few offenders.

In 2003 the national Persistent Offender Scheme was implemented with the aim to more effectively catch, bring to justice and rehabilitate this core group of prolific offenders who are responsible for a disproportionate amount of crime.

The scheme ensures each criminal justice agency has an enhanced focus concerning persistent and priority offenders (PPOs) at every stage of the process and is part of the Crime and Disorder Reduction Partnerships with a series of mandatory actions.

The national framework has three strands:

1. Prevent and Deter—has the overall objective of preventing those most at risk from becoming prolific offenders and focuses on the target groups of young offenders who are not yet prolific, older children and young persons at high risk of criminality, children who need early intervention programmes.
2. Catch and Convict—requires the criminal justice agencies to work together to ensure effective investigation, charging and prosecution of PPOs; specifically it refers to the timeframes within which offenders are brought to justice.
3. Rehabilitate and Resettle—presents PPOs with the opportunity to reform or face a swift return to court should they re-offend or fail to comply with the conditions of court orders. This is supported by locally agreed and implemented rehabilitation plans which manage statutory and voluntary interventions to prevent reoffending.

From an investigator's perspective the identification of a person as a PPO means they may be under active supervision, being tracked and monitored or possibly prioritised for proactive targeting via the Tasking and Coordination Group under the NIM. A final stage is the removal of a PPO from the list of priority offenders because of their reduced risk to the community.

## 12.9 **Multi-Agency Risk Assessment Conference**

A Multi-Agency Risk Assessment Conference (MARAC) is a single meeting involving representatives of all agencies that have a role in a particular case. The aim is sharing information to increase the safety, health and well-being of victims and others by combining current risk information with an assessment of the victim's needs.

The MARAC process establishes whether the offender poses a significant risk to an identified individual or to the general community; it produces a multi-agency risk management plan for implementation which should provide professional support to all those at risk, thus reducing harm and repeat victimisation.

## 12.10 **Multi-Agency Public Protection Arrangements**

Multi-Agency Public Protection Arrangements (MAPPA) is the process through which the police, probation and prison service, known as the responsible authority (RA) work together with other agencies to protect the public by managing the risks posed by violent and sexual offenders living in the community.

Three categories of offender are managed through MAPPA:

- Registered sexual offenders required to notify details to the police under the terms of the Sexual Offences Act 2003
- Violent offenders sentenced to 12 months or more in custody (or to detention in hospital) who are living in the community subject to probation supervision
- Dangerous offenders who have committed a sexual or violent offence in the past and are considered to pose a risk of serious harm to the public

These offenders are managed within three MAPPA levels based on risk, but they can move up and down the levels:

- Normal agency management applicable to most MAPPA offenders (Level 1)
- Local inter-risk agency management for offenders assessed as high or very high risk of harm (Level 2)
- Multi-Agency Public Protection Panels (MAPPP) appropriate for the small number of offenders assessed as posing the highest risk of causing serious harm, or whose management is so problematic and unpredictable that they require oversight at a senior level and the commitment of exceptional resources (Level 3)

The MAPPA encourages cooperation from other authorities who, under section 325(3) of the Criminal Justice Act 2003, have a duty to cooperate with the RA. These include local authority social care, health, local authority housing, registered social landlords, Youth Offender Teams and Jobcentres and local education authorities.

The structured process enables formal information sharing which is lawful, necessary, proportionate, accountable and secure to formulate risk management plans for proactive multi-agency management of offenders, particularly on their release from prison, eg by securing suitable accommodation away from perceived risks and triggers to offending.

Details of all MAPPA nominals are held on the ViSOR[2] database along with another category called potentially dangerous persons (PDP), who are persons who have not been convicted or cautioned for any offence which would place them into one of the MAPPA categories, but whose behaviour gives reasonable grounds for believing there is a present likelihood of them committing an offence or offences that will cause serious harm.

Inclusion of a PDP on ViSOR requires a Superintendent's authority and should be considered by investigators when dealing with and submitting intelligence on persons who fall within the definition.

# 12.11  **Threats to Life (Osman) Warnings**

The police have a positive obligation to preserve life under ECHR Article 2 (right to life), which is supported by case law. Any threat to someone's life that comes to notice through intelligence must be carefully considered. This includes any information which the police know or ought to have known concerning future activity where a person's life may be put in danger.

The basic principle is that if there is a real and immediate threat to the life (TTL) of a named individual, that person should be informed of the threat unless there is a justifiable reason for not doing so. Such a reason could include:

- causing serious risk to an identifiable third party by informing the victim
- protection of the life of the source of the intelligence

---

[2] ViSOR is a UK-wide system used to store and share information and intelligence on those individuals who have been identified as posing a risk of serious harm to the public.

---

- likely pre-emptive attack/retribution, with serious risk of loss of life
- escalation of gang warfare with consequent serious risk to third parties
- test of a police source

The 'immediacy test' is decided by conducting an objective assessment of all the facts on the capability of the threat being carried out; this may include considering an escalation of a series of incidents which when considered together trigger the ECHR Article 2 obligations.

Police action to minimise a known threat to life will depend on the nature of the threat, the intent and capability of the perpetrator and the wishes of the individual concerned. Action should be determined on a case-by-case basis ranging from warning the person of the existence of the threat (often called Osman warnings), providing personal safety advice, implementing target hardening measures and temporary removal of the person from their home, to proactive covert and intrusive tactics.

Another element of threat to human life warnings is what is often called a 'reverse Osman'. This relates to occasions where a warning is delivered to the alleged perpetrator indicating the police are aware of the threat and basically 'warning them off'. Again this involves complex decision making, including protection of covert sources and tactics and managing the consequences. Local force policy must be complied with at all times regarding authority levels and action required.

Failure to take appropriate measures (within the scope of police powers) could have catastrophic consequences for the victim and lead to litigation against the police. Such threats should be treated as a priority and potential critical incident. Operational decisions to manage threats to life can be complex, possibly involving the management of sensitive information (CHIS related) and covert tactics. Investigators should familiarise themselves with their own force 'threat to human life policies'. These include authority levels for issuing warnings, tactics to be considered (which are not appropriate for publication), delivering and documenting the warning, placing warning markers on intelligence databases and producing a documented audit of the threat to life risk management.

The principal current case law concerning threats to life is *Osman v UK*[3] and *Van Colle and Others v CC of Hertfordshire Police*.[4]

---

[3] [1998] EHRR 101.
[4] [2008] UKHL 50.

# Chapter 13

# Case Management, the Crown Prosecution Service and Court Procedures

## 13.1 **Introduction**

Once a suspect has been charged the case is far from over for the investigator. A number of additional important requirements need skilful management before and during any court hearing. Generally speaking the Crown Prosecution Service (CPS) has the responsibility for prosecuting cases and investigators need to work in collaboration with the CPS to achieve the best results.

This chapter sets out particular areas that need considering during the phases at the top end of the pyramid of investigation.[1] Investigators require a good working knowledge of the processes and procedures that come before a defendant appears at court. Matters such as knowing about threshold tests and charging policies, dealing with specific evidential points, powers to give cautions, national file standards, and last but not least the importance of giving and presenting evidence all come under the general scope of case management. Alongside court procedures, they become highly relevant and important responsibilities for a lead crime investigator. Mistakes and poor practice in this phase of the investigative process can work against any chances of mounting a successful prosecution.

---

[1] See Figure 2.1 in Chapter 2.

---

## 13.2 **Responsibilities of Police and Prosecutors**

The responsibilities for the police are:

- diverting, charging and referring cases as directed by the guidance
- assessing cases before referral to ensure the Full Code or Threshold Test can be met
- taking no further action in cases that cannot meet the appropriate evidential standard, without referral to a prosecutor
- referring serious cases, such as those involving death, rape or serious sexual offences for early advice
- completing pre-charge reports and prosecution files in accordance with national standards
- completing action plans and providing key evidence within agreed time periods
- ensuring responsibilities under the Criminal Procedure and Investigations Act 1996 (CPIA) (disclosure of evidence) are carried out effectively
- ensuring that cases appropriate for out-of-court disposal are identified at an early stage and dealt with prior to charge

Prosecutors are responsible for:

- charging decisions and providing advice
- deciding whether it is appropriate to apply the Threshold Test
- recording decisions on forms MG3 and MG3a
- ensuring pre-charge action plans only require the gathering of key evidence with agreed timescales for completion of any work
- ensuring cases appropriate for out-of-court disposal are identified prior to charge, and in police-charged cases, prior to the first hearing

## 13.2.1 Operational arrangements

The police will undertake investigations and pursue all lines of enquiry, which ensures any evidence or material likely to undermine the prosecution case or assist the defence is included within any referral for investigative or charging advice.

The police initially decide whether there is sufficient evidence to charge and assess key evidence ensuring the appropriate test can be met before proceeding to charging, or referring the case to a prosecutor.

If the appropriate test cannot be met and the case cannot be strengthened by further investigation, the police will take no further action.

---

### KEY POINTS

Where the police proceed to charge the following will have been assessed:

- Evidence that supports the charge
- Justification in treating the case as an anticipated guilty plea suitable for sentencing in the magistrates' court (where applicable)
- Reason(s) why the public interest requires prosecution rather than any other disposal

---

## 13.2.2 Referred cases

When cases are referred to the CPS for a decision, the Custody Officer will determine whether the suspect should remain in custody or be released on bail to facilitate the referral.

The prosecutor, whilst making charging decisions, will assess the evidential material. They will identify and suggest how to rectify evidential deficiencies and identify those cases that cannot be strengthened by further investigation, or where prosecution is not in the public interest.

### 13.2.3 **Early investigative advice**

Prosecutors provide advice in serious, sensitive or complex cases. Specific cases involving death, rape or other serious sexual assault should always be referred to a local area prosecutor as early as possible, and in any case once a suspect has been identified and it is clear that the investigation will provide evidence requiring a charging decision.

---

**KEY POINTS**

- Early investigative advice takes place wherever possible within 24 hours where a suspect is being detained in custody and within seven days where released on bail
- Seeking early investigative advice from a prosecutor does not negate the investigator's responsibility to identify and pursue relevant lines of enquiry

---

## 13.3 **Full Code Test**

Police decision makers should identify and stop cases where the Full Code Test cannot be met. Such cases should not be charged or referred to prosecutors unless a charging decision is required and is justified in line with the Threshold Test.

The Full Code Test has two stages: (i) the evidential stage; followed by (ii) the public interest stage.

### 13.3.1 **Evidential stage**

Prosecutors must be satisfied there is sufficient evidence to provide *a realistic prospect of conviction* against each suspect on each charge. They must consider the potential defence case and how it is likely to affect the prospect of conviction. A case which does not pass the evidential stage must not proceed, no matter how serious or sensitive it may be.

A realistic prospect of conviction is an objective test based solely on the prosecutor's assessment of the evidence and any information available about the defence that may be put forward by the suspect. It means that an objective, impartial and reasonable jury or bench of magistrates or judge hearing a case alone, properly directed and acting in accordance with the law, is more likely than not to convict the defendant of the alleged charge. This is a different test to the one that the criminal courts themselves must apply; a court may only convict if it is sure the defendant is guilty.

Prosecutors, when deciding whether there is sufficient evidence to prosecute, must consider whether the evidence can be used and whether it is reliable. There will be many cases where the evidence does not give any cause for concern, but there will also be cases where the evidence may not be as strong as it first appears. In particular, prosecutors consider the following issues:

- Can the evidence be used in court?
- Is the evidence reliable?
- Is the evidence credible?

### 13.3.2 Public interest stage

In 1951, Sir Hartley Shawcross, the then Attorney General, made the classic statement on public interest which has been endorsed by Attorneys General ever since:

> It has never been the rule in this country—I hope it never will be—that suspected criminal offences must automatically be the subject of prosecution.

He added that there should be a prosecution:

> wherever it appears that the offence or the circumstances of its commission is or are of such a character that a prosecution in respect thereof is required in the public interest.[2]

---

[2] House of Commons Debates, Volume 483, 29 January 1951.

Where there is sufficient evidence to justify a prosecution or to offer an out-of-court disposal, prosecutors must go on to consider whether a prosecution is required in the public interest.

A prosecution will usually take place unless the public interest factors tending against a prosecution outweigh those tending in its favour, or unless the prosecutor is satisfied that the public interest may be properly served by offering the offender the opportunity to have the matter dealt with by an out-of-court disposal. The more serious the offence or the offender's record of criminal behaviour, the more likely it is that a prosecution will be required in the public interest.

Each case must be considered on its own facts. Although there may be public interest factors tending against prosecution in a particular case, prosecutors should consider whether nonetheless a prosecution should go ahead and for those factors to be put to the court for consideration when sentence is passed.

Some common public interest factors should be considered when deciding on the most appropriate course of action to take. The public interest factors in the section that follows are not exhaustive and each case must be considered on its own merits.

## 13.4  Diversion from Prosecution

The police should consider at an early stage whether cases can be dealt with out of court.

The appropriateness of such an outcome will depend on:

- seriousness of offence
- results of offending behaviour
- antecedents of offender
- likely outcome at court (particularly when it may be a nominal penalty)

> **KEY POINT**
>
> Where an out-of-court disposal is considered, the views of the victim should be obtained and taken into account wherever possible

When the police consider that a conditional caution is an appropriate route for disposal, the case must be referred to a prosecutor. This will require:

- completion of form MG5 Case Summary containing:
  - proposed conditions
  - previous convictions

## 13.5 **Threshold Test**

Prosecutors will apply the Full Code Test unless the suspect presents a substantial bail risk if released, and not all of the evidence is available at the time they must be released from custody unless charged.

The Threshold Test may be applied to a charging decision for a suspect who may be justifiably detained in custody to allow evidence to be gathered for the Full Code Test.

The four requirements of the Threshold Test are:

1. there is insufficient evidence currently available to apply the evidential stage of the Full Code Test; and
2. there are reasonable grounds for believing that further evidence will become available within a reasonable time period; and
3. the seriousness or the circumstances of the case justifies making an immediate charging decision; and
4. there are continuing substantial grounds to object to bail in accordance with the Bail Act 1976 and in all the circumstances of the case an application to withhold bail may be properly made.

Where any of these four conditions are not met, the Threshold Test cannot be applied and the suspect cannot be charged. Such cases must be referred back to the Custody Officer to determine whether the person may continue to be detained or released on bail, with or without conditions

There are two parts to the Threshold Test:

(1) Reasonable suspicion

The prosecutor must be satisfied that there is at least a reasonable suspicion that the person to be charged has committed the offence.

In determining whether reasonable suspicion exists, the prosecutor must consider the evidence which is currently available. This may take the form of witness statements, or other material or other information, provided the prosecutor is satisfied that:

- it is relevant; and
- it is capable of being put into an admissible evidential format for presentation in court; and
- it would be used in the case.

If this part of the Threshold Test is satisfied, the prosecutor should proceed to the second part of the Threshold Test.

(2) Realistic prospect of conviction

The prosecutor must be satisfied there are reasonable grounds for believing the continuing investigation will provide further evidence, within a reasonable period of time, so that all the evidence taken together is capable of establishing a realistic prospect of conviction in accordance with the Full Code Test.

The further evidence must be identifiable and not merely speculative and in reaching a decision under this second part of the Threshold Test, the prosecutor must consider:

- the nature, extent and admissibility of any likely further evidence and the impact it will have on the case
- the charges that all the evidence will support
- the reasons why the evidence is not already available

- the time required to obtain the further evidence and
  whether any consequential delay is reasonable in all the
  circumstances

If both parts of the Threshold Test are satisfied, prosecutors
must apply the public interest stage of the Full Code Test
based on the information available at that time.

### 13.5.1 Reviewing the Threshold Test

A decision to charge under the Threshold Test must be kept
under review. The evidence must be regularly assessed to
ensure that the charge is still appropriate and that continued objection to the granting of bail is justified. The Full
Code Test must be applied as soon as is reasonably practicable and in any event before any applicable custody time
limit or extended custody time limit expires.

---

**KEY POINTS**

- The Threshold Test may NOT be used to charge a summary only
  offence that does not carry imprisonment
- Where it is used by the police to charge an imprisonable summary only offence, the reason will be recorded on the form
  MG6 and provided to the CPS with the file for the first hearing

---

## 13.6 **Guidance on Charging**

### 13.6.1 Police charging decisions

The police may make a decision (without referral to the
CPS) to charge a summary only offence (including criminal
damage when the value of loss or damage is less than
£5,000) irrespective of plea, and any either way offence
anticipated as a guilty plea and suitable for sentence in a
magistrates' court provided it is not:

- a case requiring consent to prosecute from the Director of Public Prosecutions (DPP) or Law Officer
- a case involving death
- connected with terrorist activity or official secrets
- classified as hate crime or domestic violence under CPS policies
- an offence of violent disorder or affray
- causing grievous bodily harm or wounding or actual bodily harm
- a sexual offence committed by or upon a person under 18
- an offence under the Licensing Act 2003

## 13.6.2 CPS charging decisions

Only CPS prosecutors can make charging decisions on indictable only offences, any either way offence not suitable for sentencing in a magistrates' court or cases where a guilty plea is not anticipated as well as the offences listed in the previous section.

In cases where any of the offences under consideration for charging include one which must be referred to a prosecutor, then all of the charges under consideration should be referred, even if not included in the categories in the previous section.

### 13.6.2.1 Anticipated guilty plea

A guilty plea may be anticipated where either:

- the suspect has made a clear and unambiguous admission to the offence and he has said nothing that could be used as a defence OR
- no admission has been made but the suspect has not denied the offence or indicated it will be contested and the commission of the offence and the identification of the offender can be established by reliable evidence, or the suspect can clearly be seen committing the offence on a good quality visual recording

### 13.6.3 Simple caution for indictable only offences

Any indictable only offence which a police decision maker considers suitable to be dealt with by way of simple caution, MUST be referred to a prosecutor to decide whether there would be a realistic prospect of conviction on the evidence available, and whether disposal by a simple caution is in the public interest.

A prosecutor will only confirm that this is an acceptable outcome in exceptional circumstances. A careful note of the rationale for such a decision must be made on the form MG3.

### 13.6.4 Police charging—prosecutor authority unobtainable

There may be times when the authority to charge a suspect cannot be obtained from a prosecutor before their relevant detention time expires. In such instances an Inspector may authorise the charging of an offence where the continued detention of the suspect is justified after charge, and it is not possible to obtain a prosecutor's authority prior to the expiration of the detention time.

This power is only to be used in exceptional circumstances so investigators should anticipate detention time limits under the Police and Criminal Evidence Act 1984 (PACE) and seek charging decisions in good time.

The police may apply the Threshold Test when charging under this provision, and any cases charged in this manner must be referred to a prosecutor as soon as possible following charge, and not later than the time proposed for the first court appearance.

The CPS will review all police-charged cases prior to a first court appearance. Cases will only proceed when all the appropriate tests have been met and the public interest has been considered, including whether an out-of-court disposal is not found to be more appropriate.

### 13.6.5 Management review of charging decisions and actions

There may be occasions when police or prosecutors disagree over decisions made or the actions proposed following referral. In such cases these matters can be escalated to the first line of management to review the disputed decision(s). First line management is:

- Detective Chief Inspector
- District Crown Prosecutor

If such a review cannot resolve the issues the case should be referred to:

- Basic Command Unit (BCU) commander
- Chief Crown Prosecutor

These reviews should take place as soon as possible.

### 13.6.6 Police compliance with decisions made by prosecutors

The police will carry out the recommendations of a prosecutor unless the case is escalated for management review.

## 13.7 Information Required for Investigative Advice or Charging Decisions

The police will provide to the prosecutor the material and evidence which is available at that time and relevant to the aspect of the case on which guidance is sought. In more complex cases this should be by way of a case report or form MG3.

The decision of the prosecutor will be set out in an MG3 and include an action plan with the agreed date for completion.

Where a case is referred for a charging decision, the police will compile a pre-charge report compromising:

- MG3 (a summary of facts may be provided on a MG5) which contains:
  - the views of the Investigating Officer
  - any issues on which the decision of the prosecutor is sought
- key evidence in the case:
  - witness statements that establish the elements of the offence to be proved
- relevant exhibits, CCTV, forensic reports
- PNC print of the suspect and previous convictions of key prosecution witnesses
- any material that may undermine the prosecution case or assist the defence

In cases where the suspect has made a full admission during interview under caution, the specific admissions will be included in the case summary.

Where an investigator considers there is no evidential value from an interview ('no comment' made or the questions answered have no evidential value) then no record of interview is required.

To ensure a speedy and responsive charging service, referral arrangements for all but the most serious and complex cases can be made over the telephone. The police will submit pre-charge reports and key evidence across the electronic exchange, by direct input, secure email or fax. The police then consult with a CPS prosecutor by telephone. During weekday office hours (9 am to 5 pm) calls will route to the local CPS group; outside these hours referral is to CPS Direct.

### 13.7.1 'Face-to-face' consultations

A 'face-to-face' meeting between the investigator and a prosecutor handling the case must be authorised by CPS supervision and will normally only take place in the following circumstances:

- any case involving death
- rape and serious sexual offences
- child abuse
- large-scale or long-term fraud
- cases with substantial or complex video or audio key evidence
- cases expected to take longer than 90 minutes' consultation
- any other cases agreed locally with CPS

Sometimes it is beneficial to have specialists present at such meetings to assist with the interpretation of evidence such as forensic or communications data.

### 13.7.2 Written advice files

Advice files should only be submitted in exceptional circumstances, such as:

- lengthy achieving best evidence (ABE) witness interviews
- complex/lengthy documentary exhibits to consider

Arrangements to submit such files should be made through the CPS Group Charging Manager.

## 13.8 National File Standards

The National File Standard (which is based on the streamlined process) provides a staged and proportionate approach to the preparation of prosecution files. It specifies material required for first hearings and identifies how file preparation should continue through the life of a case.

### Anticipated Guilty plea cases

| 1A—Pre-charge report | 1B—Post-charge national file standard |
|---|---|
| For charging decision to police supervisor or CPS Prosecutor | 1st court hearing |
| **Must include:** | **Must include in addition to pre-charge report:** |
| • MG3—report to prosecutor | • MG4— charge sheet |
| • MG3a—further report to prosecutor | • MG5—police report |
| • PNC print of suspect and key prosecution witnesses' pre-cons | • MG9—list of witnesses |
| • Any material that may undermine the prosecution case or assist the defence | • MG10—witness availability |
| • Disclosure schedules are NOT required at this stage | |
| **If applicable include:** | **If applicable include:** |
| • MG11s—key witness statements or ROVI if applicable | • MG2—special measures assessment |
| • MGDD A/B drink drive forms | • MG4A/B/C—bail sheets |
| • Other key evidence: CCTV (copy only when it is the sole evidence to be relied upon) | • MG7—remand application |
| • Other relevant material: domestic violence/hate crime, incident reports etc | • MG8—breach of bail conditions |
| | • MG11s—all key witness statements or ROVIs if applicable |
| | • MG15—interview record (only to be compiled in serious and complex cases) |
| | • MG17—POCA review |
| | • MG18—Offences TIC |

## Anticipated NOT Guilty plea cases

| 2A—Pre-charge report | 2B—Post-charge national file standard |
|---|---|
| For charging decision to police supervisor or CPS prosecutor | 1st court hearing |

| **Must include:** | **Must include in addition to pre-charge report:** |
|---|---|

- MG3—report to prosecutor
- MG3a—further report to prosecutor
- MG11s—key witness statements or ROVI if applicable
- PNC print of suspect and key prosecution witnesses' pre-cons
- Any material that may undermine the prosecution case or assist the defence
- Disclosure schedules are NOT required at this stage

- MG4—charge sheet
- MG5—police report
- MG9—list of witnesses
- MG10—witness availability
- MG11s—all key witness statements or ROVIs if applicable

| **If applicable include:** | **If applicable include:** |
|---|---|

- MGDD A/B drink drive forms
- Other key evidence: CCTV (copy only when it is the sole evidence to be relied upon)
- Other relevant material: domestic violence/hate crime incident reports etc

- MG2—special measures assessment
- MG4A/B/C—bail sheets
- MG7—remand application
- MG8—breach of bail conditions
- MG15—interview record (only to be compiled in serious and complex cases)
- MG16—bad character/dangerous offender
- MG17—POCA review
- MG18—Offences TIC

### Contested and indictable only cases

**3A—Upgrade file**

Magistrates' court trial or committal or sending to crown court for trial

**In addition to the post-charge National File standard, the file must include:**

- MG6C—schedule of non-sensitive unused material
- MG6D—schedule of sensitive material
- MG6E—disclosure officer's report

**If applicable include:**

- MG2—special measures assessment
- MG6B—police officers disciplinary record
- MG11—other relevant key witnesses
- MG12—exhibits list
- MG15—interview record (only to be supplied when relied upon and summary on MG5 is deemed insufficient for trial)
- MG19—compensation form plus supporting documents
- MG21/21A—forensic submissions

**Plus for Crown Court Trial:**

- MG11—all statements including corroborative, continuity etc
- MG15—interview record

## 13.9 Specific Evidential Points

### 13.9.1 Identification evidence

Where a suspect's identity is disputed, sufficient evidence to prove this will be a key requirement of the prosecution case. Although 'silence during an interview' does not challenge involvement in an offence, it does not remove the necessity for proper identification by the prosecution when not admitted. Each case will need to be considered on its own merits. The strength of witness testimony or CCTV evidence regarding the identification of an offender considered against their silence or no comment replies will assist in deciding whether identity procedures are necessary.

Investigators in consultation with prosecutors should ensure that identity procedures as required by Code D of PACE are conducted when they are necessary and justified. Full reasons for considering and requesting identification procedures should be recorded on the form MG3 including details of the issues in dispute.

### 13.9.1.1  Cases involving the forensic identification of a suspect

Where cases involve the forensic identification of a person such as comparison of DNA, fingerprint or other forensic material, confirmation of the identification by an expert's witness testimony, accompanied by other supporting evidence, is sufficient to meet the threshold test for charging purposes, and for the initial magistrates' court appearance.

Preliminary information on fingerprints must include their location and position found, plus details of other lifts taken, whether they have been identified and, if so, whether that person has been eliminated from the investigation. A comprehensive evidential statement (as opposed to the preliminary abridged report) is only required if the matter goes to trial and aspects of the preliminary report are challenged by the defence.

### 13.9.1.2  Cases involving identification of controlled substances

In offences where a controlled substance has been identified through use of a drugs testing kit (or in the case of cannabis by an experienced trained identification officer), further scientific evidence is usually only required in straightforward possession cases if the identification is challenged. The use of the equipment should be mentioned in the case summary.

## 13.9.2  Dealing with medical evidence

In most cases involving minor assaults (ie common assault or assault occasioning actual bodily harm (AOABH)) which are suitable for sentencing in the magistrates' court, evidence of a medical practitioner is not usually required. A medical statement will be required in cases of AOABH where the injuries can only be proved through the interpretation of medical records or X-rays by a medical practitioner, and during their interview the suspect does not accept the nature and extent of the injuries caused.

Reliable eyewitness evidence or good quality photographs accompanied by a description of the injuries can suffice for other summary assault cases. However, where the victim has sought medical attention this must be brought to the attention of the prosecutor.

## 13.10 Summaries of Visually Recorded Evidence

Generally there is no substitute for the prosecutor viewing passive data recordings (eg CCTV) or photographs when making charging decisions. Where this is not practicable (eg due to technical limitations), the prosecutor may consider accepting a summary of what can be seen on the recording, providing:

- the summary is a factual account provided by an officer who has viewed the recorded material
- the images displayed are of sufficient quality to clearly identify the suspect
- where practicable the material was shown to the suspect during interview and their response recorded

The prosecutor must then exercise judgment, taking the following factors into account:

- Does the recorded material provide a continuous account of the alleged offence, taking into account any witness statements provided?
- Is the recorded material consistent with other evidence available?

- Has the suspect put forward a defence which requires interpretation of the recorded material?
- Has the suspect put forward a defence including actions that are not referred to in the summary?

A summary will not be accepted by the prosecutor if they conclude they must view the material before making a decision.

The summary should be provided in report form on the form MG3 or on a separate report form attached to it and should contain:

- a clear factual account of what can be observed
- actions of the suspect
- actions of others present
- clear descriptions of the suspect, including clothing
- a clear reference point for the start and end of the relevant parts
- an indication of other parts of the recorded material that have been viewed

## 13.11 Prepared Defence Statements at Police Interviews

Prepared statements produced by suspects during interview under caution which do not include any form of admission do not form part of the prosecution case. Their production should be referred to in the case summary (MG5). A copy should be retained and listed as unused material for the purposes of cross-examination in court should an alternative explanation be offered during trial.[3]

---

[3] Dealing with prepared statements during interview is described in Chapter 9.

---

## 13.12  **Out-of-Court Disposals**

### 13.12.1  **Conditional cautions**

A conditional caution is a statutory development of the non-statutory simple caution and the basic criteria for use are:

- offenders aged 18 or over
- who have made admissions to the offence
- and there is (in the opinion of the CPS) sufficient evidence to charge the offender

The scheme is aimed at cases when public interest might be met more effectively by offenders carrying out specific conditions, as opposed to being prosecuted. The conditions applied to the caution must help to rehabilitate the offender and/or ensure that the offender makes reparation for the effects of their offending on the victim or the community.

The CPS is responsible for deciding whether to offer an offender a conditional caution in certain cases which must meet the Full Code Test. Prosecutors will offer a conditional caution where it is proportionate to the seriousness and the consequences of the offending, and where the conditions offered meet the aims of rehabilitation, reparation or punishment within the terms of the Criminal Justice Act 2003.

Prosecutors must follow the Code of Practice and the DPP's Guidance on Conditional Cautioning when deciding whether to offer such a caution to an offender. They may offer a conditional caution where, taking into account the views of the victim, it is considered to be in the interests of the suspect, victim or community to do so.

A conditional caution is not a criminal conviction but it does form part of an offender's criminal record and may be cited in court during any subsequent proceedings. It may also be taken into consideration by prosecutors if the person re-offends.

The offer of a conditional caution which is accepted and complied with takes the place of a prosecution. If the offer is refused or the suspect does not make the required admission of guilt to the person who seeks to administer the conditional caution, a prosecution must follow for the original offence.

If the terms of the conditional caution are not complied with, the prosecutor will reconsider the public interest factor and decide whether to charge the offender; usually, a prosecution should be brought for the original offence.

### 13.12.2 Simple cautions

A simple caution can be issued by the police in cases where admission is made by the offender and consideration has been given to the seriousness of the offence. The simple caution has no conditions attached to it. As previously described, in exceptional cases prosecutors (not police) can authorise the offer of a simple caution to an offender for indictable only offences (only triable in the Crown Court).

In all other cases, prosecutors may direct a simple caution is offered in accordance with CPS and Home Office Guidance, or suggest, eg the issue of a Penalty Notice for Disorder. Issuing a Penalty Notice for Disorder is, however, a decision for the police.

Prosecutors must be satisfied that the Full Code Test is met and there is a clear admission of guilt by the offender in any case in which they authorise or direct a simple caution to be offered by the police.

The acceptance of a simple caution or other out-of-court disposal which is complied with takes the place of a prosecution. If the offer of a simple caution is refused, a prosecution must follow for the original offence. If any other out-of-court disposal is not accepted, prosecutors will apply the Full Code Test upon receipt of the case and decide whether to prosecute the offender.

## 13.13 **Youth Offenders**

Prosecutors must consider that in all cases involving youths[4] the UK is a signatory to the United Nations 1989 Convention on the Rights of the Child, and the United Nations 1985 Standard Minimum Rules for the Administration of Juvenile Justice. They must have regard to the principal aim of the youth justice system, which is to prevent offending by children and young people, and must consider the interests of the youth when deciding whether it is in the public interest to prosecute. Prosecutors, however, should not avoid a decision to prosecute simply because of the suspect's age; the seriousness of the offence or the youth's past behaviour is very important.

Cases involving youths are usually only referred to the CPS if the person has already received a reprimand and final warning (these are the same as 'simple cautions', just using different terminology when dealing with youth offenders, and are intended to prevent re-offending, and the commission of a further offence may indicate these disposals have been ineffective). The public interest will usually require a prosecution in such cases.

## 13.14 **Reconsidering a Prosecution Decision**

Occasionally there are special reasons that allow the CPS to revisit and overturn a decision not to prosecute, or, having dealt with the case by an out-of-court disposal, allow the re-start of a prosecution, particularly in serious cases. These reasons include:

- rare cases where a review of the original decision not to prosecute concludes it was wrong and to maintain

---

[4] For the purposes of the criminal law a youth is a person under 18 years of age.

confidence in the criminal justice system, a prosecution should be brought despite the earlier decision;

- cases which are stopped so that more evidence which is likely to become available in the fairly near future can be collected and prepared. In these cases, the prosecutor will tell the defendant that the prosecution may be restarted;
- cases which are stopped because of a lack of evidence but where more significant evidence is discovered later; and
- cases involving a death in which a review following the findings of a coroner's inquest concludes that a prosecution ought to be brought, notwithstanding any earlier decision not to prosecute.

There may also be exceptional cases where, following acquittal for certain serious offences, a prosecutor may, based on new and compelling evidence with the written consent of the DPP, apply to the Court of Appeal for an order quashing the acquittal and requiring the defendant to be retried (known as double jeopardy cases).

### 13.14.1  Making appeals

The CPS may consider exercising the right of appeal when it believes the court has made a wrong legal decision. The prosecution has limited rights of appeal and can consider appealing court decisions in the following circumstances:

- immediately, where magistrates grant bail in serious cases and it is considered the defendant should be remanded in custody pending re-consideration of the bail decision by a Crown Court judge;
- within 24 hours, with the approval of a Chief Crown Prosecutor or Head of the relevant Headquarters Division (CPS), where a judge stops a case before a jury is allowed to consider the evidence, so the decision can be re-considered by the Court of Appeal as soon as possible; and
- within a strict time period after sentence in a limited range of cases where the Attorney General can be requested

to refer a potentially unduly lenient sentence to the Court of Appeal (members of the public, victims and their families can also submit cases which they consider have unduly lenient sentences for consideration of appeal by the Attorney General using an online process).

Other forms of appeal may be considered where it is believed the court has not followed procedure correctly, made a decision that is very seriously wrong, or the law needs clarifying by a higher court.

If a defendant appeals against a decision of the court, the CPS instructs an advocate to represent them or assist the court, except in appeals against sentence in the Court of Appeal, when the CPS could appear itself if there is a compelling reason to do so.

A Court of Appeal decision may be appealed further by the CPS if the Court of Appeal upon request certifies there is a point of law of general public importance in the case that should be decided by the Supreme Court. The CPS should keep victims informed of the progress of any appeal (often facilitated with the investigator), and explain the effect of the court's decision to them.

## 13.15 **Giving Evidence in Court**

Although giving evidence in court comes towards the end of the case management phase, it is nonetheless as important as all the other phases of the investigation. Poor presentation of evidence or a poor performance by an investigator in the witness box can have a detrimental effect on the prosecution case (and damage the reputation of the investigator and organisation).

Investigators should present their evidence in a professional, confident, impartial and efficient manner. This will help ensure that all the good and extensive work conducted during the investigation is not undone.

### 13.15.1  Mental preparation

Investigators should prepare for their court appearance by reading all relevant statements and documents. This will assist in appearing before the court with a detailed knowledge of the case.

---

**KEY POINTS**

- Explanations (eg job description) should exclude police jargon
- Be prepared to discuss the rationale behind decisions made
- Know your police powers
- Deal with facts—evidence is facts NOT assumptions

---

### 13.15.2  Physical preparation

These may seem simple examples, but if adhered to and added to the mental preparation they will lead to the professional effective delivery of evidence.

---

**KEY POINTS**

- Arrive in plenty of time
- Familiarise yourself with the surroundings of the court and witness box
- Report to the court usher and the prosecutor
- Do not speak to the defendant or their legal representative(s) without CPS approval
- Portray a professional appearance at all times, even when out of the courtroom. Defence teams are looking to spot inappropriate comments and unprofessional behaviour to discredit the police handling of the case
- Be careful when liaising with or speaking to witnesses at court who may be involved with the case, as this could be construed as an abuse of process, particularly as investigators may also be required to give evidence

---

### 13.15.3 Taking the oath

When an investigator takes their place on the witness stand they will be asked by the usher whether they wish to take the oath or affirm. Deciding in advance which is preferred is the best policy; and even if known, it is advisable to READ from the card provided as it helps to settle nerves and retain confidence and composure.

The giving of the oath or affirmation is a chance to settle nerves, breathe slowly and be relaxed. It is important to appear professional and confident, even when feeling slightly nervous or apprehensive.

---

**KEY POINT—OATH AND AFFIRMATION**

**Oath**

I swear by almighty god that the evidence I shall give shall be the truth, the whole truth and nothing but the truth.

**Affirmation**

I do solemnly, sincerely and truly declare and affirm that the evidence I shall give shall be the truth, the whole truth and nothing but the truth.

---

### 13.15.4 The golden triangle

When in court it is an unnatural situation where questions are asked by one person (prosecution/defence lawyer) and answers are directed to a completely different set of people (magistrates/jury). This is known as the 'golden triangle of communication'.

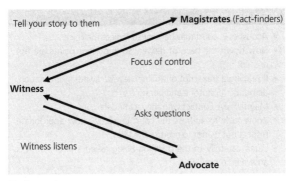

**Magistrates' court**

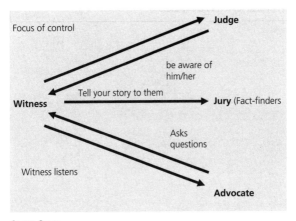

**Crown Court**

**KEY POINTS**

- Acoustics in court may be poor so project the voice
- Slow down the pace of delivery so important points are not missed
- If reading a transcript of an interview be aware of intonation, do not be monotone and boring
- Maintain eye contact with the fact finders
- Know how to address the court correctly, show appropriate respect but try not to overuse the titles
- Listen carefully to the question being asked and ensure it is answered properly
- If you don't know the answer or want the question to be repeated then say so
- THINK before speaking, consider the answer
- Keep answers simple and short and do not volunteer any unnecessary information while not appearing evasive
- Honesty is the only policy—straightforwardness and integrity make for a credible witness

# Checklist—Crime Investigator—
# 50 Initial Considerations

1. Record information, options, decisions, reasons/rationale, actions taken/not taken and timings (eg time of arrival at scene), resources etc.

2. Incident log—obtain and analyse, debrief call taker/resource despatcher.

3. Establish date, timeframe and location of the incident.

4. Establish person currently in charge at the scene, contact number and resources already involved, check decisions made and actions taken.

5. Take control and assume responsibility for investigation. Record/time all decisions.

6. Scene visit—attend as soon as possible.

7. Environmental conditions—record weather, lighting/visibility.

8. Consider health and safety and welfare of all involved including self.

9. Identify type of incident/offence and consider local procedure (rape, missing person, suspicious/unexplained death, critical incident, major incident etc).

10. Identify/interview person reporting incident to the police.

11. Obtain recordings and accurate transcripts of related calls/messages (eg 999/101).

12. Hot-debrief initial responders including other emergency services (out of earshot of witnesses/friends/relatives/public), collate statements/notes/exhibits.

## Appendix

13. Establish what is known/not known, facts/information gaps (use of 5WH).
14. Develop early hypotheses as to what may have happened and why, when, who by etc.
15. Apply ABC rule—Assume nothing/Believe nobody/ Challenge/check everything.
16. Victim(s)—identify location, personal details, injuries, medical attention, welfare, initial account, background information, possible FLO deployment, 'victimology', forensic considerations, (sensitively recover clothing, phones, other evidential items).
17. Identify, secure and protect (ISP) and sequentially number all crime scenes (eg vehicles, weapons, attack sites, people including suspects arrested).
18. Cordons—RVP, CAP, scene log(s).
19. Prevent cross-contamination—victims/scenes/witnesses/ suspects.
20. Identify parameters and prioritise all activities (eg scene, search, H-2-H, CCTV).
21. H-2-H—arrange within line of sight/hearing of scene(s) and produce questionnaire.
22. Resources—assess/request further/brief staff on roles/ responsibilities.
23. Specialist resources/equipment required (CSI/FME/ PoLSA/dogs/scene tent).
24. Searches—determine type and coordinate (forensic/ physical/house/open air/route/water/vehicles).
25. Consider suspending refuse collection in area.
26. Fast track actions—identify/instigate/review/monitor.
27. Action management—begin numbered list of actions raised and allocated.
28. Set objectives for the investigation.
29. MLOE and investigative strategies—plan, prioritise and progress.
30. Suspects—identify/obtain description/circulations/ locate/plan arrest and interviews. Treat as crime scenes.

31. TIE/TIs—establish categories and elimination criteria.

32. Witnesses—trawls, obtain first accounts, categorise (significant, vulnerable or intimidated), welfare, interviews, special measures, support and intermediaries.

33. Geography—survey area/location, check environmental and local community surroundings in context of scene(s) and offence information.

34. Intelligence gathering—research victim(s), suspect(s), location(s), closed and open source checks, prioritise and exploit information-gathering opportunities, intelligence officer/cell.

35. Identify linked or precursor incidents (CPA, incident logs, local knowledge).

36. Other agencies—notification/joint investigation (fire service, social care, coroners).

37. Exhibits—properly record processes, preserve integrity, consider use of dedicated Exhibits Officer.

38. Passive data collection (CCTV/ANPR).

39. Data communications—mobile phones/social media network usage/photos and video.

40. Proactive overt enquiries (physical searches/road checks, search warrants).

41. Communications strategy—internal/external, briefing/debriefings, team members, key personnel, supervisers, other agencies.

42. Community impact assessment (maintain trust and confidence), consider if major or critical incident.

43. Diversity management—human rights, ethical behaviour and respecting the needs of others.

44. Media management—consider initial holding statement, monitor journalistic reporting.

45. Proactive covert tactics—exploit early opportunities (consider authorities).

46. Check/update status and accuracy of crime recording and any linked incident logs.

## Appendix

47. Disclosure—retain, record, reveal all relevant material.
48. Keep victims, families, witnesses and communities updated.
49. Prepare current situation reports.
50. Consider plan for further crime prevention.

# Index

# Index

# Index

# Index

# Index

# Index

# Index

# Index

# Index

# Index

# Index

# Index